54060000015098

THE
PAUL HAMLYN
LIBRARY

DONATED BY
THE PAUL HAMLYN
FOUNDATION
TO THE
BRITISH MUSEUM

opened December 2000

TRADE AND INDUSTRY
IN
CLASSICAL GREECE

ASPECTS OF GREEK AND ROMAN LIFE

General Editor: H. H. Scullard

TRADE AND INDUSTRY IN CLASSICAL GREECE

R. J. Hopper

With 55 illustrations

THAMES AND HUDSON

To Professor Sir Frank Adcock
and
Professor Max Cary
In Grateful Memory

330. 949507 ITOP

Any copy of this book issued by the publisher as
a paperback is sold subject to the condition that
it shall not by way of trade or otherwise, be lent,
resold, hired out or otherwise circulated, without
the publisher's prior consent, in any form of
binding or cover other than that in which it is
published, and without a similar condition
including these words being imposed on a
subsequent purchaser.

© 1979 THAMES AND HUDSON LTD, LONDON

All rights reserved. No part of this publication
may be reproduced or transmitted in any form
or by any means, electronic or mechanical,
including photocopy, recording or any
information storage and retrieval system, without permission in writing from the publisher.

Library of Congress Catalog card number 78-62802

PRINTED IN GREAT BRITAIN BY
LATIMER TREND & COMPANY LTD PLYMOUTH

CONTENTS

LIST OF ILLUSTRATIONS

PLATES

MAPS

PREFACE

THIS BOOK IS INTENDED to give a picture of the economic activity of Classical Greece. As a preliminary to such an account a survey is made of the historical, economic and archaeological developments which, in Archaic Greece, led up to the Classical period.

The study of Greek trade and industry very clearly shows that for the Classical period of the fifth and fourth centuries BC, to the time of Alexander the Great, it is the Athenian economy which is most extensively and clearly revealed in literary texts and in inscriptions. Consequently, for the greater part of the book, Athens forms the basis, though where possible other Greek states and their concerns have been taken into consideration.

The term 'industry' is not so easily fitted into the Classical Greek economic framework, and what in modern times would be called minor or house-craft has been included here in this survey. The same term, rather more boldly, is applied to land cultivation, the main Greek productive activity.

As an important issue, consideration is given to State preoccupation with the legal regulations to control and to facilitate trade in general, and particularly in essential commodities. Something is also said on financial matters and banking, and account is taken of materials, craft organization, wages and costs. Particular attention is paid to mining, the only industry of its kind of which the organization is at all well known.

Despite the fact that the economic concerns of Athens are central to the theme of this book, a variety of details are known relating to other Greek states, which seem to show that their preoccupations were the same as those of the Athenian State. These are considered in a final chapter, together with some brief examination of the post-Alexander (Hellenistic) period, which reveals aims and problems similar to those of earlier times.

Two other studies in this series deal with more specialized economic topics, but from different angles. Thus, Alison Burford's *Craftsmen in Greek and Roman Society* (1972) is concerned with the social aspect of her subject and J. F. Healy's *Mining and Metallurgy in the Greek and Roman World* (1977) considers mainly the technical problems of its subject. Technology and slavery are touched on only incidentally in the present work. These are themes more appropriate to separate treatment; the same is largely true of transport, quarrying and the timber trade.

The Notes give ancient literary and epigraphical references with modern scholarly discussions kept to a minimum. The Bibliography is not exhaustive; it consists of the works which the author has read and found useful. Where the spellings of names are concerned inconsistencies are unavoidable. In general 'Latin' forms have been given preference, particularly in personal names; the rendering of place names is, however, based on the author's individual preferences. Greek forms are used in the translations of inscriptions.

For the translations of Herodotus which come from George Rawlinson, *The History of Herodotus*, Everyman, 1912, and the translations from Thucydides, *History of the Peloponnesian War. Done into English by Richard Crawley*, Everyman, 1926, I am indebted to J. M. Dent and Sons, Ltd.

To all those who have helped to advance my studies over the years I extend my grateful thanks, and, for unstinting interest, aid and patience, particularly to Professor H. H. Scullard, general editor of the series.

Sheffield 1978   R. J. HOPPER

INTRODUCTION

THE TITLE OF THIS BOOK places the subjects, trade and industry, in the traditional order. In relation to political history and inter-state connections trade – in effect import trade – was, in ancient discussion, the dominant element, especially the corn trade, in the Classical period certainly, and possibly earlier. Industry and crafts directly had a purely internal significance, not connected with inter-state affairs.

When what, in modern times, would be called industrial products were exported, as distinct from 'natural' products such as the olive-oil, lead, silver or marble of Attica, and comparable commodities elsewhere, we hear little of any problems connected with them. There was nothing like the inter-state problems, ramifications of industry and industrial investments that have developed so extensively today. This certainly applied to the Classical period. There were changes in Hellenistic times, but they were not great.

Trade, internal and foreign, is readily defined, either as a form of developed barter, or of transactions carried out by means of a universally acceptable means of exchange – a precious metal, used as bullion or struck as coin. The term 'industry' is much harder to define. In fact, in Classical Antiquity, as far as the Greeks are concerned, we are hard put to it to produce any serious evidence of 'industry' in the modern sense unless agriculture and other food production are so called. It is an odd situation which places the Classical Greek economy well down in the scale of industrial development. The absence of machinery, meaning the supplementation of direct human effort by devices other than of a simple sort, which increase its effectiveness, the lack of power, except that directly of the human operator and a limited use of animal power, meant that productive activity was on a small scale: something like 'cottage industry' as pursued still in the remoter parts of Great Britain – the much-used German term is *Hausindustrie*, as opposed to *Grossindustrie*. It would appear that where slave labour was employed there were difficulties of supervision. A curious feature of the pursuit of crafts, and all Greek industry even in the Hellenistic period took, in effect, the form of a craft, was that investment for expansion, as we know it, was conspicuous by its absence. It is clear, however, that while the concept of 'capital' was poorly developed, the idea of 'labour' as a commodity was represented by the existence of slaves. The effect of this was the inhibition of industrial technological development by the attitude of the upper-class free Greek to 'slave pursuits'. An overall principle in relation to trade, and affecting industry directly, as made clear by Aristotle, is that imports and exports were, indeed, both the concern of the statesman, but exports, as a means of paying for imports, were of indirect importance, while the latter were the vital concern. In reality the truly desirable aim was *autarkeia* (self-sufficiency).

In 'industry' an important factor – as it appears in the tradition, though whether it was so in reality is difficult to establish – was the attitude to trades and crafts. This is significantly expressed in the statement concerning Corinth that 'there craftsmen are *least* despised'.[1] What was in origin an aristocratic attitude survived in Classical Athens as a philosophical one. For the rest of Greece ideas on this matter are totally obscure except in the case of the Spartiates. Even where Athens was concerned the attitude of the philosophers may not have reflected the reality. There appears to have been present an idea that some crafts, at least, deformed men's bodies (the 'pale cobblers' who also suffered from distorted, that is, radical minds, for example).[2] It was arguable that some activities prevented men from partaking in the full life of a citizen in the Athenian democracy (implicit in the idea of pay for public service), though no objection to agriculture seems to have been raised in this connection. In fact, for those Athenians who were able to reach the Agora (market-place) and Assembly (the Pnyx) in a reasonably short period of time, accustomed as they were to starting at dawn or before, the pursuit of trades and crafts was made easier by the practice of piece-work. A Greek was in general free of the servitude of daily or weekly terms of employment and subservience to an employer. Slaves, representing labour in terms of a commodity, were not. On the other hand, slaves as capital had to be maintained even in idleness, while free labour would be turned off when not wanted. From this view of the free man came the view of the desirable state of things, independent economic activity free of a master (still apparent in Greece today); but also the failure to develop capital investment and co-operation. What follows relates mainly if not wholly to the Classical period.

LITERARY SOURCES

The problem in dealing with both production ('craft', 'industry') and exchange ('trade') in Classical Greece is that we know little of states other than Athens, who captured the historical tradition. The conditions of 'industry' and 'trade' of other city states receive only marginal consideration in the literature, which is almost exclusively Athenian, so no explanation need be made when 'Greek' turns out to be 'Athenian' for the most part. The Hellenistic period, however, shows a much greater abundance of material. On the other hand, the Archaic period is in a quite different category. A great deal of obscurity prevails, and the contemporary sources are for the most part non-literary.

Even in the case of Athens there is, for the Classical period, little direct writing on industrial, craft or mercantile themes, except the curious treatise *On Ways and Means* which appears among the works of Xenophon.[3] The Pseudo-Aristotelian *Oeconomica* is barely worth consideration except in so far as it demonstrates the conviction of the Greeks that, especially in the fourth century, they were economically in difficulties and reduced to shifts and devices of a puerile and ineffectual sort. There are the incidental references in the historians, far fewer than might have been expected, and when forensic oratory develops, from the end of the fifth century into the fourth, there seems to be a promising source of information, which, on closer inspection, shows certain disadvantages. How far is this random selection of speeches and fragments dependable evidence for economic activity? How far do they represent the exception or the norm, and how far are they affected by rhetorical and partisan exaggeration? Except for the corn trade the concern of these speeches is with inheritance, mortgage, trusteeship and the like: and, in the case of foreign trade, with borrowings on ship or cargo.[4] Then there are the Comic writers, especially Aristophanes. It is inevitable that the humour is heavy-handed. A first reaction to this source is that it provides a good deal of trivia, uncertainly related to reality. None the less, further reflection must show that, discounting the exaggeration, it provides a certain background of detail acceptable to those contemporaries whose daily experience was its source, while the slight distortion formed their entertainment.

INSCRIPTIONS

Another source of contemporary information is provided by inscriptions, frequently much fragmented. They increase in number as time passes: very few in the sixth century, more in the fifth, a considerable number in the fourth century, and a great many in the Hellenistic period. The Greeks were concerned to inscribe on stone or bronze certain types of record for which they sought a measure of permanence. 'A measure' must be stressed; for after a certain interval such records were melted down, burned for lime, used as building material, or put to base uses as drain-covers and the like. Anything to do with the gods was deemed worthy of record in durable material, as a manifestation of piety. Thus, religious regulations, temple inventories, temple building inscriptions, loans to the State from the sacred treasuries, and leases of sacred land are common. It is significant that the Tribute Lists of the Delian League, with the exception of the reassessment of 425 BC, give the sums due in the form of a tithe to Athena. Since they were intended to last, honorific inscriptions were carved on stone; so also were lists relating to the socio-political organization of the State (for later reference), and mortgages, records of confiscated property and fines, together with boundary stones and mining leases because of the long duration of some of them. Many of these have an obvious importance for economic affairs, but the kind of record which would most interest the economic historian, such as tax lists and the like were in the eyes of the Greeks of only ephemeral significance, and appear to have been recorded on perishable materials, such as wooden boards. These could be stored, but need not be publicly available. Aside from all this, individual inscriptions on durable materials are frequently defective, and even where there is a sequence or something like it, as in the mining records of the *Poletai*, there are many obscurities.

MATERIAL OBJECTS

(a) *Coins*

Where material objects are concerned, a most obvious source of information would seem to be coins, and particularly coin hoards. These can be indicative of trade or trade connections, but of a maritime link only, which might have existed once for an individual, but was not necessarily consistent and repeated over the same route. No class of evidence is more subject to chance discovery than coin hoards, and a few new finds may entail a reassessment of theory and in some cases make more enigmatic the presence of the coins involved. Difficulties are presented by the dispersal, total or partial, of hoards, and subsequent attempts at reconstitution. In general, then, the evidence of hoards for economic purposes[5] must be approached with caution. But the origins and early development of coinage by the Greeks is one of the most important aspects of early economics.

The over-striking of the coins of one state on those of another must have some economic significance, and will also suggest problems of the supply of silver, and the connections between the state or states supplying the coins for over-striking and the state using them for this purpose.[6]

(b) *Pottery and bronze-work, etc.*

Chief among the categories of material evidence is that of pottery, especially in the Archaic period, which is dealt with in Chapter I. There are two reasons for this: the possibility of identifying the place of manufacture, distinguishing an original group, such as Corinthian or Attic, from local imitations elsewhere, and its imperishable character. The latter characteristic applies universally, but local conditions such as burial practices determine to a very large extent the volume of pottery preserved and the survival of whole vases. From the standpoint of artistic achievement the evidence is satisfactory enough; from others it is not. From the 'craft' aspect, that is what the Greeks would call 'crafts' – in modern times they would be called 'artistic activities' – we can see, in vase-paintings, how the Greeks represented potting and vase-decoration, bronze-working and weaving (Pls 31–33; 37; 40–43; 45–47). This latter pursuit, it may be said, seems generally domestic, but even so, might be called a cottage or home industry. These representations, however, give no indication of the size of the labour force in the workshop. Such information derives, as far as it is available, from the speeches of the Orators, and only for the Classical period.

Portable metalwork presents more problems than does pottery. Artistic objects in bronze are common enough (gold and silver objects hardly come into consideration), but they were peculiarly vulnerable to decay in the earth and to being melted down, and it is impossible to judge how numerous they were originally, as, for instance, in the case of bronze vessels and mirrors. It is hard to view their production as an 'industry' or their export as a significant element of 'trade' in the broad sense. If they could be so regarded, there is the problem of identifying their place of origin; the distinguishing of 'schools' of three-dimensional figurative art in metal is notoriously difficult, increasingly so in the Classical period, given the mobility of the artist-craftsman travelling from one city state to another. This is also true of the Archaic period (see p. 37). For the commoner objects of everyday use the problem of centres of manufacture, and thus of trade, is even greater and for the most part find-place must be equated with place of manufacture, but it is not always true of the Hellenistic period, and it may not be true of the Classical.

Pottery shows a certain advantage in that it can be identified as produced in different centres. There is a natural desire on the part of economic historians to use this material for dating trading contacts, and to estimate the volume of trade. The latter point may be taken first. All travellers in Greece have seen, particularly on the quays of island harbours, assemblages of pots for at least regional export. They will also have noticed the kind of vessel, the caïque, into which the cargo is to be loaded, and that the pottery is common stuff for everyday use. A trade in such ships, suited for coasting, also characterized Classical Greek Antiquity. This type of pottery must have been produced in considerable volume, and included clay containers for solids such as pickled fish, and liquids, olive-oil and wine. Until recently archaeologists have failed to preserve and study this material, since the tradition of the preservation of 'museum-worthy' objects only has died hard, and consequently the view of the pottery trade and particularly the container trade has been distorted.[7]

It must also be pointed out that we are less well informed by the literary sources concerning the pottery industry than could have been wished. In Classical times there was the shadow of the 'banausic'[8] over the manufacture of even fine painted pottery, so that an achievement of Greek and particularly Attic art, much admired in modern times, gets almost no mention in Antiquity. This should not, perhaps, surprise us when the same can be said, for example, of the architectural sculptures of the Parthenon, and of the craftsmen who converted the designs of Phidias and other artists into marble sculpture. It is true that the rivalry of Attic potters manifested itself on occasions on an outstanding painted pot, but a proverb converted this into something less flattering: 'potter is angry with potter'. A low and cantankerous crowd they were seen to be – not so much different from the pale and radical shoemakers.[9] And some of them were aliens of a barbarous sort, even slaves or ex-slaves, as some names indicate: Amasis, Lydos, Kolchos, Skythes.

The price inscriptions (*graffiti*), as opposed to *dipinti* which must have been produced in the pottery, provide puzzlement rather than information. They could have been done in the pottery at the end of the process, but it is more natural to suppose that they are the marks of middlemen. The striking thing is that they sometimes represent prices wholly inadequate to the quality of the pot on which they appear.[10] They underline what is apparent from other sources, including account inscriptions, namely that a low, indeed a very low, standard of wages was the lot of the urban worker, a state of affairs borne out by Aristophanes and his Jurymen in *The Wasps*. The small cultivator will probably have been better off.

On the volume of trade as far as pottery is concerned, it is true that the surviving amount of, say, Corinthian or Attic black- and red-figure pottery looks impressive at first sight, but reflection shows that the Corinthian has to be spread over two centuries, which include the Archaic period, and Attic over a century and a half or more. This represents relatively few cargoes[11] and suggests that its export value was small (compare the prices on the vases) and unimportant, certainly in the fourth century, when the problem of the means whereby exports paid for imports presents itself most acutely.

The economic historian faces another temptation – to try, by studying the location of pottery finds, and their dating, to determine changes in commercial relations. This is a particular temptation in the Archaic period, and is a form of exercise to be engaged in with caution. The problem is clear in the case of Corinthian, seemingly forthcoming to a much greater degree in the better explored West in the past, now increasingly found in the East as archaeological exploration expands. As far as Attic black- and red-figure pottery is concerned, the great work of the late Sir John Beazley produced universally accepted identifications of pot-painters and schools of pot-painting within the Attic context, but the problem is how far these can be dated, as individual pots or groups, sometimes in the long life of a painter, in terms of years in a period when, for co-ordination with political history, the necessary dating margin is ten to twenty years.

Finally, there is another problem. The distribution of pottery does not tell us how the product was conveyed to the regions where it is found. The position of the East Greek states, Phocaea, Samos, Miletus and Rhodes, and in Greece proper the location of Athens and Corinth, point to the passage-ways of commerce, where the pottery products of these and other states were collected and carried in diverse directions; but no indication is thereby given of the carriers, who must at all times, as in the fourth century, have been a motley lot.

For the rest, industry and trade were concerned either with natural products or with manufactured articles in perishable materials, and these have not survived. In particular textiles must have been an important element in industry and not always 'home industry'. There were not only such mass-produced articles as the slave garments manufactured in Megara (an interesting example of specialization), but also heavy textiles and those of high quality, of which only rare examples have been preserved. There were, for example, the products of Amorgos, Cos and Miletus which will be mentioned again later. For these categories we have to fall back on the literary texts and inscriptions.[12]

PHILOSOPHICAL AND SOCIOLOGICAL ATTITUDES

Such attitudes to trades, crafts and trade in the fifth and fourth centuries B C, and probably earlier, have conditioned the nature of the information available from ancient literary sources. First, there is the question of the occupations which best become a 'gentleman'. There was little doubt about this. He must concern himself with his estate and its cultivation, and, in favourable circumstances of politics, conservative not radical, show active participation in State affairs, including military matters, after the manner of the great Cimon in Athens. Every effort, it was felt, must be deployed to preserve that state of physical and moral quality which was summed up in the phrase *kalos kai agathos*, typified by the poet Sophocles. For leisure, field sports were the desired pursuit, and so in the *Knights* of Aristophanes[13] the reformed Demos declares that he will henceforth make the demagogues take to hunting and give up concocting decrees for the Assembly. If the political conditions were not suitable for a gentleman's participation, there were the joys of *apragmosyne*, something like the *otium cum dignitate* of the Romans, which some might interpret as the sulky withdrawal of the disgruntled man in opposition. The same idea, coupled with suitable employment for the poor and lower orders, is expressed by Isocrates[14] in describing nostalgically 'the good old days' of Athens, and the supposed fitting of 'fair pursuits and congenial labours' to men according to their circumstances, in an effort to keep them out of mischief. Isocrates says: 'They turned the needier towards farming and trade, knowing that poverty comes about through idleness, and evil-doing through poverty . . .'; on the other hand 'they compelled those who possessed sufficient means to devote themselves to horsemanship, athletics, hunting and philosophy . . .' The statement is interesting not only for the mixture of 'aristocratic' activities, which at any rate as far as philosophy is concerned need not be taken too seriously, but also for 'farming and trade' as the pursuits of the poorer class. Farming came first – that mother of sturdy men and soldiers – and here 'trade' means crafts.

The reality was no doubt different from the ideal expressed by Isocrates. It is also obvious that the ideas of extremist philosophers were quite unpractical. Thus Plato proposes[15] that citizens be excluded from the pursuit of crafts, though it must not be forgotten that the citizens in the *Laws* were of a special sort. In the same passage he lays down a number of principles which have the same import: in his ideal state, the exclusion not only of citizens, but also of the servants of citizens, from the pursuit of handicrafts, and the banning of any one individual from engaging in a multiplicity of arts and crafts. The rule is to be one man one craft, here presumably applied to aliens and slaves – and, what is of great interest, there is to be no capitalistic organization. The same attitude, in what might be called the same Socratic tradition, is expressed by Xenophon in rejecting the 'banausic' activities,[16] since they do harm both to bodies and to minds in cramping and distorting them, though in an emergency,[17] and for the womenfolk, they might be tolerated even as a source of profit from which a man could live. Another argument was put forward by Aristotle:[18] 'Again, it is noble not to practice any sordid craft, since it is the mark of a free man not to live at another's beck and call.' (It may be pointed out in parenthesis that there still exists the same Greek intolerance of partnerships and subordination in employment.) A related phenomenon is the Platonic contempt for the technicalities and terminology of the day-to-day pursuits and services which formed a large part of arts and crafts.

All this was theory, far removed from what was practical, but influencing attitudes in discussion and the sort of descriptive account on which modern writers depend for their information. It was understandable in its aim – not to deflect the citizen from his true duties and activities in the service of the State and the securing of his own moral and spiritual welfare. It was extended to the practice of trade, more particularly to retail trade rather than wholesale, because of the corrupting influence of competition and the market-place; but it led also to the condemnation of contact with the sea and mercantile trade, since mercantile communities, in part because of their pursuits and in part because of their association with foreigners, were notoriously disorderly and corrupt. Here, of course, a contradiction crept in, for while Plato would remove his community from the sea and contact with trade, Aristotle admitted that the statesman had to concern himself with such matters as imports and exports, though it was desirable to reduce this preoccupation as much as possible by aiming at self-sufficiency. Here philosophical ideas and what might have been best for Athens went hand in hand. The attitude was very different from that of Pericles, as represented by Thucydides in the speech on the greatness of Athens, which he ascribes to the statesman at the beginning of the Great Peloponnesian War.[19] In this Athens is described as the centre of a great nexus of trade-routes, and the freedom of Athens and its contacts with the rest of the Mediterranean world are contrasted with the self-imposed seclusion of Sparta. Yet even here there is a subtle suggestion of a difference, of which account must be taken, between those who administer and those who judge and approve only.

This aristocratic attitude was absorbed by those who were steeped in the philosophical tradition, even if they came many years after, and it must have impaired both their judgment and their choice of information about the Classical period. This is unfortunate since we depend so much on them. Thus Plutarch,[20] in his description of the artisan class who profited from State expenditure in the period of Pericles' building projects, calls them 'the disorderly and banausic mob'. Since little distinction was made between the practice of the arts and that of crafts, as is clear from the building inscriptions and the inclusion in them of payments to piece-workers who converted into stone the ideas of great artists, there was difficulty in reconciling the aristocratic concept with the glory and reputation, and indeed greatness, of those artists who played their part in creating the cultural distinction of Athens. It was comparatively easy to place Phidias, who, in his statue of Zeus at Olympia, not only added something to the established concept of the god, but was also a friend of the statesman Pericles. Nor were architects like Ictinus, the designer of the Parthenon, 'banausic', for they could express in their work, as musicians also could, profound philosophical and mathematical principles, which must surely approve the quality of their minds and souls. In general, however, the artist-craftsman did not readily fit into this mould. So those who had this attitude of mind were forced to adopt shifts and devices of the most patent sort. Thus in Plutarch's description[21] of the great painter Polygnotus it is said: 'He was not one of the banausic class of craftsmen, nor did he decorate the portico with paintings as a matter of paid employment, but without payment, being desirous of securing esteem from the city.' So payment is the debasing element.

Elsewhere the doctrine is propounded that admiration of a work of art does not necessarily entail admiration for the artist or craftsman who produced it. To such an attitude we owe, perhaps, the fact that though from the proverb mentioned above we know of the rivalry of potters, our knowledge of the exponents of vase-shaping and decoration comes wholly from the actual vases, except for a contemptuous reference to the makers of funeral *lekythoi*. And, despite the great artistry which Attic black- and red-figure pottery displays, the potters and painters were regarded as nothing more than minor craftsmen beneath the notice of literature.

On the other hand there is a suspicion, first, that this aristocratic attitude was noted and perhaps resented, and, second, that there was a contemporary joy in craftsmanship and a conviction of the importance of 'banausic' tasks which offset the primitive and aristocratic prejudice that was so strong even in democratic Athens. 'Even in democratic Athens' is to be stressed, because there is little or nothing, even in the Attic Comedy as it has come down to us, to offset the impressions given by the other literature. Yet, as it has been seen, potters and vase-painters could be conscious of their worth, and show their pride and rivalry with contemporaries, as the inscription 'Euphronios never did anything like this' on a vase of Euthymides appears to show. A much restored inscription from the Acropolis,[22] which recorded and accompanied the offering of a tithe to Athena perhaps in the form of a sculptured figure (compare Pl. 44), seems to refer to the advantages of having a craft (though the dedicator was unsure of his aspirates), and many years later the great poet of the New Comedy, Menander, makes an interesting comment: 'Chance sometimes makes away with our patrimony, but leaves us with our bodies; there is certainty of a livelihood in a craft.'[23] As in the case of the arts and crafts, so too in the pursuit of trade, those who gained their livelihood thus must, if they thought about it at all, have been sustained by a conviction of the importance of their activities for the life of Athens, and, indeed, may have viewed the aristocratic tradition as something outmoded and contemptible, or belonging to a different world, but they were not vocal in the literature.

CHAPTER ONE

TRADE OF THE PRE-CLASSICAL ERA

THIS PERIOD MAY BE TAKEN as commencing with the transition from the Bronze Age Mycenaean culture, therefore excluding what may be called the 'Linear B period', and ending with the first intrusion of the Persians into the Aegean.

THE SUB-MYCENAEAN AND PROTOGEOMETRIC PERIODS

The end of the thirteenth century BC and the twelfth, commonly called Late Helladic IIIC, saw the transition from a bronze- to an iron-using culture, a change not unconnected with a series of disasters which also saw the end of the elaborate form of organization of the Mycenaean period, and the destruction of its palaces.[1] Whatever the nature of the disasters which afflicted Greece – invasion, attack by roving peoples, epidemic, drought – they had wide ramifications, and the face of the eastern Mediterranean and Near East was changed. The Hittite Empire in Anatolia was destroyed, eastern Mediterranean areas were invaded by migrants, Egypt was threatened and with difficulty repelled her attackers. There was a disruption of the Bronze culture common to Greece and the eastern Mediterranean, and increased danger for land and sea travel, and an interruption of trade-routes and organized life (for how long is a moot point). There are apparent, largely from later evidence, movements of refugees from Mycenaean centres to peripheral areas of the Greek mainland or to the eastern Mediterranean, from the Peloponnese, for example, to Cyprus. In the sequel this meant improved possibilities of communications and commerce. It has also been argued[2] that communications across the Aegean were not wholly interrupted, and even that a memory of Mycenaean connections westward was retained. On the other hand, there appears to have been a decline in population and building activity, and a change in burial rites from chamber tombs to cist graves.[3] There were changes also in items of equipment that might indicate the incoming of new people, related to those of the Bronze Age. There was a tradition in Greece that a new 'invasion' or infiltration of Greeks took place at this time, the so-called

'Dorian Invasion' or 'Return of the Children of Herakles'.[4] It was once customary for archaeologists to couple this legend with the appearance of a certain form of pottery-decoration, of narrow bands, panels, stylized leaves, concentric circles and ultimately silhouette figures; also with small stylized bronze figures of men and animals, and fibulae for the fastening of woollen garments. It used to be thought that there were also certain religious innovations, with Zeus and Apollo replacing the Mother Goddess.

In recent years it has become evident that this connection of legend and material objects is illusory. It is now apparent that there is a continuity between the poorly shaped and decorated Late (Sub-) Mycenaean pottery and what followed (Pl. 1). There is a gradual development in pottery shapes and decoration from Sub-Mycenaean to Protogeometric, the preliminary stage of the 'Geometric' style, and on to Geometric, best represented by the splendid eighth-century pottery of Attica (Pl. 7). Pottery is indeed so important (it might cynically be said 'faute de mieux'!) that the successive cultural and historical periods are called Sub-Mycenaean, Protogeometric and Geometric.[5]

For trade and industry there are naturally no contemporary literary sources. In their absence they have to be replaced by inferences based on material remains, and, for the eighth and early seventh centuries, by what can be made of the Homeric poems, the *Odyssey* in particular, and Hesiod's *Works and Days*.

The pottery called Protogeometric, with its tauter outlines, in comparison with Sub-Mycenaean, and more skilfully drawn linear decoration, including compass brush-drawn concentric semi-circles, presents some problems. Formerly the material from Attica suggested that this area of Greece, traditionally dissociated from the 'Dorians', was the originator and main producer of Protogeometric pottery.[6] Consequently, when the same pottery forms and decoration appeared elsewhere, it was natural to think of Attica as the centre from which actual Attic Protogeometric pottery was disseminated. This could be related to a contemporary phenomenon, extensively treated in later historical writing: the progressive emigration of Greeks for various reasons from mainland Greece into the Aegean and across it to Asia Minor, and especially Ionia.[7] Consequently Protogeometric pottery was taken as an index of migration and trade, either being conveyed by emigrants to the coastal regions of western Asia Minor, or imported and imitated by native communities. It penetrated, for instance, as far as Sardis.[8] So it came about that this Protogeometric pottery, and Athens as its putative centre, provided the first evidence of a number of related phenomena:

a certain Athenian pre-eminence in the revival of crafts, in commercial transport and other maritime activity, and in a revival of overseas connections. Later Athenian assertions of her rôle as leader of the Ionian migration helped to strengthen these ideas.[9]

This evidence from pottery is the principal index for movement and trade in this early period from c. 1000 BC on. Other evidence, for industry, is scant. Trade in metals and the pursuit of metallurgical techniques present a confused picture. At a time when bronze metallurgy was particularly well developed and flourishing in Central Europe (and continued to be so even in the late eighth century), the Greeks are characterized for a considerable period by a limited number of iron tools and weapons.[10] The question then arises: whence came the iron and knowledge of iron metallurgy? From the North, Macedonia and beyond, formerly the prevailing view, or from north-eastern Asia Minor and the eastern Mediterranean?[11] If this latter view is accepted, it is reasonable to think of reviving trade connections, after the disasters of the end of the Mycenaean period, promoted by the settlement of Greeks along the south Asia Minor coast and in Cyprus.

The picture given here has been to some extent modified by more recent excavation and research. It appears that there were other independent centres of development of Protogeometric;[12] and that the Attic claim to pre-eminence in promoting Ionian migration must be modified in view of the literary assertions of a wide diversity of other migration across the Aegean.[13] It seems that a number of Greek states produced this Protogeometric pottery, and that many Greeks began to push abroad. Detailed study of the pottery shows at times interinfluence, and at times isolation and separate development.[14] Despite all doubts as to detail, there clearly was very appreciable progress and development in all fields, and in this Athens may have played a significant part.

THE GEOMETRIC PERIOD

The progress which marked the Protogeometric era characterized also to an increased degree the Geometric.[15] This period displays a number of important features. The basic one, of considerable relevance here, was the increased technical and artistic skill shown in some centres such as Athens and Corinth, in pottery production, with a diversification of shapes and decoration. Towards the end of the period there was also an impressive redevelopment of bronze-work,[16] especially the great three-legged tripod cauldrons with hammered bowls and cast legs[17]

(Pls 2–3). A mould for such was found at Lefkandi in Euboea. In the case of the pottery fluctuating inter-influence and contact, or isolation, can be detected. Another important feature was the increased appearance of the products of one centre at another, both in Greece, in the case of close neighbours and more distant communities, and in the wider Mediterranean world outside. So the problem which will also appear in the seventh and subsequent centuries presents itself at this earlier time. If at certain periods Attic Geometric pottery, for example, is found abroad,[18] as on the coasts of the eastern Mediterranean and inland, or in Cyprus,[19] what does this signify? Given the element of chance in its survival (and this applies later in the case of coin hoards), how far are we justified in balancing the products, mainly pottery, of one centre against another, Euboea, for example, against Attica, when seeking to determine economic developments? Do imports of pottery represent the presence of members of the state producing it in foreign parts, who wished to use the familiar products of their home state, or trade in the conventional sense? Over and above these considerations we must ask ourselves how much material justifies the use of the term 'trade', rather than the more vaguely conceived 'contact'.

With these caveats, especially the last, it is not unreasonable to attempt some form of economic interpretation. For technical skill there is the evidence of preserved objects, especially the breakable but basically indestructible pottery. For the rest we are not very well served: in metalwork, in terms of the volume of what survives, because of the menace of the melting pot and of corrosion, and in wood and textiles because of decay. For technical organization, economic practices and policy there is no real substitute for a written account, and such could not exist before the coming into being of a system of writing and the development of a historical sense. It is possible, however, with due caution to make some reasonable conjectures.

As time progresses in the Geometric period certain other important phenomena appear. The Greeks were not alone in the pursuit of trade, in the broader sense, and they were not the only craftsmen. There were other peoples. In their homeland the Greeks were subject to certain stresses. Greece was a poor country, and life was hard for the Many (hence the proverb 'Poverty is ever our familiar companion'). Political oppression of the Many by the Few existed (witness Hesiod's 'crooked counsels of princes').[20] Thus economic and political issues were inter-related. There were also the developments, due partly to increase of population, whereby a more powerful central community expanded to swallow up its weaker neighbours; while, on the other hand, two powerful states expanded their boundaries to meet in hostile confrontation.[21] In the earlier period of more limited population states could expand from a polis-centre to the surrounding more thinly occupied countryside, but ultimately communities met at frontiers, as did Boeotia and Attica, Attica and Megara (and Eleusis), Megara and Corinth, Corinth and Argos, and Argos and Sparta. So there was inter-state rivalry as well as internal strife, equally disturbing for populations. There is, on the other hand, no clear evidence of trade rivalry, as distinguished from rivalry for fertile or otherwise rich territory, the most potent means to economic advantage.

These problems could be solved by the greater production of essentials, which indirectly also touched political problems. It might be attained in two ways. The first was by the improvement of technical methods in both cultivation and manufacturing crafts. There are, perhaps, some indications for the Classical period and later, of improvements in agriculture, as seems demonstrated by the *Oeconomicus* of Xenophon (see Chapter VIII). For other aspects of economic activity there was little or nothing to show. Throughout the whole period under consideration, there is no conspicuous change or development in technological skills, except an elaboration in the division of labour produced by the needs and desires of the wealthy class, which could encourage the pursuit of luxury crafts. But such a wealthy class was limited in numbers, and, indeed, resources. There were no changes in terms of new sources of power, new tools or new materials; had there been, there would have been no possibility of the accumulation of capital to use them before the development of coinage. Even later, in the Classical period, there was no inclination to devote capital to the development of such resources as were available.[22]

If there was no prospect of improvement in this way, it might be possible for the politically and economically deprived to take themselves off elsewhere, from their native land to other areas (of the Mediterranean, for this period), where conditions were more favourable: where natural resources and fertile land were more abundant, and where those oppressed in their homeland might in turn act as oppressors of the natives. This had already happened earlier, in the Ionian Migration, and in this way one suspects that much may have been learned about increased trade and the concomitant problems of co-operating with the natives or exploiting them. There was also the possibility of producing a surplus in these areas of greater fertility, to be exported back to Greece.

Thus a period of colonization of the Mediterranean coasts developed, from the eighth century (at what point in it is disputed) into the sixth or indeed the fifth.[23] The primary purpose of this colonization is clear – to get away from Greece. The earliest area to be involved was the West, the middle Mediterranean. The impulse was different from that to the south-eastern coast of Asia Minor, Cyprus and the coast of the eastern Mediterranean, with its access routes to the Middle East and the eastern peoples. In this direction the purpose was to found trading stations, and, for the more ambitious, to carve out a principality.[24]

The situation in the middle Mediterranean was thus colonization in a substitute area for the homeland, though settlements could be trading stations with a hinterland, or staging points on a trade-route. Everything known about the Greeks in southern Italy and in Sicily[25] underlines the importance of natural commodities, in what were very fertile areas – witness the cereal grains represented later on coins. There were also timber, wool and hides. At first these resources undoubtedly served the needs of the settlers, to replace those so conspicuously meagre in Greece proper. It is arguable in what measure and how soon a surplus was exported. Then there is the question: how were they paid for, in a period before the use of coinage, although there could be silver bullion? The olive was a late arrival in Italy at any rate, though certainly exported from Attica in the seventh century. There were other things in the late eighth and seventh centuries for which Greek centres acted as importers and forwarders, from the East in particular. The iris perfume of the Adriatic might be mentioned.[26] Then there were manufactured goods – container pottery certainly. A limited amount of painted pottery makes a brave showing in an archaeological context, but represents a luxury if exported over a long distance.[27] As for other manufactures, transport problems would make it easier to export craftsmen than goods. In the case of transit commodities and manufactures, unless they were passed on at vastly inflated prices like the eastern spices and other goods of a later age, Greece would not benefit much from this trade.

It would, none the less, be difficult to deny the existence of trade, if rather haphazard in nature. Since Pithecussae (Ischia) and Cumae (on the mainland north of Naples), the earliest Greek colonies in the West, were the farthest away, they must have been determined by some factor other than settlement in a new and more favourable land. So it has been suggested[28] that Etruscan minerals provided the attraction – iron (ore) from Elba and copper from the bronze-producing area of Vetulonia. There are indications that smelting took place at Pithecussae,[29] if not at Cumae. This trade may have served only the needs of Sicily and South

Italy, but could have been extended back to Greece, though metal cargoes are heavy and Greece was not ill-provided in this category.

There are obviously sea passages, which could be 'trade-routes', determined by geographical circumstances – the easiest routes or the shortest, the best provided with transit anchorages sheltered and with water. In Antiquity, to use modern terms, sea-routes were always 'tramp-shipping' routes, disposing of cargo or picking it up wherever opportunity offered, not 'liner' routes. In addition there were land-routes, profiting from isthmus crossings, to avoid enemies entrenched on narrow seas, or difficult sea passages through such narrow seas or around dangerous headlands. There were one or more of these overland isthmus routes in South Italy from the south coast to the west coast, avoiding, possibly for political reasons and certainly for weather reasons the passage of the Straits of Messina.[30]

How the Greeks knew of these Central Mediterranean lands is a question that has frequently been debated. Too much stress in this particular case need not be laid on storm-driven mariners like Odysseus. There were no doubt bold adventurers, who cut straight across the Ionian Sea, but again too much must not be made of the Columbus image. Geography was helpful in this western passage, out of the Corinthian Gulf northwards to Ithaca and Corcyra (Corfu),[31] north of west to the heel of Italy, then south-westwards to the Straits of Messina and eastern Sicily, or through the straits and north, or by portage across Bruttium, to the west coast of Italy. It might require greater boldness to sail up the Adriatic beyond Corfu, in an area where there were few ports on the west, and where the Bora wind blew and there were pirates. In this region there might not have been a great deal of mercantile activity (trade with the Po Valley came later). On the other hand, in the later eighth century, a renewal of skill in bronze technology[32] appears (cf. the Argive panoply, Pl. 10), which could have come by way of the northern Adriatic from Central Europe, which implies travel if not trade. In the seventh and sixth centuries the west Balkan coast and interior were connected with Corinth through Apollonia and Dyrrhacium. This coast was later very notorious for piracy, but pirates did not have to prey on extensive long-distance trade, and therefore need not imply the existence of the latter; piracy could be directed at first to coastal trade, of the Hesiodic type, which of necessity existed in areas where travel by land was made difficult by mountainous and indented country.[33] For the most part this northern Adriatic connection belongs to a later period.[34]

The Greek knowledge of the route to southern Italy and Sicily was acquired by coastal exploration via Ithaca and Corcyra, which was pushed gradually farther west. Some bold spirits may have ventured or been blown straight across the Ionian Sea, but adventures like those of Colaeus the Phocaean belong rather to the open Mediterranean and to its western part beyond Sicily, Italy and Sardinia (always of interest to the Greeks), to the south coast of France and the east coast of Spain. These areas, however, like Emporium in North Spain, resembling the more attractive parts of Greece, were not opened up until the foundation of Massilia (Marseilles) *c.* 600 BC by the Phocaeans. The chief attraction may have been true trade – for instance the trans-Gaul tin-route, not just colonial settlement – particularly up the Rhône, until the Carthaginians and Etruscans applied a kind of *mare clausum* ('closed sea') policy. By this route, possibly, the Vix krater came to Burgundy.[35]

A much debated issue, perhaps of inflated importance, in this western movement is that summed up in the catch phrase: does 'the flag follow trade', or 'trade the flag'? In other words, does the limited amount of early pottery either carried from Greece or imitated in the West represent pre-colonial exploration?[36] It will be seen that the conclusion depends on the date accepted for the earliest colonization.[37] Otherwise it has to be admitted there was no more than exploration, a conclusion based on logical grounds. The terminology used is a good illustration of Professor Finley's contention[38] that modern politico-economic terms are wrongly used for Early and Classical Greek economics. There was no 'flag'; and the primitive conveyance of goods, the nature and volume of which are really unknown, cannot be dignified by the term 'trade'.

The contact of 'pre-colonial' Greeks and 'colonial' Greeks with the natives of Italy and Sicily is more interesting.[39] 'Pre-colonial' explorers or pioneers, as they might better be called, must have encountered the natives, and this contact could be registered by the influence on native crafts of the products which the pioneer 'explorers' brought with them. When, in their wake, colonists arrived, it was natural for the natives to withdraw into their own communities, some into the interior, and to trade with the incomers to the advantage of both. In one case this appears not to have happened to any great degree – the Spartan colony of Tarentum seems to have made little contact with the natives of their area of South Italy.[40] This was an importation to the West of Spartan exclusiveness and contempt of 'natives'.

These questions are perhaps less important than the appearance of an alien people, the Phoenicians, who developed their activities and influence in the Mediterranean side by side with that of the Greeks, from the ninth century, or before, into the seventh.

The Phoenicians[41] were a Canaanite people strategically placed north of the kingdom of Israel and on the Mediterranean, but connected via Ezion-Geber with the Red Sea, whence came 'ivory, apes and peacocks'.[42] From the Red Sea and East Africa came the clam shells (*tridachna*) and ostrich egg-shells which, widely distributed, seem to indicate a Phoenician connection. The Old Testament tradition made of them skilled craftsmen, traders and shipmen, aiding Solomon in the building of his temple. The later (eighth–seventh century) *Odyssey* spoke of them as traders, pirates and kidnappers, dealing in luxury goods. They were skilled in metalwork, ivory-carving, textiles and embroidery. Important examples of their skill were silver-gilt bowls (Pl. 5) with concentric bands of figure and landscape decoration, reflected in the Homeric Shield of Achilles,[43] which have Assyrianizing and Egyptianizing motifs reflecting the geographical position of Phoenicia between them. Later tradition,[44] which should be treated with reserve (see below nn. 62, 64), represented them as early voyagers in the Mediterranean, establishing themselves *c.* 1100 BC at Utica, well before the traditional foundation of Carthage in 814 BC, at Hadrumetum at some early date, and at Gades outside the Straits of Gibraltar.

The best of Phoenician products are connected with the Assyrian palaces[45] and others elsewhere,[46] but ivory-carving and metalwork also travelled west to the great religious centres such as Olympia, to Samos and north to Thasos (witness the ivory lion-heads, from a throne? found there).[47] This carving was imitated in Greece in the same precious material by Greek craftsmen or produced by immigrants from the East. Examples, probably of adapted Greek style, are the nude female figures found in late Geometric Attica.[48] The craftsmen who made them travelled farther west to Etruria. Here, in addition to ivory-carving, there is splendid metalwork, to be dated to the late eighth and earlier seventh centuries, suggesting a Phoenician, east Anatolian and north Syrian/Assyrian connection. This bronze-work, also present in Greece and some of it coming from Cyprus, takes the form particularly of cauldrons to be set on separate conical supports, unlike the Greek Geometric tripods mentioned earlier (Pl. 2). These cauldrons had ring-handles carried in mounts, some in the form of bulls' heads, others with human-headed birds ('sirens'). Other cauldrons had attachments with long-necked lion-heads or griffin-heads (Pl. 4), which present a number of archaeological problems,[49] especially concerning eastern originals and Greek imitations. For the present theme the originals and the imitations represent an important artistic and trade link between the Orient and the Central Mediterranean. The nature of this link requires consideration.

Phrygia in west-central Asia Minor was an important bronze-working area in touch with those just named.[50] Some of the bronzes from the East may have come to the Greeks through Phrygia until its overthrow by the Cimmerians *c.* 700 BC, and subsequently through the Lydians who replaced them. This would be a stage on what was later the Royal Road of the Persians, westward through Sardis to Ephesus. Exports from eastern Anatolia (Urartu), at any rate, could also pass across the Pontic Mountains to Trapezus on the Euxine (the Black Sea in modern terms), and so by sea to the Aegean and possibly up the Danube into Europe. Finally, there was the most important route from Urartu south-westwards by way of Bitlis and Diyabakr, and through northern Syria to the region of some of the later Hittite principalities, across the Amanus Pass to the north-western part of Syria and so to the Mediterranean. There contact was made with the Greeks coming from the West[51] who could convey these eastern products in parallel with the Phoenicians via Cyprus to Rhodes, Crete and Greece proper. This route and its continuation farther west to Italy and Sicily was not the open sea one of the Roman period (what might be called 'the route of St Paul'), but that through the Aegean and across the isthmus of Corinth. It is easy to exaggerate the importance of the Corinthian device (the *diolkos*) which was used from the beginning of the sixth century BC to transport small ships across the isthmus. A depôt at Corinth for Phoenician and other oriental goods between the eastern Corinthian port of Cenchreae and the western port of Lechaeum was the natural arrangement, with Corinth as a nodal point. Corinth clearly acquired some oriental characteristics, from dealing in perfumes to sacred prostitution!

Cyprus, with the Semitic settlement of Citium on the south coast, established probably in the latter part of the ninth century,[52] had considerable significance on the route westwards from the eastern Mediterranean. It was a centre of Phoenician influence, which appears elsewhere in the island. On the east coast was Cypriote Salamis, traditionally a very early Greek foundation, with chamber-tombs of the eighth–seventh centuries containing Greek pottery, including Attic Geometric.[53] Not very far away was Enkomi-Alasia with its horned god, believed to be another early foundation of the thirteenth century. Cyprus, from the tenth century or earlier down to the Classical period, was divided between Semite and Greek, as it is now at the present day between Greek and Muslim Turk. Here, if anywhere, there would be commercial rivalry. On the mainland of Cilicia was Tarsus, also affording evidence of the trade-route,[54] in an area (like north Syria and the region southward), open to Assyrian aggression and domination. Farther west were the outstandingly important centres of Rhodes and Crete.[55] Rhodes has clear oriental connections; probably the Phoenicians got this far at an early date. In Crete the finds from the Idaean Cave show a particular oriental link; they consist of ivories and bronze ornamental shields.[56] Some of the shields are clearly oriental – imports or the work of expatriate oriental craftsmen (the same is true of some Cretan jewellery), others Greek, of eastern style or wholly Greek.[57] Here there are problems of date, and we may be moving into the seventh century. For the artistic importance of Crete the Cretan Protogeometric, Geometric and 'Orientalizing' periods are equally significant. It is difficult to think they do not reflect a craft and trading activity.

How far west the Phoenicians penetrated and when is debatable: by the beginning of the seventh century, probably, to Crete and Rhodes.[58] They, and no doubt other east Mediterranean seagoers, made their impact on Greek tradition at this time. This is excellently illustrated by the story of Eumaeus, Odysseus' faithful swineherd,[59] son of the king of Syrie, somewhere in the West. He was kidnapped by Phoenicians with the connivance of his Phoenician nurse. In the story there are many touches which reflect what has been said of the activities and character of the Phoenicians. They bring 'countless jewels in a black ship'. These rare works of art appear elsewhere in the *Odyssey*, such as the silver bowl with gold rim which Menelaus promised to Telemachus at Sparta.[60] It was, indeed, the work of the divine smith Hephaestus, but this was the measure of its quality as a gift to Menelaus from a king of Sidon. We may also believe that Phoenician or related work was in mind in the description of the gifts which the Suitors brought to Penelope: a splendid embroidered robe with gold fastenings, a gold necklace with amber beads, ear-rings 'with three globes in mulberry fashion' and another necklet.[61] The stress is on craftsmanship in precious materials, a taste displayed also in the eighth–seventh centuries by the Etruscans.[62]

The Phoenicians must have made their way to the western Mediterranean, to areas other than North Africa. There is perhaps a tendency to put this western penetration too early (even for the Aegean and Greece). To the west the foundation of Carthage was placed in 814 BC; however, the earliest finds are nearly a century later, but possibly subsequent occupation has obliterated the earlier.[63] The finds of incised ivories in Spain at Carmona (Pl. 6) near Seville[64] are not as early as some would put them; an example of the same style (by the same hand?) has been found at Samos in a seventh-century context.[65] The Phoenicians were also very interested in Sardinia where, apart from representations of warriors who look much like the Shardana of late Bronze Age Egyptian reliefs, much 'oriental' material has been found. Scarabs which may have been carried by them have also been found in Pithecussae.[66] Probably Phoenicians and Greeks ran neck and neck in a western direction; but in some cases the Greeks were first, as in Sicily, and it was later that the Phoenicians established themselves in the west of the island through pressures in their homeland.

The Greeks were particularly interested in the Phoenicians. It was in their remote past that they placed the legendary figure of Cadmus, who, in his quest for his sister Europa, came to Greece, founded Thebes and introduced the alphabet. The mythological date was incorrect, but the Greeks had in fact obtained their alphabet from the Phoenicians. They regarded the historical Phoenicians as having frequented places in Greece indicated by the worship of the Tyrian Herakles. They also connected them with mining activities as in the island of Thasos in the north Aegean. The *Odyssey* reflected their attitude. They were not admirers of the Phoenicians, who must often have outsmarted them. As pirates themselves, on the other hand, the Greeks could hardly have disapproved of the easterners' activities. They certainly admired their craft skills. It would be wrong to speak of trade rivalry, except possibly in Cyprus. It was not really a characteristic of the Greeks who understood that seafaring and trading constituted a free-for-all with no holds barred.

The Phoenicians, because of their geographical position, moved westwards, by sea. The Greeks, centrally placed, moved both east and west. Later came their movement to the northern Aegean, to the Black Sea and its approaches, to Egypt and North Africa. The western movement has been discussed, and the Greeks in the northern Adriatic and in the far west will be considered later.

In the other direction the routes in the eastern Mediterranean used by the Phoenicians could also be followed eastwards by the Greeks. That was particularly true of the route which went across the Aegean and by way of Crete, Rhodes, Cyprus and Cilicia (Tarsus) to the Syrian coast. The presence of early Greek pottery does not necessarily mean the presence of Greeks; Phoenicians and others returning to their homeland could have taken it back with them. There is, however, sufficient evidence from points on the east Mediterranean coast and inland to indicate the actual settlement of Greeks (there is Assyrian reference to them).[67] It has been suggested that an upper limit of date is given by the site of Tell Sukas for the presence of Greek traders on the north Syrian coast.[68] The site also underlines the particular hazard in the eastern Mediterranean presented by the Assyrians, whose shadow lay not only over Syria, but also over Cilicia and ultimately Cyprus. Tell Sukas was destroyed *c.* 850 BC in the campaigns of Shalmanezer III in 853–844 BC.[69] These were followed by peace until the reconquest of Tiglath – Pileser III in 746–727 BC. There was another interval until the revolt of the Levantine cities and its suppression by Sargon II in 720 BC, and the revolt in Cilicia in 696 BC, supported by the Greeks at Tarsus, which was followed by its destruction by Sennacherib. If it be borne in mind that around 700 BC and later, eastern Anatolia suffered from the nomadic Cimmerians and the Assyrians, it will be apparent that life and commerce in the eastern Mediterranean was from time to time extremely disturbed, and it is surprising that some success attended the enterprises of the Greeks in this area.

The site of Al Mina at the mouth of the Orontes in Syria is particularly important.[70] It was characterized by warehouses rather than habitations, which have not survived, and by important pottery finds, the earliest of which come from Euboea and the Cyclades, showing Attic influence; there is also some Attic pottery.[71] The settlement, therefore, matches the Euboean activity in the West, but might be somewhat earlier. The Euboeans were clearly pioneers in both directions. In Level VIII at Al Mina there is destruction to be connected with the revolt and its suppression by Sargon II mentioned above, which seems to be marked by two other phenomena: the disappearance of the import of Greek pottery inland, and the foundation of Phoenician Motya in western Sicily, *c.* 720–710 BC, as a refugee settlement arising from these east Mediterranean events.[72] Again, warehouses were reconstructed at Al Mina soon after 700 BC, which might be connected with the punitive action of Sennacherib.

Around the end of the eighth century ceramic evidence pointing to the presence of the Euboeans seems to disappear, perhaps as the result of the Lelantine War between Chalcis and Eretria over the plain between them, in which other Greek states may have participated, in a series of 'colonial' and other rivalries.[73] Euboean pottery was replaced by Corinthian and East Greek, and certainly in East and West there now begins a period of prominence for the ceramic products of Corinth. This is abundantly clear in centres such as Syracuse, especially involving the perfume vessels or *aryballoi* (Pl. 11). These, coming from burials particularly at Syracuse, coupled with Thucydides' relative dates for the

Sicilian colonies from the earliest one (Sicilian Naxos),[74] have provided an archaeological framework which could also be applied to other areas, colonial and non-colonial. Some of the Sicilian dates have been called into question, with the placing, for instance of Megara Hyblaea earlier than Syracuse,[75] but this does not materially affect the present theme. These perfume vessels contained aromatic substances coming from the east via Rhodes or the well-known iris root (orris) perfume which probably came from the Adriatic.[76]

The problem of the Euboeans, Al Mina and the Lelantine War underlines an important issue. The effects of the war on trade links should not be admitted without reservations. There may have been a shift of trade-routes, or a further development of Corinth as a centre of maritime exchange. Pottery styles may come and go as a result of changes of fashion or other factors hard to define: witness the reduction of Attic pottery abroad which characterizes the seventh century except in the case of Aegina; while in the sixth century Corinthian pottery is greatly reduced abroad and Attic is increased. This can hardly be ascribed to a reduction of the importance of Corinth as a centre of trade. There is a tendency also to think of maritime trade as to and from Greece, yet there is no reason to think that Greeks did not engage in carrying trade in certain areas, particularly the eastern Mediterranean, which were entirely divorced from Greek lands proper. Such is the explanation which best accounts for the storehouses of Al Mina.[77]

Before discussing the problems of the seventh century, there is one important question in relation to Athens and Attica to be considered. Something has been said about oriental products and craftsmen in Greek lands,[78] not only bronze work and ivories but also jewellery, such as that from the Khaniale Tekke tomb near Cnossus.[79] Fine objects were not confined to Crete: there are the dedications found in the sanctuary of Hera on Samos and the splendid ivory lion-heads found on Thasos, to mention only two sites. They belong mostly, but not exclusively to the seventh century. The presence of oriental objects and craftsmen inspired local Greek craftsmen in bronze-work, ivory-carving and possibly wood-carving, and in the production of fine jewellery, especially gold head-bands, the earlier of late Geometric style, the later of seventh-century orientalizing.[80] The occurrence of impressive gold jewellery in later eighth-century burials in Athens and Attica[81] is of great interest. The contents of these burials, including the gold jewellery, are indicative of wealth. From what source did it come? Attica, it has been seen, had long been prominent as a centre of the manufacture of Geometric pottery, which, in the last third of the eighth century, particularly in Attica (to a lesser degree in Corinth), showed not only linear decoration but also silhouette figure pictures[82] (Pl. 7). These comprise scenes of lying-in-state, chariot processions, files of warriors, dancers and the like. In addition there are what appear to be sea-battles (Pl. 8), men swimming in a fish-infested sea, and in one case a man bestriding an overturned ship (Pl. 9). A later parallel is the Aristonothos krater, with a sea-battle of warriors. Some of these pictures are of everyday life, others may be epic themes. The largest of these Attic Geometric vessels were used as grave monuments. It seems they were 'custom-made', and it has been suggested that the subjects somehow related to the activities in life of the dead noblemen.[83] In certain cases the maritime scenes indirectly have trade as their basis. Some ships look like warships and suggest a form of naval activity. So piracy has been suggested as a pursuit of the Athenian nobles on occasions; hence their wealth. If there was piracy, then there was maritime trade to prey upon, though it need not be more than coasting trade of the Hesiodic type. However this may be, these Attic representations subsequently disappeared and Attic seventh-century pottery knows them no more. Athenian maritime strength suffered some reverse, perhaps defeat in a war with Aegina.[84] From the late eighth century – if pottery found abroad means trade – then Corinth was supreme as trader, or as a transit centre, and even as a naval power – witness a Corinthian mixing bowl depicting an oared ship (Pl. 12) (there is also a picture of a two-masted ship). Athens, on the other hand, had no part in the colonizing or other overseas activity in either the western or eastern Mediterranean.

THE SEVENTH CENTURY

The eighth century saw the development of the Greek city states. This continued in the seventh. For this period an increased number of sources become available, some contemporary, but most of later date. With the beginning of the seventh century comes the *Odyssey* – in effect as a source backward-looking; while the *Works and Days* of Hesiod, the poems of the great Archilochus (sadly fragmentary), the elegiac and lyric poets of the late seventh century, including Alcman of Sparta, provide contemporary evidence.

Historical themes characteristic of the seventh century[85] consist of the development of the hoplite battle line with its middle-class, property and other socio-economic implications, and the appearance of tyranny in the leading Greek states, but not yet in Athens. Whilst the

development of the hoplite soldier organization is only indirectly connected with trade and industry, the tyranny is generally thought to
have more bearing on it. Also characteristic of the seventh century,
and continuing into the sixth, is the further great development of
pottery; followed by three-dimensional works of art in bronze,
filling out the Geometric austerity, wood, ivory and terracotta, and
there was incised decoration on metal, like the celebrated Crowe
corselet (Pl. 16) with its floral patterns and human figures. 'Source-
investigation' (*Quellenforschung*) in art history can frequently be as
suspect as in literature or history. It is, however, impossible to deny the
mixture of styles which can be detected in the seventh century and on
into the Classical period. They argue the mobility of craftsmen. The
Crowe corselet, the work of a Cretan artist operating in the Peloponnese,[86] is a case in point. Furthermore, it symbolizes the increased
complications of inter-state relations in the seventh century.

This is also indicated by a multiplicity of pottery styles in leading
centres in Greece, in Italy and Sicily, in the islands of the Aegean, as
well as in coastal Asia Minor. These include the 'Wild Goat Style' in
Asia Minor, 'Melian', 'Naxian', and 'Parian', with Cretan in the Aegean,
together with Protocorinthian and Corinthian (Pls 14–15), Argive,
Laconian, Protoattic (Pl. 13) and the earliest Attic black-figure (Pl. 18),
on the mainland. These groups of pottery with their inter-relations
reflect the influence of oriental art – contrast the austere Attic Geometric (Pl. 7) with the following Protoattic (Pl. 13). These pottery
styles or most of them[87] appear particularly in burials throughout the
Mediterranean world, especially Etruria, and in temple dedications.
Corinthian is predominant; Attic as yet appears rarely outside Attica.

It would be foolish to overstress the 'trade' aspect of this pottery
evidence, but some significant points can be made. Corinth, where an
aristocracy replaced an enfeebled kingship, became a centre of industry
and trade. This does not necessarily imply that the Corinthians themselves travelled abroad, but it does indicate that they were entrepren-
eurs at home. There is very clear evidence of mass production in
pottery, some of it quite execrable, and so, doubtless, in other things.
Then, around the mid-seventh century, the Bacchiad aristocracy was
overthrown by the tyrant dynasty of the Cypselids (657–584 BC), and
some of them went into exile, like Demaratus.[88] They displayed their
interest in the West and, by implication, in trade. They were involved
with Corcyra, and other centres in the Adriatic, and later Corinthian
connections with the east coast of that sea and inland are demonstrated
by the bronze vessels from Trebenište[89] and other sites in what is now

Yugoslavia. At Perachora, on a peninsula north of Corinth across the gulf, there were shrines of Hera of the Headland and Hera of the Harbour, where shipmen, before they set out on their voyage to the West, may have consulted an oracle,[90] and certainly dedicated Corinthian pottery, and other styles in a much lesser degree, sometimes of a very cheap and nasty sort! They need not have been Corinthian merchants; they were seafarers who passed across the isthmus from Cenchreae to Lechaeum, the two ports of Corinth. If their ships were small enough they could be drawn over the isthmus on a sort of 'railway' (the *diolkos*; see above p. 28), thus avoiding Cape Malea in the south, from the rounding of which there might be no return. Too much importance, however, should not be attached to this device, since it may rather have been intended to switch warships from the Saronic Gulf to the Corinthian and thus husband a limited fleet.

In this Corinth-dominated period there is extensive evidence of mass-production in Corinthian pottery (Pl. 15) with an eventual disappearance of that good taste which characterized in a large measure the period down to about 625 BC (Pl. 14). Throughout the seventh century and into the sixth there is the abundant production of perfume containers, but also a large amount of pottery devoted to drinking: mixing-bowls, amphorae, cups, especially cups in the earlier sixth-century slipshod style, and *skyphoi*. There is little or no information on plain pottery containers. As noted above this period sees the appearance of a great variety of other fabrics, East Greek and Aegean. Some of these display, as time passes, the same decline in quality as Corinthian pottery does; elongated animals obviously show the same urge, as in Corinthian, to fill space with the least possible effort.

A feature of the second half of the seventh century was a widening sea-going activity: a continuation of the opening-up of the north Aegean; intensified penetration of the Black Sea and its approaches; the securing of a Greek foothold in Egypt, and the establishment of Cyrene and subsidiary settlements on the coast of North Africa. At the turn of the century Athens once again comes into prominence.

In the northern Aegean area a number of settlements were established in Macedonia and Thrace; the dates of the foundations are frequently uncertain. The interest of Paros in the northern island of Thasos and the mainland opposite, as reflected in the fragmentary works of Archilochus belongs to an early date in the century. However unlikely it may seem that at this early date, long before the introduction of silver coinage, the concern was with mining, it could have been so, since in Attica mining activity can be pushed back much earlier than was formerly believed. Later, mining was important in Thasos and on the mainland among the native tribes of Macedonia and Thrace.[91] There was probably a quest for fertile land, in abundance on the mainland, though Archilochus sounds a great deal less than enthusiastic about Thasos. Later corn and timber were exported from the mainland, and there was wine in Thasos and elsewhere. A particular part in this northern colonization was played by Chalcis, so that the three-pronged peninsula in eastern Macedonia was called Chalcidice; the Greeks from Asia Minor also participated. Corinth, probably at the end of the century, founded Potidaea in Chalcidice at the eastern end of a trans-Balkan route from Corinthian centres on the Adriatic. This north Aegean area was later affected by hostility between Thasos and Athens, and between Greeks and the native tribes. This tension appears earlier in the poems of Archilochus, as do other hostilities, e.g. between Paros and Naxos, and involving certain of the northern settlements.[92] It would be an error to call these 'trade wars'. They were, rather, struggles for 'living space', which the Greeks badly needed.

The Black Sea area may have been entered first overland (by an isthmus route in fact), if the original foundation dates of the south Black Sea colonies are to be accepted.[93] In that case they must have been overrun by the nomad Cimmerians and refounded. Miletus was the main pioneer in this activity, for which the reasons are debatable. The Ionian Greeks possessed fertile land of their own, and it is not certain they required corn from abroad. There was, probably, an expansion of population in Ionia, both Greek and native, and consequently a need for more living space. There was also pressure from the interior, from the Lydians. In this particular example of colonial activity requirements of trade cannot be discounted even from the beginning. Some of the Asia Minor cities were the natural out-ports of the interior. The Milesians, even at this early date, were active in the production of woollen goods, and required in addition the natural products of the Black Sea area, for instance iron; and, if they did not themselves require the product of the rich cornlands of the western and northern Black Sea, they could trade corn with other needier areas of Greece. Whatever the reasons this colonization assumed a remarkable magnitude.

Trade clearly gave the impetus in the eastern Mediterranean. Activity continued at Al Mina. An important East Greek presence is apparent until 600 BC, but after that date the evidence of occupation is slight.[94] The reason may have been a development at Tell Sukas, or the events of the latter part of the seventh century in the Middle East – yet the fall of Assyria and its replacement by the Babylonians can hardly have been anything but an advantage. At Tarsus and other sites Corinthian and East Greek pottery appears.

The important new venture was in Egypt. In the sixties of the seventh century Carians and Greeks, 'the bronze men from the sea', had entered the country to aid the establishment of the Twenty-sixth Dynasty under Psammetichus I.[95] About the same time the Milesians established a trading post, 'the Milesian fort'. Somewhat later, perhaps in the thirties, a number of Greek states from Asia Minor, together with Aegina, developed Naucratis in the Delta as a trading centre.[96] In 631 BC Battus, from the island of Plataea off the coast, founded Cyrene, ultimately, in effect, from Sparta and Thera.[97] This was a colony proper, not a trading post, in a fertile area of North Africa. Subsequently other settlements were established to form the Libyan Pentapolis. This area flourished under the Battiad dynasty, and it is significant that a cup in the Laconian style shows a king of Cyrene supervising the loading of a ship, probably with wool (Pl. 21).

As well as this colonization of North Africa, Greeks turned their attention to the far west, into which Colaeus of Samos had been blown against his will as he sailed in the southern Mediterranean in the second half of the seventh century. He ultimately got to Tartessus outside the Straits of Gibraltar, where, we are told,[98] he discovered 'an untouched market' and, we may suspect, guileless natives. It should be pointed out here that, if this is true, he got there before the Carthaginians or Phoenicians (see above, p. 32) He brought back a fine cargo of silver to Samos, and the indication of his success was the dedication of a great cauldron in the temple of Hera – the type of monument which facilitated the recording of these early adventures.

Herodotus,[99] in his account of the attacks of the Persian general Harpagus on the Greek cities of Asia Minor after the defeat of Croesus of Lydia by Cyrus the Persian, says of the Phocaeans: 'Now the Phocaeans were the first of the Greeks who performed long voyages, and it was they who made the Greeks acquainted with the Adriatic and with Tyrrhenia, with Iberia and the city of Tartessus.' The main comment on the Phocaeans must, however, come in an account of the sixth century.

Before discussing the problems of the sixth century, there are three points to consider. First, the idea of a merchant class has often been particularly linked with the rise of tyranny: a class seeking to assert itself against aristocratic rule, under the leadership of an individual without kingly antecedents. But such an idea lacks all logic: in a transitional period whence could merchants, their goods and their capital come, except from the aristocratic families of the pre-tyrant stage, 'the younger sons' in fact? And it is to be suspected that trade, except in connection with certain crafts, meant to a very large extent the disposal of surpluses from aristocratic estates.

However this may be, one notable development, ultimately of great economic importance, had its inception in the seventh century. This was the introduction of coinage:[100] the stamping of portions of a precious metal of standard weight and fineness with the device of a recognized authority. It is generally agreed, in accordance with the Greek tradition, that it was first introduced in Asia Minor by the Lydians, or some of the Greek cities, in the second half of the seventh century (Pls 17a–c). The invention was taken up in mainland Greece at some later date by the Aeginetans (Pl. 17d) and Corinthians (Pl. 17e) but not so early as was once believed.[101] In Asia Minor the earliest coinages were of electrum (an amalgam of gold and silver), but in Greece of silver, and it is a nice point how far Attica or North Greece supplied the metal. The Aeginetan and Corinthian coinages came into being probably some time in the first half of the sixth century, earlier than that of Athens which may have started in the second half of that century under the Pisistratid tyranny. To what extent the use of coinage led to internal economic difficulties is debatable. Indeed the reasons for its introduction are obscure:[102] payment of mercenaries, the means of levying on merchants dues on imports and exports, or the facilitation of trade in general, but whatever the reason the development of coinage made possible the accumulation and transmission of wealth in a way previously impossible.

The third point concerns the situation of Athens and Attica.[103] Athens, which had played some ill-defined part in maritime affairs in the latter part of the eighth century, fell into obscurity in the seventh, apart from a splendid pottery style, mainly funerary, and hardly ever exported except to Aegina.[104] The decline does not seem to be connected either with the development of the hoplite army or with tyranny. Athens appears to have played no part in colonization, and to have become an inward-looking agricultural state, particularly suited to the growing of the olive, and possessed of a great asset in the form of argentiferous lead ore.[105] Her potters and vase-painters possessed great skill.

Then, in the third quarter of the seventh century and later, problems appeared: attempted tyranny, an oppressive codification of the customary law, and war with neighbouring Megara. It is apparent from the poems of Solon[106] that there were economic problems. He was a statesman of the earliest sixth century, a man of the middle way, and concerned himself with these troubles arising from issues of land tenure and personal debt-bondage, which inflamed relations between the nobility and the rest. Why a relatively sudden crisis of this sort should come upon Athens has been much debated. Apart from the effects of the war with Megara, the noble landowners of Attica were perhaps anxious to increase their estates at the expense of their poorer brethren – the intention being to export as much corn as possible to infertile states like Aegina and Corinth, to add to the supplies which, it is supposed, were imported from Egypt, particularly by the Aeginetans. An export issue, therefore. It is generally agreed also that olive oil in the plain clay 'SOS' amphorae was exported from Athens. It appears increasingly clear that Attic silver from the Laurium mines acquired importance earlier than was once thought.

THE SIXTH CENTURY AND THE EARLY FIFTH
(TO THE PERSIAN INVASIONS)

At this point (c. 600 BC), thanks largely to the survival of considerable fragments of Solon's verse dealing with the problems he faced and his attempts at solving them, Athens very largely takes the front of the stage and retains it throughout the Classical period. Many efforts have been made to interpret Solon's economic policy; it need not be supposed that he himself clearly understood the trend of economic processes. The fact that he forbade the export of all natural products except those of the olive would seem to connect with the previous undue export of corn mentioned above. He clearly regarded olives as an important cash crop suited to the soil of Attica. Attic wine, it may be added, was of little account. Olive planting and cultivation were something of a rich man's or moderately rich man's investment. For the rank and file of the Athenian populace he did what he thought right, freeing them by 'the shaking-off of burdens' from the oppression of debt, serfdom and slavery, but he took no notice of the cry for a redistribution of land (gēs anadasmos). It could well be that he regarded small-holding cultivation as uneconomic and small-scale corn-production as equally so; they none the less remained as the basis of the Athenian economy. Consequently the impoverished people among the Athenians, if they would not serve as hired labourers, had to find some other source of livelihood, in the pursuit of crafts. Solon apparently imported craftsmen. He certainly imported non-Athenians whose citizen status was later held to be dubious. These craftsmen may have produced, and taught Athenians to produce, a variety of manufactured goods. As ever, only pottery survives. In its development from Proto-attic (Pl. 13) in the earlier seventh century to the early monumental black-figure (Pl. 18), there is an increasing suggestion of Corinthian influence, and this is augmented to such an extent that Attic pottery of the latter part of the seventh century and the early sixth shows strong Corinthian characteristics (Pl. 19). The next stage (Pl. 20), from the time of the artist Sophilos,[107] was for Attic pottery to appear abroad, in Greece, and farther afield, for instance at Caere in Etruria. From about the seventies of the sixth century to an ever-increasing degree Attic pottery replaced in foreign markets what were more and more slipshod Corinthian products, clearly mass-produced. There are some large figured pots with mythological scenes made in Corinth, which show quality, but some of these significantly adopt the red-ground character-istic of Athenian pottery from the mid-sixth century or even earlier, just as later Corinthian vase-painters imitated Attic red-figure. The linear-decorated pottery, however, could still maintain a high standard.

This growing presence of Attic pottery overseas, a fine example of which is illustrated in Pl. 22, from the second quarter of the sixth century to the earlier part of the fourth will be further discussed when dealing with the Classical period.[108] It is important to see its significance clearly. A high degree of skill in craftsmanship, of aliens in some cases, and possibly even of slaves, is indicated, which one must suppose was paralleled in other crafts where the products have perished. It does not mean that Athenian merchants carried the wares of Athens to all parts of the Mediterranean world, to the Black Sea, into Asia Minor and the east Mediterranean, to Italy, Sicily, Gaul and Spain. It does mean that merchants passed by way of the Piraeus, collected wares there and pas-sed on farther to East and West.[109] In the Classical period there was a great diversity in these merchants, not all reputable (witness the scoundrelly Phaselite traders in the fourth century), and in their ports of call. The situation was certainly similar in the earlier period.

In the late seventh century, and in the sixth, the interest in the far west and the north Adriatic is of considerable importance. While it is true that the mention of 'Enetic coursers' in the *Partheneion* of Alcman of Sparta[110] does not refer to the horses of the Veneti at the head of the Adriatic, it would be surprising if bold Greeks did not penetrate so far. In the next generation the choral lyric poet Stesichorus of Himera[111] composed his *Geryoneis* which dealt with a far-western Labour of Herakles (the Oxen of Geryon). Stesichorus is also said to have known of the silver mines of Tartessus (beyond the Pillars of Herakles). The adventure of Colaeus of Samos in this direction has already been mentioned, and the reference of Herodotus[112] to the far-western interest of the Phocaeans of Ionia: 'it was they who made the Greeks acquainted with the Adriatic and with Tyrrhenia, with Iberia and the city of Tartessus'. Around 600 BC they founded Massilia in southern Gaul and other settlements such as Nicaea (Nice). To a certain extent this was land-settlement and the same would be true of Ampurias (Emporium) in Spain, perhaps the result of a desire on the part of the Eastern Greeks, to get away from their oriental neighbours. They must, however, have perceived the trade possibilities up the Rhône and through various portages to the other Gallic river-routes and from Ampurias into the interior of Spain.[113] Thus a Phocaean trade-route from Asia Minor led across the Aegean and the Isthmus of Corinth to the West. Later, possibly in 564 BC, the Phocaeans founded Alalia in Corsica (Cyrnus), and later again, as a result of the defeat of Croesus by Cyrus and the campaign of Harpagus, more Phocaeans went to Alalia, where 'five years of plundering and pillaging' provoked attack from the Carthaginians and Etruscans, resulting in what was effectively a defeat (539 BC) and retirement, first to Rhegium and then to Velia in southern Italy. This hostility may have been provoked by the plundering propensities of the Phocaeans: later, after the defeat of Lade inflicted on the Ionians by the Persians in the Ionian Revolt, Dionysius of Phocaea fled to Sicily and directed his piratical activities against the same adversaries.[114] The plundering may have been provoked by the Carthaginians and Etruscans seeking to operate a *mare clausum* policy against the Greeks, which ended in the battle of Himera (Sicily), 480BC.

Such a trade-route between East and West with many potential mercantile centres accounts for the pottery which comes from temple dedications and grave groups, and provides an index of other goods conveyed. In the second half of the seventh century and in the sixth it shows an amazing diversity. The main constituent is first Corinthian and then Attic, but there is a variety of other styles in a lesser degree: East Greek 'Wild Goat Style', Cretan, Chiot, Samian (Fikellura), Laconian (Pl. 21), including the curious black-glazed spherical perfume vases which appear frequently but in small numbers, and a variety of moulded vases. Two striking examples of such assemblages have been found, at Tocra (Teucheira)[115] in Cyrenaica and at Catania in Sicily,[116] to match the variety found at Syracuse and Taranto. It should make us wonder what complex comings and goings of merchants and other travellers and what casual trade carried all this material from the places where it was made. On the other hand two groups, Aegean ('Melian', 'Naxian', 'Parian' and the like), and Italian (such as 'Caeretan' and

'Chalcidian') rarely if ever appear; the same is true of Etruscan material except for a limited number of *bucchero kantharoi*. It is difficult to see a reason for this.

The pottery was originally accompanied by a variety of other objects, in various materials, of use and ornamental, including bronze vessels which more than any other category show the combined artistic and metallurgical skill of the Greeks. They include the splendid Vix krater, either Laconian, Corinthian or Tarentine, as remarkable for its transport as for its artistry; it may have come to eastern France by way of the Adriatic and Switzerland, or up the Rhône like the diadem buried with it, which must have followed the route mentioned above from some oriental area such as Persia, through Asia Minor to the West.[117]

A most important consideration arises from this diversity of cargoes: that producers did not insist on carrying rights even for imports. They sat at home, as the Corinthians and the Athenians did, and many merchants traced a path to their ports, and to others not so important. On the other hand, some Greek states clearly perceived that there were isthmus crossings, or portages from one river to another as in Gaul, and that considerable profit could be gained from the exploitation of these geographical phenomena – in short the exploitation of other people's trade. The major example was the Isthmus of Corinth; another was a trans-Attica route from north-east to south-west. This was to avoid Cape Sunium in the face of adverse winds, and there were other examples, such as the channel between Rhodes and the mainland of Asia Minor or the rounding of the tip of the Cnidian peninsula. The Hellespont with adverse current and wind was a special case; witness the importance of Çanakkale in modern times as a refuge. The leading principle, therefore, was the control of passage-ways and safe havens. Policy was little concerned with trade in the modern sense, except later in the import of certain essential commodities, but control of it from the land. Thus, land issues were the important ones in inter-state politics. This was true in the case of neighbouring states, where it is wise to keep 'trade' issues out of the question: the hostility of Megara and Attica, of Argos and Sparta or Athens and Thebes may have had an economic significance based on a quest for land, but not on trade. The enmity of Athens and Megara concerned Salamis; that of Athens and Aegina ('the eyesore of the Piraeus') rested on the capacity of the one to dominate the other. However, in the case of these two states there was a maritime (and naval) rivalry; the latter was a long-established trading centre having connections with Egypt and the Hellespont, the former a nascent trade centre, which, from the time of Pisistratus and before, was established at Sigeum, and later in the Thracian Chersonese (the Gallipoli peninsula). There was a clear issue, not exactly 'commercial' rivalry: did merchants frequent the port of Aegina, where, no doubt, they could benefit from Aeginetan expertise and overseas connections, or the port of Piraeus, for the sake of the goods there available for export, including silver, and because of Athens' control at the Hellespont? The same was true of Megara and Corinth, offering alternative routes across the isthmus, though the Megarian was not so convenient as the Corinthian. On the other hand there could really be no rivalry in this connection between Athens and Megara or Athens and Corinth since the isthmus had to be crossed. It must be reiterated that frequently where commercial rivalry is superficially apparent, enmity arose from the fear of political domination; later, for instance, between Athens and Corinth over the entrance to the gulf. It is most unlikely that Corinth as the state controlling the isthmus would object if merchants purchased Attic rather than Corinthian pots, which would infer a state policy on exports.

A similar nice problem in the later sixth and earlier fifth centuries arises in connection with the east Mediterranean. It has sometimes been suggested that in the first decade of the fifth century the revolt of the Ionian Greeks was in part provoked by an anti-Greek and pro-Phoenician Persian policy, so that Greek interests suffered in Naucratis. It would be difficult to discover an anti-Greek Persian mercantile policy – the Persian would have scorned to have any sort of mercantile policy. The Aeginetans feared Persian pressure on their trade routes when they submitted in 491–490 BC, but this was not competition, rather a military danger. It is not even clear that the Phoenicians saw the Greeks as trade rivals, for Dionysius of Phocaea got ships from the Phoenicians. At Al Mina[118] there is no evidence of discrimination. For Persians and Greeks alike a general 'trade policy' in the modern sense was non-existent, except, in the case of the Greeks, for the promotion of the import of necessities.[119] This will emerge clearly later on, where Athens appears paramount because of her political power when this existed, her central trading position, and her dominance over the historical tradition. Despite this, all the states described above continued to have their interests, and play their part.

CHAPTER TWO

GREEK TRADERS AND TRADING –
THE CLASSICAL PERIOD

UNDER THE GENERAL HEADING of 'Trade', there are some rather diverse aspects of economic activity to be considered which cannot always be neatly separated out.

WHOLESALE TRADE

The first category is that of trade on a scale larger than domestic, which every economy but the simplest must have, the domain of the whole-sale trader. Sometimes, if his trading took him abroad, he was called an *emporos* as distinct from the ship-owner who was called a *naukleros*, or else, if he specialized, as he often did, he was given a generic name that indicated the nature of the goods in which he traded. Thus, in particular, the corn-dealers, or *sitopolai*, were well known in Athens and the Piraeus for their shady ways. Other names of the same type include Eucrates, the rope or tow merchant,[1] Lysicles, the cattle merchant,[2] and Cleon, the leather merchant.[3] These were men who made their way into politics, as did Hyperbolus, the lamp-seller.[4] The fact that they won notoriety in politics seems to indicate that they did not belong to the lowest level of economic activity or social status (there were no trade unions to facilitate the passage, through the holding of full-time office, from craftsman to politician). They may well have been men of some substance, and it was their origins and their line in politics which distinguished them from Pericles, while it would have been difficult to distinguish them economically from Nicias with his mine-working slaves. In ancient times it was found convenient to represent them as low types (note that Plutarch[5] conveniently calls Lysicles a *probatokapelos*, using the more pejorative term, as if we were to use 'huckster' instead of 'merchant'), as Aristophanes and the philosophers do, though Demosthenes has nothing to say against Cleon. And this has been misunderstood and accepted *au pied de la lettre* by some in modern times. But it is worth noticing that Eucrates, after the death of Pericles, married Aspasia, the latter's mistress and commanded a squadron of warships.[6] In the same fashion it seems that Cleophon, the 'lyremaker', the later demagogue, was not so low in the social scale as is often inferred (his father was probably a general). If he was a lyre-maker, so might Demosthenes' father, if he had lived at the time of the Old Comedy, have been called a 'cutler' or a 'bedmaker', and re-presented as working himself at the crafts in question. It is clear that there were well-to-do merchants, as there were manufacturers; middlemen, collectors and redistributors of the products of others, and the negotiators with the merchants who took the commodities abroad. Some of them were undoubtedly men of substance, and indeed of considerable wealth. However ignorant we may be in detail of the dimensions of Athenian import and export trade, its volume was very impressive.

We can form some idea of the extent of the trade in corn. Other commodities must have been imported, such as timber and hides, some textiles or the raw materials for their manufacture. These had to be paid for: in part, perhaps, by the export of silver. But Athens also produced some natural commodities such as the products of the olive,[7] and, no doubt, some manufactured goods, vases (as is well known) among them, though we should not inflate the importance of these as an element in export trade. Apart from the specialized sphere of the corn trade, the impression is gained from what little information we have that cargoes were mixed. A ship carried small parcels of this or that, variously owned and destined for a number of ports of call. Indeed the very nature of the Aegean and its islands would produce a mixed type of trading cargo, and probably require only small ships. This was less likely to be true of trade with the major ports of the Asia Minor coast, with the Black Sea and the West, but since sea traffic was to a considerable degree coasting, if not completely so, very mixed cargoes, except for timber and corn, would again be the rule. Thus many individuals were concerned who might call themselves *emporoi* or operate more or less on the fringe of the trading world. There was a multiplicity of individuals who served as middlemen, to gather the goods, whether natural or manufactured, from the small producer or craftsman, whether free, or slave working on the so-called *apophora* system.[8] It will later be seen that neither in cultivation nor in manu-facture were there establishments of any considerable size. Their dimensions were modest, and there was, therefore, more scope for the middleman. We do not hear of him as an oppressive and distasteful element in mercantile operations. So many are likely to have operated in this way that their profit margins were thereby reduced to a mini-mum; though at work behind the small operator was the man of capital, who lent money and facilitated the operations of his lesser brethren, not greatly different from the mode of operation in eastern Mediterranean ports today.

LOCATION OF TRADING

The export trade and the whole process of the collection of cargoes was also facilitated by the markets which, in Classical Athens, appear to have reached a high degree of specialization. There was the wine market,[9] where wine might be purchased by the amphora. It looks as if porters could then be hired to carry it (Pl. 23). This was no doubt true of all port and market transport tasks, for which labour must have been available after the fashion of the Turkish porters of Istanbul. The wine was given a preliminary tasting (note the *geusterion* ('tasting place') mentioned in Aristophanes (frag. 299)). What was true of wine also applied to olive-oil (Pl. 26). We hear of the cheese market, and indeed of a further specialization, 'the soft cheese market', used as the place of resort of the Plataeans in exile in the fourth century BC. It is clearly difficult to distinguish market and quarter, the latter being a combination of residence and place of business – of the tanners, the honey-sellers, the cheese-sellers.[10] These were the place of trade of those who acted as middlemen in natural commodities, and the place of resort of those who came in with their products from the country. Yet there were also the country towns of Attica, in which the same thing took place on a minor scale, and where the middleman for the supplies to the great city and for the export trade met the producer. In similar fashion there were the quarters of the manufacturing craftsmen and their markets. There was the 'bedding market'[11], where the frames (*klinai*) of couches and beds were sold, the coverlets, rugs, pillows – everything included in the term *himatismos* ('bedding') – could probably be bought too, and the costly fabrics imported from cities such as Miletus. They were not all necessarily concentrated in the market-place (*agora*) of Athens *par excellence*, or even in its immediate vicinity, and certainly not under one roof like the Great Bazaar at Instanbul. But the division by categories there present was followed also in Athens. Ultimately, with the construction in the Hellenistic period of the great *stoai* or porticoes, a certain measure of concentration was attained. It is by no means clear, however, that it existed already in the Classical period.

On the other hand, the great diversification and specialization both in trading and in manufacture was a matter of comment in Antiquity, as characteristic of the city of Athens and the multiplicity of its economic requirements. There appears to have been quite a degree of specialization within one category, such as the manufacture of shoes, and a corresponding elaboration in the terminology of trade. The Classical period, as can be seen from the American excavations of the Agora and its surroundings, witnessed a large development of craftsmanship and small industrial establishments. This took place, appropriately enough, in the vicinity of the temple commonly called the Theseum, though it was in fact a temple shared by Hephaestus, the patron god of craftsmen, and Athena Ergane, equally the patroness of crafts pursued by women (somewhere in the background was Prometheus). It extended to the Areopagus and the south side of the Acropolis. Until the restoration of the public buildings on the west side of the Agora, which remained long in ruins after the Persian sack, these industrial establishments included the borders of the market-place itself (Pl. 39).

They were not, however, confined to this particular area. They appear elsewhere, and one of the most famous districts of Athens, both within and without the walls, takes its name from industrial or rather craft activity – the Kerameikos, the Potters' Quarter (see p. 131). The craftsmen lived where they worked. There were no factories in the proper sense of the word. The material remains are for the most part poorly preserved, much of the area was overlaid by larger and finer houses of the Roman period, but sufficient remains to show that the houses of the Classical period, of mean enough construction, with rooms and court, also incorporated workshops. Some, like the bronze-casters' shops, are easily identifiable by their installations. Likewise, a house which has a part fitted out with pipes and vats may have belonged to a fuller. *Koroplastai* and potters can be identified by kilns and wasters. There were others again, such as weaving establishments, which have nothing to identify them except perhaps an excess of loom-weights.

It is, indeed, clear that there was the same concentration of craft establishments in this area as of traders in natural products and manufactured goods here and elsewhere. Even more extensive excavation of other parts of Athens within the walls is not likely to modify this impression. On the other hand, just as there was an area of the Kerameikos outside the walls, so there may have been other quarters of craftsmen in the suburbs of Athens, as well as in the country towns. And what was true of Athens was also true of quarters in other Greek cities. These would have been modest, but certainly present, as in the small towns of the Middle East today. For Attica Thucydides[12] points out that in the later years of the Peloponnesian War, from 413 BC, when the adversaries of Athens were in possession of a permanent base at Decelea, more than twenty thousand 'craftsmen' fled to the enemy there (see p. 154). These can hardly have been cultivators. Nor is it likely that so many 'craftsmen' (if the word has its normal meaning) found employment in the Laurium mines (see p. 178). Many, therefore, must have been slaves engaged in crafts: not so much like the slaves of the father of the Orator Demosthenes, working in the house of their owner and under close supervision,[13] but more like the specialist slaves belonging to the Orator's acquaintance and political aide, Timarchus, and his father. In connection with them we hear of slaves who worked on the *apophora* system.[14]

It is very likely, too, that a number of the small houses which were in the vicinity of the Theseum and the Agora and on the slopes of the Areopagus, with their attached workshops (the ever-recurring *ergasteria* of *horos* incriptions),[15] belonged to free craftsmen. These were not always on a very small scale, since coupled with *ergasteria* in mortgage documents we sometimes hear of groups of slaves, though others no doubt were inhabited by slaves working on their own. The same may be said of traders. Both categories could pursue their callings and, indeed, live in the great *stoai* which were later erected; though it must be admitted that these at first sight appear to have been too splendidly organized to be occupied by the small trader or craftsman.[16] Be that as it may, the principle of concentration was followed both early and late. In modern Athens a feeble remnant of a bazaar, destined soon to disappear, survives in the Odos Pandrosou ('Shoe Lane') and a craft area in the metalworking and repair shops of the appropriately named Odos Hephaistou. Both are still on the edge of the ancient market place and not far from the industrial quarter of ancient Athens. The important and elaborately organized purveyors of materials in Antiquity lived in the same region, as is clear from the Athenian building inscriptions. A supplier of olive wood[17] has his place of business in the vicinity of the Theseum. These inscriptions, again, impress the reader with the elaboration of the trade in building materials and related commodities: ruddle, nails, iron, wood, tiles, tow, and many other such commodities. It was at establishments of this kind that such materials, many of which had in fact already been imported from abroad, could be purchased.

Rather different from these markets and 'quarters' in the city itself was the establishment in the Piraeus known as the Deigma or 'Show-place', set up by the State to enable foreign merchants to display samples of their commodities, such as corn, and wine, possibly in sample bottles.[18] The wine merchants of Chios, Thasos and other wine-producing regions, when they brought their wines to the Athenian market, would send up samples doubtless in bottles of a special size or shape, to the Deigma in the Piraeus, there to be tested and, if approved, purchased by the Athenian wine-merchants. The word *deigma* itself means 'sample', and so the term was extended to the building to which in-coming merchants brought samples of their cargoes, and to which, it might be suggested, merchants from Athens could bring samples of the wares they had for export. To judge from the references to the Deigma[19] it lay in a part of the Piraeus particularly accessible to the sea. It was a resort and negotiating place for merchants, and also one where bankers did business, and where those loans could be raised on ships and their cargoes, which in the fourth century made the port of Athens such an important centre of mercantile activity. The Deigma was the hub of the port of Athens, to which, as Pericles could proudly say,[20] the products of all the world came: an advantage at once to her culture, and to her wealth and well-being.[21] Thus Isocrates,[22] in the fourth century, refers to 'one *accustomed* to sail to the Pontus'. In the same speech[23] there is reference to the colony of (? Athenian) ship-owners in Pontic Bosporus, to banking connections,[24] to judicial arrangements probably existing between the South Russian rulers and Athens,[25] and to a centre of information on international affairs and events, and on shady practices and persons.[26] The commodities dealt with in the port of Athens were various in the extreme, ranging from the homely anchovies and pottery, referred to half jokingly by Aristophanes[27] as a likely line for export, to the embroidered and plain fabrics of Thrace mentioned *en passant* by Thucydides[28] and the long lists of foreign specialities which it sometimes delighted the Athenian Comic poets to insert in their plays.[29]

TRADE-ROUTES

Not all trade passed through the Piraeus and the Deigma. We should not take too seriously the humorous picture in the *Acharnians* of Aristophanes of the Boeotian and Megarian in search of trade. It is commonly supposed that transport by sea was easier than transport by land, and so it might seem that trade with Megara could go through the Piraeus or Eleusis, and with Boeotia by sea from one of the east coast ports of Attica. But this ease of transport by sea was not always so clear, especially when a sea voyage meant the rounding of a cape in the face of an adverse wind, with all the consequent delays. Cape Sunium was a case in point, and it appears, as we are informed by Thucydides, that before the occupation by the Peloponnesians in 413 BC of Decelea, commodities came from the north-east overland from Oropos instead of round Cape Sunium, which the historian says was 'more expensive'.[30] So it is likely enough that there was traffic across Attica, over the land frontiers, much of it local and relatively unimportant; and also sea traffic, especially from Salamis and Eleusis, with Megara, and from the east coast of Attica with the ports of Boeotia, Euboea and the nearer Aegean islands. But such traffic could not compare in volume or importance with that which went through the Piraeus. This we know was very considerable. The exact extent of it is, on the other hand, difficult to assess, since we have but one solitary indication of the sort of sum which might have been raised from the one percent tax on imports and exports at the end of the fifth century or the beginning of the fourth. It is to be regretted that the Athenians, and indeed the Greeks in general, were so uninterested in economic statistics. There was also the undoubtedly considerable volume of the corn imports, on which we are just a little better informed. These were of public importance, as were the diplomatic relations of Athens with the rulers of those regions, and especially South Russia, which provided the great bulk of Athens' corn imports. Athens, it will be seen, and Attica produced a certain amount of grain. This, because of the lightness and shallowness of the Attic soil, was only a small proportion of the total requirement, and the bulk was barley, suitable enough for human consumption but only half as nutritious as wheat.

There is something of a problem here. How soon did Athens start to import corn to improve her standard of life and to sustain an increased population? It is not generally felt that this expedient was adopted as early as the seventh century BC, even though, towards the end of that century, Athens' agriculture ran into difficulties (see Chapter I above). It is a common view that Athens did in the sixth century become interested in trade-routes (ibid.), and frequently the idea is propounded that this was on account of her need to import corn. It is difficult to prove both this need for corn and the reason for it (an increasing population?) until after the PersianWars of 490–479 BC, and even then the arguments are not very convincing until well on into the fifth century.Whatever her need for it, the hold exercised by Athens over the Delian League, which later became the Athenian Empire, gave her control of corn supplies in the eastern Mediterranean. And Athens learnt to use such control of corn, and ship-timber, as instruments of domination over other states. The final episodes of the

Peloponnesian War demonstrated her vulnerability in this matter, and in the fourth century the problems of the supply of corn and the protection of the routes by which it came to Athens, with the cultivation of the good will of those who produced it and of those who conveyed it, bulk large in the foreign and domestic policy of Athens.

The corn trade, with its organization and protection, was a thing apart. From time to time the Athenians sought to control other commodities such as the ruddle of Ceos, or timber, both important for the construction of warships, but never with such interest or under the pressure of such necessity as in the case of corn. In the fifth century Athens viewed the problem of corn both from the standpoint of feeding her citizens and of controlling her subject allies. When the Peloponnesian War came in 431 BC there was the added problem of intercepting supplies of corn being shipped from the eastern Mediterranean to the Peloponnesian allies of Sparta. The availability of it would undoubtedly allow them to keep their armies longer in the field. Hence, the interest of Athens in the island of Cythera as a station on the route from Egypt, Cyprus and Crete to the Peloponnesus. The same purpose in part accounted for the Athenian interest and intervention in Sicily. It was an extension of political influence, to be sure, but also, as Thucydides points out,[31] an effort to prevent corn from this superlatively fertile island being imported by her enemies.

Athens' second interest in corn was no less important. Early in the Peloponnesian War, at the time, for instance, of the revolt in Lesbos (428/7 BC), there appears to have been no close control over imports by the allies of Athens, or at any rate by Mytilene, which held a privileged position, of corn from the great corn-producing area of the Pontus, as the Greeks called it, meaning the Euxine (Black Sea). This was in effect South Russia, where a stable power had existed since the middle of the century, with which the Athenians under Pericles established firm relations and thus tapped the corn production of the Black Earth region. As long as Athens controlled the sea – or at any rate the Aegean – she was in control of the approaches to the Black Sea, and to the coast of Thrace, a region of considerable fertility between the Maritsa (the modern boundary between Greece and Turkey) and the Struma to the west. This area was important not only for corn but also for timber and precious metals. For Athens the regions of Thrace and the Black Sea seemed far more accessible and controllable than distant Sicily with Corinth and the isthmus or dangerous Cape Malea on the way between; or distant Egypt under the shadow, if not always in the control, of the Persians. The mid-fifth century period, when there was disturbance both in South Russia and in Thrace, saw the increased interest of Athens both in the West and in Egypt. Though in impulse it was mostly political and imperial, we need not exclude a concern with the corn trade. But this interest seems, to the present writer, to have been temporary. When settled conditions came in the north-east, Athens turned in that direction still more strongly – even though Egyptian rebels against Persia might dangle the bait of free gifts of corn before her. Thus, Athens was master of the trade-routes to these regions. Her control was as much essential to her very existence as the 'linked fortresses of Athens and the Piraeus'. But, as the clandestine preparations for revolt of the Mytilenaeans show, Athenian control of imports by others was not close.[32] No doubt the Athenians, as in their own public life, relied on the infinite capacity of the Greeks to watch their neighbours. Sure enough, the inhabitants of Tenedos, near neighbours of the Lesbians, and even nearer to the Hellespont, told tales of their activities.

Later, however, in the Peloponnesian War Athens applied a much more strict control over the movement of both corn and ship-building timber. After the Athenian disaster in Sicily, with the renewal of hostilities by Sparta and the intervention of Persia, attended by the revolt of most of her subject allies, Athens found herself fighting a naval war in large part to defend the vital trade-route to the north Aegean and the Black Sea. Her ultimate defeat at the Hellespont in 405 BC meant that the Spartans could impose a blockade and starve the Athenians into submission.

The great importance of the north-eastern corn trade-route is apparent in all the actions of fourth-century Hellenic Athens, which had learned from her experiences in the fifth century. In part it lay at the back of her interest in a renewed maritime league, and seemed justification for securing and maintaining the naval strength of Athens. It was a prime factor in her attitude to events in the Greek world. Manifestly 'the man in the Athenian street' knew that if any enemy defeated Athens on the sea, or sought to coerce her, he would make for the narrow seas which lay between the Aegean and the Black Sea, or seek to dominate that area of the central Aegean through which all merchant ships to and from Athens must perforce pass (in effect the Doro Channel). In times of war or uneasy peace the price of corn at Athens was the barometer of her success and influence abroad. Thus hostile relations with Sparta, with Boeotia, and above all with Philip II of Macedon involved the corn trade, and the speeches of the fourth-century Orators leave us in no doubt of it.

There were other difficulties in that century which Athens had not experienced in the fifth, when she had the military predominance to control these routes. Athens was now one among many. There were more eager customers for corn at the source, for factors not very easy to determine seem to have increased the dependence of city-states on imported corn. There were more markets open to corn carriers who would, if unconstrained, seek the best profit possible (as with some modern oil-producing countries). There were, from time to time, local emergencies in which communities on the Aegean seaboard, faced with shortage and a hungry populace, compelled, as far as they were able, corn ships to come into their port, or if they were there already, to disgorge their cargoes to the benefit of the local market, and against dubious promises of repayment. Naval power and inter-state agreements on the protection of sea-borne trade could in some measure deal with these difficulties. As far as the sources in Thrace or South Russia were concerned, something could also be done. It was a main principle of Athenian policy to secure her position of influence in the northern Aegean, though it involved her in hostilities especially with Philip II. South Russia, with its curious mixed Hellenic and Scythian culture, was far away, and exposed to local dangers which Athens could not hope to control, even if she aspired to control the way thither. But the evidence seems to indicate that there was a close connection between Athens and what was called the Bosporan Kingdom. This is clear in particular from Isocrates' speech, the *Trapeziticus*, which is concerned with the financial difficulties of a young man who was a member of the South Russian nobility, and from Demosthenes' speech *Against Leptines*, concerned to preserve for the South Russian rulers those honours and privileges which a grateful Athens had accorded them. In its beginnings this connection went back to the sixth century BC, but the period of Athenian dominance in the fifth century had seen the Bosporan Kingdom even more firmly connected with the Piraeus as a great centre of trade. Thus a tradition of mercantile relations and friendliness had grown up which was strong enough to survive the vicissitudes of the Peloponnesian War.

The South Russian rulers seem to have preserved a sentimental friendship for Athens, not uninfluenced by the consideration that she was among the greatest importers of corn, and from time to time, though not as strongly or as consistently as in the fifth century, controlled the Black Sea approaches. Thus Greek merchants going with a return cargo to Athens were accorded priority over others and favourable treatment in the local courts. In times of distress Athens received corn at a cheap rate or as an outright gift from these rulers of a distant outpost of a half-Hellenic culture. The Athenians, for their part, sedulously cultivated the South Russian rulers. How important the connection was is clear from the anxious and unctuous tone of the speech of Demosthenes mentioned above. Honours which were cheap, and reciprocal privileges both mercantile and judicial, were bestowed by the Athenians: a practice which had already started, in the case of the barbarous Thracians, in the fifth century. So speaks an Athenian envoy to the king of Thrace:

> I all that time was drinking with Sitalces:
> A most prodigious Athens-lover he,
> Yea such a true admirer, he would scribble
> On every wall My beautiful Athenians!
> His son, our newly made Athenian, longed
> To taste his Apaturian sausages,
> And bade his father help his fatherland.[33]

To such difficulties as have been outlined above were added others. In the later fourth century there was the disruption of trade and shipping by the operations of Alexander the Great against Persia and the manoeuvres of his minister Cleomenes in Egypt. Another possible cause of complications was the quest for other sources of corn when the demand was great: Cyprus and Egypt, the Adriatic. All of which added to Athens' strategic and political preoccupations in particular, in what was in any case a difficult period. In the Adriatic it involved Athens in the establishment of an anti-pirate base. The multiple difficulties with the corn supply meant that those merchants who shipped it and those dealers who dealt in it at Athens (and no doubt elsewhere) developed a particular and important relationship with the State. The actual seafarers, who transported the corn from South Russia and elsewhere did not have to be Athenians, and indeed rarely were. Such, at any rate, is the picture we get from the Orators of the fourth century, whose speeches on occasions have to do with the corn trade. The great majority of these seafarers were foreigners, and as such the natural object of suspicion, or resident aliens (metics = *metoikoi*), who tended to turn to such activity because their status precluded them from land-owning or the possession of any form of real estate. Some were therefore elusive in the extreme, with the whole eastern Mediterranean open to them. On the other hand, the good will of the Athenian authorities and any privileges they might be inclined to grant were very welcome. From time to time the arm of Athens might be long enough to reach a defaulting merchant outside the territory of Athens herself, but never again was it so powerful as in the period of her fifth-century empire, when such a ban might virtually close, for an individual, the majority of the Greek ports of importance in the eastern Mediterranean. Thus, the Athenian state was concerned to control, but at the same time to encourage and conciliate, the international merchant class; for as long as the port of Athens could be made to remain a centre of trade, and even more, an *entrepôt*, though the Athenians did not evolve the idea of a free port, this essential trade in corn would benefit, and among so many competing markets for corn the merchants would favour Athens.

The private provision of capital for mercantile ventures, which itself was promoted by the burdens laid on other investment in real estate and industry by the State, was one of the attractions of Athens. Many an Athenian anxious to conceal his wealth, and at the same time profit from it, would advance loans to ship-owners or merchants on the bottomry principle. If ship and cargo returned safely the loan was repaid with very high interest – often more than thirty percent, and in the case of the dangerous and pirate-ridden Adriatic, as high as one hundred percent. If the ship was lost, the capital was not repaid. It was in effect a sort of insurance. Bottomry, as might be expected, begot barratry, the criminal sinking of ships to avoid repayment. In the speeches of the Orators we hear only of the seamy side of all this. It constituted, however, an important aspect of Athenian life, involving all the refinements of ship's papers and book-transfers, helped also by the excellent Athenian coinage of silver drawn from the mines of Laurium. The State also did what it could: granting legal facilities to encourage merchants. Over and above the arrangements negotiated between two sovereign states (*symbola*) for the settlement of disputes between individuals of each, Athens provided special courts to deal with mercantile cases, held during the winter months when shipping was at a standstill, and characterized by unusual expedition in settlement (within the month). There was every reason for seeing to it that foreigners were not penalized in the Athenian courts, even if Athenians suspected that they were all scoundrels (especially the Phaselites!). If they showed favour to Athens and carried corn thither when they might have carried it elsewhere, if they sold it at a price lower than that which prevailed elsewhere, or, better, treated it as a gift, the once great imperial city showed herself pathetically willing to grant the honour of *proxenia* (a sort of honorary consulship) or even of citizenship to individual merchants *pour encourager les autres*. There were also other less striking privileges, such as freedom from imposts, and the right to acquire a house or other real property at Athens. These were so many breaches in the wall of exclusiveness which surrounded the city-state. There was also the grant of freedom from judicial or military seizure (*asylia*), no small advantage in the troubled times of the fourth century, if, in fact, it could be implemented. So many states, in that period, made grants of such immunity that it is to be wondered whether they amounted to anything more than an empty gesture. The Athenian State did what it could, painfully conscious that its power was not as it had been and that its control over seafaring merchants was imperfect.

There were, however, two classes of persons involved, over whom the State could exercise rather more control in the interest of its citizens and their daily bread. First, there were those who lent money on mercantile ventures. If corn was the cargo on the return voyage, the destination must be Athens and a stated proportion of the cargo must stay there, otherwise the offending lender would be liable to denunciation and punishment. A certain element of harbour control was here involved. It was unlikely that the return voyage would be to another place unless the lender went with the ship, though the charge of illegal diversion was sometimes brought, but in certain circumstances cargoes might go elsewhere. Not all the comings and goings took place within the lawful boundaries of the Piraeus harbour proper. We hear of a 'Thieves' Harbour' where odd transactions might take place away from the supervision of the harbour superintendents.

The other class comprised the middlemen corn merchants, of whom we hear much to their discredit, since they were in the earlier fourth century the objectives or victims of a speech of the Orator Lysias. Just as the seafaring trader, using what appears to have been an extraordinarily efficient intelligence system, might divert his cargo to a port where a better price could be obtained, so too the purpose of the corn-dealers was, not unnaturally, to make money: to buy cheap and sell dear, the dearer the better. It was unfortunate that the well-tried devices of the 'ring' and the 'corner' were inimical to the well-being of the citizens, and especially of the poor citizens. The result was the picture of the corn merchants as the unprincipled enemies of the *demos*. Yet the fluctuation of supply which they manipulated was the result of political and military events in the Aegean. It is odd that there is no suggestion that the State should step in, and by the purchase and storage of corn (in the manner of Gaius Gracchus at Rome), and its release in times of crisis, get round this problem. That the State did not do so was not so much a matter of dislike of intervention in this sector of the citizen's life, as of a lack, in the primitive organization of Athens, of the necessary financial and administrative machinery. The price fluctuations must have been disturbing to the economy of the individual. On the other hand high prices seem not to have lasted long, and in any case economic, like military, crisis was part of what seemed to be the order of nature.

Of other major commodity trades we hear nothing or next to nothing. They did not touch the individual citizen as closely as the corn trade, nor were they quite so much influenced by or exposed to political vicissitudes, though the timber trade because of its connection with the construction of warships was of vital importance. The efforts of the Athenian State to regulate and restrict the traffic in ruddle or red ochre (*miltos*) from Cea, by reason of its importance for the waterproofing and preservation of ships' hulls, rather than for vase manufacture, suggests that other things than corn were organized and could be controlled. The same was true of certain exports, but we know little of the intervention of middlemen between the Laurium miners and the mint or the exporter of silver, or between the individual olive growers and olive-oil manufacturers, or the individual potteries and the actual exporter: that is, the cargo owner, who so often travelled with the ship, when he was not represented by a supercargo or the ship's captain. We can only guess how other goods, whether luxury items or mass-produced, were collected from their producers and assembled for the bulk purchase of exporters; or how far cargoes were homogeneous, except in the case of corn. Certainly it was not always clear that shippers, by which are meant shipmen, could obtain in any given port the sort of cargo they wanted. One of the suggested advantages of the port of Athens was the great multiplicity of goods for re-shipping. If these failed there was always the excellent Attic silver which could be exported as bullion.[34]

It is difficult for us, used to seeing the great modern ports and their activity, to form a true picture of ancient Athenian or any other export trade. It is probably necessary to banish ideas of modern Piraeus or Salonica, and to think rather of something like a smaller modern Greek port, on some island, for instance: with the caïque at the quayside, the modest horse or mule-drawn transport, the heaps of diverse merchandise and, in some places, the serried ranks of domestic pots set out on the quay. In Antiquity there would be the pointed amphorae (Pl. 23) for oil and wine, the bales of wool or bolts of cloth. Something of all this is recaptured for us in the lively scene in the tondo of the celebrated Arkesilas Cup, of the earlier sixth century (Pl. 21).

LOCAL AND RETAIL TRADE

A contrast to our limited knowledge of foreign trading on a large scale (the sphere of the *emporos*) is provided by retail trade at Athens. Here 'trade' is involved, not 'trades'. By this is meant the function of distributing in small amounts to individual purchasers the food and other natural products and manufactured goods which they require for their daily life. The retail trader was either the actual producer, such as the country people who came to market in the town, often travelling considerable distances, to sell their own fruit and vegetables and the like,[35] or the true middleman, whose function appears to have been the handling not only of natural commodities which he purchased from the primary producer (as, for instance, Pericles found it convenient to sell the produce of his estate, which must imply the existence of traders) but also of what might be called prepared commodities, such as bread, and, we might add, the wares of Aristophanes' Sausage-seller, for to this category of retail trade belong not only the cook-shop but also the itinerant vendor. For foodstuffs the picture is not quite a clear one: vegetables, fruit and fish (Pl. 24), and possibly a little meat, were the commonplaces of the market, and lent themselves to what might be called stall traffic (Pl. 25). Grain, as in the matter of its import, and perhaps oil (Pl. 26), were in a rather different category. It was not necessarily in the form of bread that grain was eaten; it was also made into porridge. All grain would be rather coarsely ground. But that bread consisting of baked dough was made is clear from the rations allowed to the Spartans shut up on Sphakteria during the Peloponnesian War. The meal or flour used for the preparation of bread was not necessarily prepared domestically. There were grinding establishments, as Thucydides makes clear[36] in mentioning the conscription of *sitopoioi* (*emmisthoi*) to go with the Sicilian Expedition. How far the same principle was followed for bread-baking, in what must have been an equally difficult operation in constricted quarters in a large town, with little opportunity for outside ovens and with limited supplies of fuel, we cannot tell. The bread would have taken much the same form as in modern Greece: the *koulouri*, the ring-shaped cake of bread sprinkled with sesame seeds, and the great loaf, of which hunks could form the staple of a man's meal. Again, how far these were the product of bakeries and the object of retail distribution is not clear; probably less so, outside Athens, than in modern times when improved transport has reduced the local or domestic production of bread. The same problem attends the production and sale of wine, that is local wine, since there is no difficulty about imported wine, and olive oil. Did the owner of every small vineyard and olive grove (Pl. 29) press his own? Present-day practice suggests that this is relatively easy for wine: in any case Attic wine has never been held in very high regard. Olive-pressing (Pl. 30) on the other hand was a complicated technical process in which the producers of Attica certainly had to maintain their high reputation. How this was carried out when so many small olive producers existed is quite unclear (there is no indication of anything like modern co-operatives), but there must have been a certain degree of organization at a higher level than the small grower. Again, it would not be far wrong to assume for ancient Attica (the circumstances in Athens itself may have been different, as will be seen) and its small towns and villages something like the commodity market of such places say a generation ago: with fruit and vegetables locally produced. Evidence of more highly organized economic procedures might appear in the sacks of grain and meal and the containers of oil (in ancient times of clay, in modern times of metal). The other commodities, as far as food-stuffs were concerned, were very marginal: some luxury cheese perhaps, to offset the local product, and dried and pickled fish.

A modern visitor to Greece will be aware of a close association between the market and the equally indispensable Greek equivalent of the village store. While larger communities will rise to a certain degree of specialization and possess a bread-shop or *artopoleion*, a *zacharo-plasteion* (cake-shop), a *kreopoleion* (butcher's shop) or even an *ichthyo-poleion* (fish-shop), the smaller communities possess only a general store, a *pantopoleion*, which does not, however, always live up to its name. Some commodities, particularly clothes (though not necessarily finer textiles, and certainly not better leather (for the preparation of this has always been a thing apart)) and footwear were until recently prepared and distributed without the intervention of the middleman, that is, by the tailor (where the clothing was not made at home) or the shoemaker (Pl. 36). In ancient times the same direct contact of the producer and purchaser must also have extended to such objects as tools, and to coarser pottery of everyday use, but not to the pottery of higher quality (Pls 45–47) which was the speciality of different centres in Greece at different times. Then, as now, salt was a staple product, produced by evaporation of sea-water in suitable places. These salt-pans often gave names to localities, which carried on a specialized trade.

This was the position in the small communities of Attica and elsewhere. A high degree of self-sufficiency was possible in food, clothing, and even housing, given suitable clay for tiles, and mud for crude brick. The necessary timbers on the other hand were not always readily available, and were therefore more costly and more liable to be plundered by invading neighbours. The members of a family had their varying competence, and mutual aid, as in all simple communities, supplemented the deficiencies of the family in strength and skill. But as there was essential trading in some commodities – though not necessarily in all that we could think of – so there were also the specializations of certain trades. This does not apply to tailoring or shoemaking in general, since these were at the earlier and more primitive level of domestic or semi-domestic operations or to weaving (Pls 31–33), but rather to the work of the smith (Pls 40–41), the carpenter (Pls 34–35), wheelwright, boat-builder, and in a lesser degree of the potter (Pls 45–47). These may well have been the *demiourgoi* ('public workers') of earlier Greek society, and with those who prepared metal from its ore and shaped it (Pls 38, 39, 42, 43), they represented a class of 'trades' into which the amateur and the idea of family self-sufficiency had not intruded. But here again, in at any rate the smaller communities, the contact was immediate between craftsman and customer.

No doubt in the city of Athens itself and other large towns, and for luxury products, there were middlemen: between the armourer, for instance, or the potter, and possibly between the tool- and knife-maker, and the customer. These, however, were, on the whole exceptional instances of what has been at times improperly dignified by the name of 'industry' rather than trades: not mass-producing industry but 'industry' of a specialized sort. Greek Antiquity was acquainted with the manufactured speciality. The chief place where such things were or had been made often gave its name to the product: so *milesiourgos* for woollen rugs or carpets, *amorginos* for fine semi-transparent fabrics probably of silk or cotton. The diligent lexicographers and their like were able to compile lists of such specialities, which were sometimes products of a city other than that whose name the product bore. The high degree of skill required for their production was often possessed by slaves, who singly or in groups worked for a master. Similar slaves sometimes worked with precious materials to produce objects of luxury, furniture, rich and highly-decorated metalwork, embroidered or woven tapestry, and splendid arms. Of these few examples have survived, but inventories of temple treasuries contain plentiful references to such objects. This is in effect the 'industry' for which the scanty evidence has been so endlessly debated, and which will be dealt with again later. It was for the most part an activity characteristic of a great city, though some of it must have been carried out in the countryside of Attica.[37]

The general theory of the simple life of the small community has been explained, but Athens was different and so, probably, were cities like Corinth. The elaboration of the life of Athens and other large towns could hardly leave the country untouched, however. Thus, a fishmonger peddled his wares not only in Athens but also in the country, so we gather from Theophrastus whose Boor[38] 'means to have his hair cut when he gets to Town, and at the same time to bring some salt-fish from Archias as he goes by'. (One cannot refrain from recalling 'going to Town to get one's hair cut and bring back a barrel of oysters', as John Buchan has it!) There is relatively little reference to the larger middlemen except in the case of the corn-dealers. On the other hand, a great deal is heard of the small trader; not unnaturally, since immediate contact existed between him and his customers, who therefore were not without their strong impressions of his character. It is true to say that 'aristocratic' prejudice disliked the idea of crafts for a reason which is made clear by Aristotle:[39] 'Again, it is nobler not to practise any sordid craft, since it is the mark of a free man not to live at another's beck and call.' To this objection to service to another, unless it was seasonal temporary agricultural labour generally for a neighbour, was added, for retail trade – and for all trade, in the eyes of the philosophers – the corrupting effect of the profit motive.

In an Ideal State such activities were better left to foreigners! The word kapeleuein, 'to engage in retail trade', was not one Plato or Aristotle used with approval. Plato clearly defines in the Laws his attitude to retail trade.[40] In his Ideal State he seeks to confine this activity to metics and foreigners[41] and to control trade and promote standards of integrity,[42] though this is not a matter on which he believed success to be attainable, as he makes clear from his discussion of the faults of retail traders and their origins.[43] After this discussion, however, he returns again[44] to questions of the restriction, regulation and 'illiberality' of retail trade. Incidentally Plato would also exclude from the market the principle of credit. Exchange shall be of money for goods and goods for money, and there shall be no redress for the trader foolish enough to give credit.[45] One of the corrupting factors, in his opinion, was the profit motive. Hence the proposal to fix profit margins in retail trade.[46] There is an air of impracticability and un-reality about these ideas, but it would be a mistake to suppose that they did not, though perhaps in an exaggerated manner, reflect common notions and prejudices relating to small-scale trading. There is the oft-repeated charge in Comedy of dishonesty (the equivalent of our modern attitude not towards the regular and respectable retail trader, but rather towards the barrow-boy and the huckster: 'huckster' being the equivalent of the contemptuous use of *kapeleuein*. Cf. *cauponari* in Latin.) It signifies such tricks as the wetting of wool and so increasing its weight;[47] the fig-dealer putting good and ripe figs on the top of the basket and poor and hard ones underneath, and selling wild figs with the pretence that they are cultivated ones;[48] the 'corner shop' where water is put into wine and vinegar.[49] Comedy is full of humorous attacks on fishmongers (Pl. 25) and their ways,[50] a staple of sometimes rather bitter jokes which have come down to us, though the selective process by which fragments of the Comic writers have been preserved might give a false picture. With dishonesty in general is coupled the sale of bad or inferior wares, and tricks with small change, and indeed other unamiable characteristics. In Comedy the equivalent of our 'fishwives' in ancient Athens were the bread-sellers (*artopolides*), women traders[51] with a reputation for abuse[52]. It may, incidentally, be noted that some hints on the bread trade thus emerge,[53] and the question of bread distribution.[54] Likewise in Aristophanes[55] the female pease-pudding-seller is characterized by violent behaviour and cheating[56] and coupled as a low-class undesirable with that figure of Comedy the female inn-keeper, the *pandokeutria*.[57] She indeed represents another example of what was in effect retail trade. We can readily see why *pandokeion* (inn) and *pandokeutria* acquired such ill-repute. In modern times the term *pandokeion* represents a place of resort implicitly of much inferior status to the *xenodokeion*. We may compare our 'lodging house' as opposed to 'hotel'. Likewise, the contrast between *mageireion* and *hestiatorion* is much the same as between our 'cookshop' and 'restaurant'. Certainly in the Classical period better class accommodation for travellers was a matter of private hospitality.

The shadow of contempt and the acceptance of the idea of knavery were not unconnected with the servile status or ex-servile status of many of the practitioners of retail trades. The reality of public contempt for these callings is illuminated by a point in a speech of the Demosthenic *corpus* of private speeches,[58] where the question of the trade of a wreath-seller arises. She is described as 'gaining a living not in the manner we desire'.[59] In this connection the general principle is propounded that engagement in trade in the market place, if made the basis of reproach (*oneidos*) to the person concerned, was liable to an action for slander.[60] Clearly commercial dishonesty and moral obloquy were associated in the public mind with such named activities. Note-worthy also in the same speech is the appeal[61] not to scorn the needy or those engaged in trade. Necessity might cover a great deal, and justify household industry or even agricultural labouring for those who would not normally have carried on such pursuits, but selling things was clearly a doubtful occupation, and sometimes, as in the case of wreath-makers, because of the association with feasts and *hetairai* (prostitutes), suggested dubious morals (as with the eighteenth-century English 'mantua-maker'). On the other hand, wreaths were associated with religious ceremonial, too, and so the making of myrtle wreaths was suitable employment even for a respectable widow, whose semi-humorous tale as imagined by Aristophanes is worth repeating,[62] reminiscent as it is of the Ephesus of St Paul;[63] it implies also horticul-ture on a commercial scale[61]

> Ladies, I've only a few words to add.
> I quite agree with the honourable lady
> Who has just sat down; she has spoken well and ably.
> But I can tell you what I've borne myself.
> My husband died in Cyprus, leaving me
> Five little chicks to work and labour for.
> I've done my best, and bad's the best, but still
> I've fed them, weaving chaplets for the Gods.
> But now this fellow writes his Plays, and says
> There are no Gods; and so, you may depend,
> My trade is fallen to half; men won't buy chaplets.
> So then for many reasons he must die;
> The man is bitterer than his mother's pot-herbs.
> I leave my cause with you, my sisters; I
> Am called away on urgent private business,
> An order, just received, for twenty chaplets.

Wreaths were certainly also associated with clandestine love and revels.[64] The reference, in the above passage, to Euripides' mother, the vegetable-woman as scandal said, and Demosthenes' to us distasteful references to the many callings followed by the mother of Aeschines, serve to confirm the reality of this contempt, humorous at times, at others pathetically snobbish, but contempt none the less. The contempt, the assumption of dishonesty, the firmly held idea of the lowness of such activities group the small trader with the keepers of the apartment houses (*synoikiai*) often used for immoral purposes, and of the low-class taverns, the *mageireia*, which likewise suffered from ill repute[65] to such an extent that it was maintained even decent slaves would not be seen in them.[66] It appears there was a later improvement of their reputation, though this is not very apparent from the reference to these *kapeleia* – the name is to be noted as indicating that this calling was yet another branch of retail trade – by Isocrates,[67] except that the claim is made that even the free youth of his day ate and drank in them.

So much for the attitude of the Athenians, mainly, to retail trade and those who engaged in it. Of its elaboration in Athens there is no doubt. There were fixed shops, of the sort which existed in the great porticoes or *stoai*, the form of which can be seen restored in the Stoa of Attalus in the Agora, now the museum of the American Excavations. There were also temporary booths, often the simplest possible, set up in the vicinity of the Agora[68] or, indeed, anywhere in the more frequented parts of the city. The modern city of Athens provides plenty of examples of such. Finally, there were the itinerant vendors: the bread-seller, like the modern seller of *koulouria*, sellers of prepared food like Aristophanes' sausage- or black-pudding-seller in the *Knights*, who carries around his little stall or table, and washes the raw material of his wares at the public fountain; a prospective rival of the leather-seller, Cleon.

NIC. (Nicias) A sausage-seller! Goodness, what a trade!
 Wherever shall we find one?
DE. (Demosthenes) That's the question.
NIC. Why here comes one, 'tis providential surely,
 bound for the Agora.
DE. Hi, come hither! Here! You dearest man,
 you blessed sausage-seller!
 . . .
NIC. Make him put down his dresser . . .
DE. Come put you down those cookery implements
 . . .
S.S. (Sausage-seller) Good fellow, let me wash the guts,
 and sell my sausages. What need to mock me so?[69]

Or there was the charcoal-seller, like other static or itinerant traders, with his cry 'Come buy'. So Aristophanes in the *Acharnians* makes Dicaeopolis say plaintively:

 Loathing the town, sick for my village home,
 Which never cried, *Come, buy my charcoal*, or
 My vinegar, my oil, my anything;
 But freely gave us all; no *buy*-word there.[70]

Here the emphasis is on the difference between the city where every commodity must be bought, and the country, where the farm or small-holding will provide the most essential commodities for its cultivator, and the rough waste of the stony upland (the *phelleus*) the necessary firing. Alternatively, it was possible to obtain a wood-gathering concession from the owners of the land (*hylasia*).[71] Or one could send a servant to steal wood from one's neighbour,[72] in which case the maid-servant might pay for it, if detected, with the remnants of her virtue. Not inappropriately does Dicaeopolis mention the cry of the charcoal-vendor. The Acharnians, who give their name to Aristophanes' comedy, not only provided the Athenian army with the largest detachment, but were the charcoal-burners *par excellence* of Attica[73] since their district lay on the wooded slopes of Mount Parnes. They were also cultivators. The *larkos*, the charcoal basket of the itinerant vendor, is mentioned in various passages.[74] But this was only one of the many categories of vendors, though very important, since there was no other source of fuel than charcoal for firing or cooking, or indeed for industrial processes, on which the urban populace could depend. In the reverse direction some traders went to the country but certainly not in great numbers, sometimes providing luxuries, like the fishmonger in the *Boutalion* of Antiphanes:[75] 'once to the country came the fishmonger, bringing sprats and mullet, and, by Heaven, how pleased we were!' (Just like those middlemen who, from Hull and Grimsby, penetrate to the inland regions of England!)

Writers like the Old Oligarch,[76] and Thucydides[77] (through the mouth of Pericles) comment on the elaboration and importance of the maritime market of Athens; others stress the elaboration of retail trade. The departments of the market are given by Pollux,[78] admittedly a late reference. The elaboration of trading terminology, *autopoles*, *palinkapelos*, *kapelos*, *emporos*, is given by Aristophanes.[79] A list of traders appears in an inscription.[80] Literature gives abundant evidence of minor callings: the garlic-seller,[81] the drug-seller,[82] the needle-seller,[83] and the wreath-seller,[84] in one case a Thracian girl, slave or ex-slave. One might add that a seller of other people's goods is also the auctioneer or *kērux*.[85] These retailers, as far as they were not itinerant, tended to foregather in the same place to form a specialized market. An amusing picture of the markets in war-time, with the soldiers doing their shopping or robbing the stalls, is given by Aristophanes.[86] These markets took their names from the commodity sold there:[87] so: 'in the fish', 'the garlic' and 'the onions',[88] a naming of the market from the commodity commented on by Pollux.[89] There were also the wreath market,[90] the myrtle market,[91] the perfume stalls[92] – more sweet-smelling than some (Pl. 27), and therefore a place of resort – and the bird market,[93] the dealer in which has a price put on his head by the birds of Aristophanes' play, for his evil trade as well as for his cheating ways.

> He who strings and sells the finches, seven an obol, at his store,
> Blows the thrushes out and, rudely, to the public gaze exposes,
> Shamefully entreats the blackbirds, thrusting feathers up their noses.
> Pigeons too the rascal catches, keeps and mews them up with care.
> Makes them labour as decoy-birds, tethered underneath a snare.

Philocrates the 'Sparrovian' is therefore both fowler and dealer. Such special markets were located in known places. So, in Aristophanes[94] reference is made to 'the gate, where the dried-fish market is'. Places of resort for categories of individuals were likewise to be recognized: thus the Orator Lysias mentions[95] that Plataeans on the first of the month foregathered in Athens at the soft-cheese market, in just the same fashion as the inhabitants or members of the deme of Decelea did at the barber's shop 'by the Hermai'.[96] Every household servant knew where to go to obtain what was needed.[97] Business started in the market at early dawn.[98] The Athenians, country people and townsfolk alike, were used to rising while it was still dark. It also seems that retail shops stayed open until relatively late: so, in Lysias[99] there is a reference to 'obtaining torches from the nearest shop'. In all, not very different, perhaps, from the ways of our not too distant forebears.

Such trading was carried on, in establishments of varying size, by free men and women, though, as we have seen, the prejudice against such activity existed. As in the pursuit of crafts, so too in trading the owner of slaves allowed them to live and trade independently of his household, granting them a measure of responsibility, for instance in the contracting of debts, and receiving from them an agreed sum from the profits (the *apophora* system). In this way something of the direct taint of trade was avoided. Thus, an issue in Hyperides' speech against Athenogenes was a perfumery operated by slaves, with its debts and what sound like deposits, and its stock of perfumes and the *alabastra* which contained them: the whole sum involved being some five talents.[100] A point of interest[101] is that the proprietor, described as 'sitting in the market-place day in, day out, owning three perfumeries, and receiving his accounts monthly', was in fact the third generation so engaged.[102] The distinction between the trading establishment and the manufacturing establishment was a small one.

The motley crowd who engaged in these trading activities clearly required close supervision in the interests of public order and of the customers. Something has already been said about the tricks of traders. There is little or no evidence that the public authorities concerned themselves with the quality or adulteration of food: here the acuteness of the customer was relied on. On the other hand those weights and measures found in the Agora excavations, marked *dēmosion*, together with tile patterns, show a concern for the interests of the customer, of which more will be said later. A decree on weights and measures[103] requires the deposit of standards. Comedy very naturally mentions dishonest ways of trading; so the curse of the female town-crier in the *Thesmophoriazusai*[104] on all who misbehave, includes the person who:

> ... being a trading man or trading woman,
> Gives us short measure in our drinking cups ...

Wine, naturally, is the basis of the humorous reference, since women in Comedy are always twitted with secret drinking, and women slaves with sneaking out to the corner shop for a whet. No doubt ignorance of weights and measures was as much exploited as the diverse currencies (e.g. the Athenian and Aeginetan obols) which circulated in Athens. Thus, when Socrates, in the *Clouds* asks Strepsiades:

> Attend to me: what shall I teach you first
> That you've not learnt before? Which will you have,
> Measures or rhythms or the right use of words?[105]

Strepsiades deliberately misunderstands the meaning of the word 'measures' and replies:

> O! measures, to be sure: for very lately
> A grocer swindled me of full three pints!

The officials who looked after this sort of thing and supplemented the natural sharpness of the Athenians were the *agoranomoi* or market superintendents whose other duties are made clear in a decree[106] of 320–319 BC. They were to concern themselves in general with the character of the market place and its state, and with the major roads associated with it. Noteworthy in this decree are the regulations against fouling the streets, and their powers to inflict floggings on metics and slaves.

CHAPTER THREE

THE IMPORT TRADE – PRINCIPALLY CORN

THE QUESTION OF THE EXTENT of Athenian trade, through its very nature, touches the heart of economic life in the capital city of Attica. The quantity and character of the imports into the Piraeus were inevitably conditioned by the dimensions of the population of Attica[1] and its economic situation; the exports were influenced by the same factors. It is a fact of cardinal importance that exports must have paid for imports, at any rate approximately, at Athens, as they do, for the most part, in the economy of every modern state. As we have seen elsewhere, emphasis tended to be laid on imports more than on exports, in as much as the former were obviously of such vital importance for the life of the State. The imports of Athens were many and various, and drawn from numerous sources, as our authorities show,[2] but the great problem which presented itself to Athens, as to many other Greek states, was the corn supply.

There were many sources of supply for cereals. In Greece itself the Spartan and Messenian regions were very fertile, but did not produce for export; Thessaly grew large quantities of corn.[3] Xenophon contrasts Thessaly exporting corn, and Athens importing it. Lemnos, Thasos and Sciathos are mentioned by Demosthenes[4] as providing corn, but no impression of importance is given. Being a considerable source of corn, Euboea was very important to Athens,[5] and the Athenians kept it exclusively to themselves.[6] According to Gernet[7] Euboea assumed importance when the western supply was cut off. The existence of the latter is a moot point. The Athenians at most envisaged the West as a possible source of supply in default of others. The occupation of Decelea must have reduced the value of Euboea (by overland route) during the Peloponnesian War, whereas the South Russian supply was always open until the last years of the war. The role played in this connection by Euboea in the fourth century is uncertain.[8] Asia Minor was of some importance[9] in the period 321–319 BC. Somewhat earlier Phrygia, Lydia, and Paphlagonia apparently supplied Artabazus, a Persian prince[10] with a fair amount of corn. Further sources were Assos,[11] Lampsacus,[12] and the plain of the Maeander.[13] We hear at various times of corn from Cyprus,[14] but Gernet[15] seems right in regarding this not so much as corn produced in Cyprus (as Strabo[16] seems to infer that the island farmed only enough for its own needs) as that which was gathered there in an entrepôt, or in corn ships which made the island a stopping place on the route from Egypt and Phoenicia to Greece. An inscription[17] mentions 'the despatch of corn from Cyprus', where 'despatch' probably means an escort, by war vessels, of merchant ships.

South Italy and Sicily were very fertile[18], and provided a source of supply for the Peloponnese,[19] particularly for Corinth, during the Peloponnesian War. There seem no grounds for the view[20] that in the sixth century Athens had close relations with the West, and particularly with Sicily, and not with the north Aegean and Black Sea regions. The capture of Sigaeum, and the establishment of the Athenian family of Philidae in the Thracian Chersonese would indicate otherwise. Not until towards the end of the fifth century was there any rivalry between Athens and Corinth, and it was in the West that their interests would clash. In support of this view it may be pointed out that in 506 BC Corinth refused to attack Athens. At the Thirty Years Peace she agreed to Athens holding Naupactus, which she would not have done if she had believed that Athens had designs in the West. She likewise opposed the proposal to support the revolt of Samos.[21] However, there is one period (the mid-fifth century) at which Athens turned her attention to the West; namely when her supplies from Thrace and South Russia were temporarily threatened. Thrace was a fertile area, and one with Athenian connections since the time of Pisistratus, and it is certainly true that (a) the Thracian corn was a surer supply than that of Pontus, since it did not have to pass through the narrow seas; while (b) Athens' alliance with Sitalces in the fifth century, and her desire for friendship with the kings of Thrace in the fourth, had the corn trade as a basis, at least in part.[22] Athens was also interested in South Russia, in particular that preeminently fertile area, the Black Earth region of the Black Sea. Both sources were probably at one time rendered precarious: the Thracian supply by the rise of the Thracian kingdom under Teres and Sitalces (c. 450 BC), and that drawn from the Crimea by the period of unrest which must have preceded the emergence of Spartocus as tyrant. This period of uncertainty may have lasted for a considerable time, perhaps for twenty years. It seems that Athens then turned in two directions for possible alternative sources of corn, to Egypt (see below), and to the West. In 453 BC a treaty was concluded between Athens, Segesta and Halicyae[23] of which the terms are unknown, but probably military aid against Selinus was asked for. In interpreting this alliance we may compare the real purpose, as given by Thucydides,[24] of the Athenian assistance sent in 427/6 BC to Rhegium and Leontini, i.e. to cut off the corn supply from her Peloponnesian enemies. Probably in the earlier alliance Athens had an idea of securing it for herself. If the expeditions of 455 and 453 BC to the Corinthian Gulf, and Athens' possession of Naupactus be borne in mind, it will be seen that Corinth would be in no position to resist Athens' western policy. It is probable that the first colonization of New Sybaris (445/4 BC) was an imperialistic venture by Pericles,[25] reorganized later, in the year of Pericles' absence from office, by Thucydides, the son of Melesias, as a Pan-Hellenic colony (443 BC). The view that Pericles' Euxine policy was in reaction and opposition to a 'western' faction, is hardly justified.[26]

When Spartocus seized power in the Cimmerian Bosporus,[27] he was no doubt very glad to give privileges to Athens in the export of corn, in return for support against his local opponents. Relations were cemented by the visit of Pericles to the Black Sea in 437 BC[28] (it is not certain that he went far north), and an Athenian garrison was established at Nymphaeum. The route was secured by the expulsion of the tyrant of Sinope, and the settlement of Athenian colonists there. Amisus was colonized and renamed Piraeus. In 435/4 BC Astacus on the Propontis was secured by an Athenian garrison (cf. the colonization of Imbros, 445–442 BC, on the route to the Hellespont). When the South Russian supply was secured Athens ceased to be interested in the West, until the Peloponnesian War.[29] The corn trade from the north-eastern area (if it existed) had been in the hands of Miletus and Megara in the seventh and sixth centuries, and these states in the great period of colonization planted colonies on the Black Sea coasts and its approaches. After the capture of Salamis by Athens, the power of Megara declined, while Athens, through her possession of Sigaeum, acquired an interest in this direction. After 494/3 BC, on the fall of Miletus, Aegina held the chief carrying trade from the Pontus.[30] Before this Aegina probably imported her corn from Egypt, her influence in the southern Cyclades and Rhodes being shown by the Aeginetan Standard there, apart from her privileged position at Naucratis. For this reason, since her interests indicated submission to Persia, she fell foul of Athens in the first decades of the fifth century. The hostility of Megara and Athens may have come into being, in part for the same reason as well as on account of Salamis, which appears to have been an important producer of barley. The north-eastern policy of Athens and her enmity with Megara became manifest when the corn problem also apparently grew serious, i.e. in the time of Solon, and in the next half-century.

After the battle of Salamis (480 BC) Athens, with the aid of her allies, followed up her victorious course by freeing the Hellespont, and Thrace.[31] She wished to secure an uninterrupted corn supply, and the timber necessary for her naval aims. Thus there was a contrast with Sparta, whose needs were supplied by the corn produced at home, and who, therefore, adopted a less active policy. The successive efforts of Athens in this direction have frequently been noticed, culminating in her securing for herself, thanks to her sea-power, the major part of the South Russian corn, an important instrument of empire. It is considered that the law forbidding the re-export of more than one-third of the imported corn[32] dates from the Peloponnesian War. It certainly proves that Athens was the centre of a corn re-export trade, and the rulers of South Russia in the fifth century might be regarded as the commercial agents of Athens.[33] All corn imported had to come to Athens before being exported to other states. Probably the view of the Bosporan tyrants as 'commercial agents' is a little exaggerated, but it is certain that corn exports from that region were in the hands of Athens. In war-time the traffic was supervised by the *Hellespontophylakes* ('Guardians of the Hellespont'), a body of officials established at Byzantium.

There is another view of the north-eastern corn trade divergent from the above:[34] that in the fifth century the documentary evidence does not show a highly developed trade, and in the case of the cities of the North, as members of the Athenian Empire, their sole interest for Athens was as sources of tribute, since the tribute of the Hellespontine cities was very large. But in this respect they were not more important than those of Ionia. In 433/2 BC the contributions of both Thrace (121 talents, 2120 drachmae) and Ionia (101 talents, 3355 drachmae) were greater than that of the Hellespont (74 talents, 1115 drachmae), as appears from the Tribute Lists.

It has also been asserted[35] that little consideration was given to Athens' economic interests in the north-east at the commencement of the fourth century, despite the fact that the downfall of Athens was brought about by the loss of this route, and despite the significance of the operations of Thrasybulus, the Athenian (the establishment of a tax station on the Bosporus), and Antalcidas, the Spartan, in that direction. A statement of Isocrates[36] mentioning 'the things which we are not now able to obtain by reason of war and great expense' does not prove a lack of interest in the Thracian Chersonese, but the problem of Athens' military weakness in the fourth century. On the other hand, Aeschines[37] refers contemptuously to places in Thrace. It would, it may be noted, be incorrect to say that fresh circumstances turned the attention of

Athens Thracewards in the fourth century, or that the north-eastern trade developed on account of the growth of the Spartan fleet and the Peloponnesian pirates. It could be claimed that the loss of Euboea, and the cutting-off of a Sicilian supply constituted fresh circumstances, but the loss of Euboea was, in any case, only temporary, while the available Sicilian supply was reduced at the end of the fifth century by the Carthaginian invasion of Sicily and its aftermath, and when Dionysius of Syracuse developed his empire he probably needed all his timber and corn. A period of anarchy followed, which was finally settled by Timoleon. By the middle of the fourth century, or even before, Sicily was again producing corn for export, but only in the last thirty years of the century does Sicilian corn seem to appear at Athens. Since Athens, as far as we know, never made use of this source of supply in the fifth century (or for a short time only), it would not be missed. The Spartan fleet and the Peloponnesian pirates may have threatened a corn supply from Egypt, but apart from our ignorance of the magnitude of this supply until the later decades of the fourth century, these two potential sources of trouble, according to all our authorities, menaced the north-eastern trade most of all (see below). Later in the fourth century, when the problem of Athens' relations in this region came to the fore, Gernet suggests that Demosthenes exaggerated the relative importance of the corn trade from the Black Sea, but such a suggestion goes against the whole trend of fourth-century policy.

An essential part in Athens' policy of utilizing the trade of the Black Sea for her own ends was played by the *Hellespontophylakes*, who seem to have been introduced some time between the summer of 428 and 426 BC. The *terminus post quem* is fixed by the fact that the Mytilenaeans, planning revolt in 428 BC, drew corn and archers from Pontus, without any check being placed on them by Athens.[38] The inscription dealing with the affairs of the Methonaeans,[39] which mentions the *Hellespontophylakes* as superintendents of the corn trade at the Bosporus, in 426 BC, provides the *terminus ante quem*.

Their existence very probably is to be coupled with the imposition of a toll of ten percent on all trade passing through the Bosporus. It has been proved conclusively that the oldest mention of a tenth appearing in a Treasury inscription[40] of 419/18 BC, or at latest 418/17, was a tax drawn from the subject states, the receipts of which passed into the treasury of the empire. It is termed 'the tenth', and therefore stood alone as the ten percent tax *par excellence*. A tenth is mentioned by Antiphon[41] and can therefore be dated before 411 BC. Aristotle[42] seems to have had some such toll in mind when using the phrase 'from the

tributes and the taxes' in speaking of the revenues from the Athenian
Empire. It must, therefore, be concluded that there was a tax of direct
character in the empire even before 413 B C, when, it is generally agreed,
one was established to replace the tribute. Some authorities identify
this tax with that mentioned by Xenophon and Diodorus[43] as established at Chrysopolis on the Bosporus by Alcibiades in 410/9 B C. No
mention is made by those authorities of a previous tax. On the other
hand Polybius,[44] in speaking of Alcibiades' action, does use the adverb
'first'. This, however, need not preclude an earlier toll, as Polybius
probably used Xenophon as his authority, and saw no mention of a
prior impost. Such a considerable tax as this could only have been
raised at the Bosporus[45] on all transit traffic. It would appear that the
appointment of the *Hellespontophylakes* and the establishment of the
tax were simultaneous. The introduction of the war-tax at Athens in
427 BC marks a financial crisis, which would in part be alleviated by
such a source of revenue. The tax was re-established in 390/89 B C by
Thrasybulus[46] and in the Hellenistic age by Byzantium under stress of
financial necessity.[47] Polybius calls the tax a *paragogion* (transit tax).

The use which Athens made of her power is well exemplified by the
decree concerning Methone. The inscription[48] consists of two parts,
dated respectively 429/8 and 426/5 B C. The earlier part deals with the
lightening of the tribute payable by Methone, and with the despatch of
an embassy to Perdiccas of Macedon, to require him to allow the
Methonaeans the free use of the sea, which is paralleled by the decree[49]
relating to Aphytis (see below), by a decree receiving back a revolted
ally[50] and another[51] concerning the founding of a colony. The Methone
decree also required unrestricted relations with Macedonia. The second
section (426/5 B C) permitted the Methonaeans to import corn from the
Bosporus to a fixed amount, without hindrance from the *Hellespontophylakes*, provided a proper declaration was made. The decree was a
war-time measure designed to assist a state badly affected by the
disturbed economic conditions.

A similar decree[52] of 428 B C survives, dealing with the mercantile
activities of Aphytis, a town of Pallene in Chalcidice.[53] It was promul-
gated either at the request of Aphytis, or spontaneously by Athens, to
define the trade rights of the state in question, and to secure its commerce against injustice. The inscription clearly demonstrates the many
limitations on trade prevalent in the Aegean (for example *asylei*
'without seizure' is mentioned, showing that Athens adopted this procedure against those whose trade she wished to check); they were
mainly imposed for the benefit of the import trade of Athens, particu-

larly the corn trade. It would seem from the decree that trade in corn was permitted within the Athenian Empire only on special conditions, and was otherwise forbidden. The Aphytaeans had an unlimited right of importation with a particular reference to Athens, and also the right to transport corn, in keeping with the regulations laid down by Athens and the allies, of which the details are unknown. The whole decree, with that concerning Methone, shows the extent to which Athens claimed to interfere in the trade of her subject allies.

Finally, Egypt remains to be considered as a source of corn. The connection of Aegina and Egypt has already been mentioned. In the fifth century, trade between Athens and Naucratis, whether direct or indirect, is shown to have existed by the abundant red-figure vase fragments from that place. The possible export of corn from Egypt is a different matter. In 455 BC a gift of corn was made to Athens by Psammetichus, an Egyptian pretender.[54] It amounted to thirty thousand medimni, and in the process of its distribution the citizen lists were revised, and nearly five thousand names removed. In one of the two accounts given by him, Philochorus uses the phrase 'there being a scarcity of corn in Attica at that time'. The aim of Psammetichus was no doubt to cement relations political and mercantile between himself and Athens, a potential connection which was not followed up. Some suggestion of the reason for this was made when the possibilities of a corn trade with Sicily in the fifth century were considered. Egypt was the other region to which Athens might turn as an alternative to the uncertain Black Sea supply, and possibly there is some hint of a general shortage as well as a failure of crops in the words of Philochorus.

In this connection Egypt is to be considered in close relation to Cyprus. The history of Athenian relations with Cyprus shows a continual failure on the part of Athens to establish her power decisively in the island. The revolt from Persia under Onesilas[55] was supported by Athens; yet Cyprus was again subdued, and supplied Xerxes with ships.[56] The Persian power in Cyprus was attacked by Pausanias (after Plataea and Mykale) with eighty ships (thirty Athenian), but the temporary success was not followed up.[57] Cimon, after the battles of the Eurymedon, sailed to Cyprus (? 469 BC) and defeated a Persian fleet.[58] On a second expedition (451 BC), he died while besieging Citium; successful land and sea battles were fought, but again the victories were not followed up.[59] Down to the year 449 BC Athens and Persia were hostile to each other. In this period Athenian intervention (460–455 BC) in Cyprus and Egypt is connected with her efforts to support the anti-Persian revolt of the Egyptians, which ultimately failed. It is true that this can be interpreted in part as stemming from the anti-Persian policy of Cimon, and also of Pericles, when Cimon was in exile (461–451), and in part it explains the final operations off Cyprus, as calculated to 'bottle-up' the Phoenician fleet. But it is possible to see more in these efforts than a desire to 'teach Persia a lesson',[60] a curious piece of policy when Athens was also fully engaged nearer home. It has been said:[61] 'It is surprising to find Athens undertaking any responsibility in western Sicily at a time when the Egyptian catastrophe had just crippled her resources, and the war against the Peloponnesian League claimed all her energies.' A nice balance of preoccupations. Cyprus was a convenient half-way house to Egypt, as in the late fourth century.[62] Athens was not, however, successful in Egypt, and the connection with Psammetichus was not followed up, when the Black Sea area was again secured. Likewise, after peace with Persia was obtained, and the possibility of trade between Athens and Cyprus existed, commercial intercourse still remained very slight, until the accession of Evagoras, as is indicated by the few vase remains from the second half of the fifth century.

This evidence goes to prove that in the fifth century, while her empire lasted, Athens had no need to make agreements with corn-exporting countries, such as the Black Sea region, relying instead on her overwhelming sea-power. Not only did Athens use this to secure her own supplies, but in the last struggle of the Peloponnesian War, as long as her naval fortunes endured, she harassed the trade-routes of her enemies as well as securing her own.

Such attacks on enemy trade-routes and trading vessels formed an important part of the strategy of Athens in the naval warfare of the Peloponnesian War. In the winter of 430 BC an expedition was sent to Caria and Lycia, to protect the merchant vessels, coming from Phaselis and Phoenicia, from the piratic activities of the Peloponnesians in that region. In the same year Phormio and twenty ships were despatched to Naupactus to close the Corinthian Gulf to all traffic ('So that no one could sail from Corinth and the Crisean Gulf or to them'). As Corinth depended very largely on imported corn and timber, and on transit trade, for her revenues,[63] these operations were evidently aimed at her. The assistance sent in 427 BC to Leontini and her allies,[64] and the attack on Cythera in the summer of 424 BC had the same end in view. The significance of Cythera for the Spartans is to be noted: 'for them it was a port of call for the merchant ships coming from Egypt and Libya; and at the same time pirates did less damage to the Laconian territory from the sea.'[65] Both had as their aim the prevention of the importation of corn into the Peloponnese. It was her sea-power also that enabled Athens in the Peloponnesian War to exert a certain amount of influence over Macedonia, in restricting exports of timber to her own advantage,[66] and blockading the coast in 417 B C,[67] which would prove disastrous to the revenues of Perdiccas.[68] Athens claimed a general dominion over the sea, as is shown by one of the terms of the truce of 422 B C,[69] which limited the Peloponnesians to sailing along their own coasts in 'rowed ships', not exceeding five hundred talents (twelve tons) burden. Permission might be given to individual traders to sail in waters under the domination of Athens, as in the case of Lycon of Achaea,[70] who was allowed to trade anywhere except in the Corinthian Gulf.

The change was a grave one when fortune went against Athens after the Sicilian expedition. The Spartan occupation of Decelea in 413 B C not only had a disastrous effect on Athenian industry and mining, on account of the defection of the slaves,[71] but the corn hitherto conveyed to Athens via Oropos and Decelea had now to be brought by sea round Cape Sunium[72] with a consequent increase in price. Sunium was fortified[73] to afford protection to the merchant vessels on their course. As Thucydides points out, the city, now an armed camp and cut off from Attica, needed to import everything.

Even so, as long as Athens still retained some part of her former naval power, she was not too badly off, as Agis at Decelea realized.[74] The toll station was re-established on the Bosporus at Chrysopolis by Alcibiades, and a squadron at the Hellespont protected the passage of corn ships,[75] destroying or putting to flight in 410 B C a squadron of fifteen ships under Clearchus, sent by Agis. At home corn proved a useful weapon in the hands of the Four Hundred (411 B C), who fortified a stoa at the Piraeus, in which all corn was stored, and from which it was sold.[76]

In the Black Sea region it was inevitable that Athens' defeat at Syracuse would result in loss of prestige. Nymphaeum in the Crimea was captured by Satyrus,[77] an exploit in which, according to Aeschines, Gylon the grandfather of Demosthenes played an inglorious part. But in reality Athens could no longer maintain her power in a region so distant. Worse was to come, however. All authorities join in commenting on the importance of Euboea, both as a source of corn,[78] and as a bulwark of Athenian power.[79] The island and Oropos on the mainland opposite were closely linked as stages of the north-eastern corn-route. In the winter of 412 B C the Boeotians captured Oropos by treachery,[80] and in 411, after the utter defeat of a small Athenian fleet by a Pelo-

ponnesian force, Euboea revolted,[81] producing great consternation at
Athens. Thus only the all-sea route remained, and that could only be
used as long as Athens retained some vestiges of her sea-power. Corn
must have been dear at Athens in the last years of Peloponnesian War,
as even the local production had ceased in war-time.[82] Public-spirited
citizens assisted in the corn trade[83] and even metics participated.[84] The
final defeat of Athens at Aigospotamoi, and the siege of Athens, the
population of which had been increased by those Athenians sent home
by Lysander, marked the complete cutting-off of the corn trade, and
the suffering of the Athenians was great.

The early fourth century was a period of gradual recovery. The
farms of Attica took some time to revive after the war-time devastation.[85] There is an honorary decree for an Athenian citizen, for services
in providing capital for the restoration of land disused after the war.
Yet corn was quite cheap at three drachmae per medimnus (as may be
deduced from Aristophanes[86]) in 390 BC.

The connection between Athens and South Russia was maintained
in the fourth century, though the relations of the two powers were
somewhat altered. The Piraeus remained the great trading centre of
Greece, but Athens, in securing her supplies, had to resort less to force
of arms and more to bargaining. A leading authority, Rostovzeff,[87]
regarded the first agreement between Athens and Satyrus as made after
the battle of Cnidus (394 BC), which resulted in the partial recovery of
Athenian naval power, and this would explain the relatively cheap
price of corn in 390 BC. This date, and the conclusion that it was not
earlier, is based on a statement of Isocrates,[88] who refers to the preference in loading corn given to Athens, as though this was not a right
secured by agreement, but a favour granted from time to time. There
was, however, a great change which characterized the fourth-century
Athenian corn trade, a change which became more accentuated as
the century advanced. It was true that Athens had favourable
relations with the corn-producing region of South Russia, but the
narrow seas through which the trade-route passed proved a source of
weakness to her, as they had been an advantage during the period of
the Athenian Empire. Furthermore, the disturbed course of the fourth
century, in which no one power was supreme for long, rendered sea
travel more hazardous than when Athens held the naval hegemony of
the eastern Mediterranean. A consideration of these two factors, and
the facts which illustrate them, form the basis of an assessment of
fourth-century trade.

The first years of the fourth century saw the corn trade flourishing enough. The refounding of the Athenian navy in 390/89 BC was attended by some successes under Thrasybulus. The toll at the Bosporus was re-established, and customs duties were imposed on some of the states of Asia Minor in order to provide funds for the upkeep of the fleet.[89] An inscription of 387/6 BC,[90] a decree of the Athenians concerning Clazomenae, also shows that some attempt was made to regulate the mercantile activities of subordinate allies.[91] The attempt to revive the empire and the naval power of Athens was, however, a failure on account of lack of money, which constantly frustrated Athenian naval efforts in the fourth century. In consequence the Spartan Antalcidas in 387/6 BC was able to cut off Athenian corn supplies and compel the acceptance by Athens of the 'King's Peace'.[92]

The great menace of the fourth century was that of piracy, which became very prevalent, and was used as a weapon of war. In 387 BC Iphicrates the Athenian and Anaxibius of Sparta used pirates as a means of offence in their operations off Abydos. Pirates were likewise established on Aegina by Sparta in 388 BC,[93] to harass the trade of the Piraeus, and despite the efforts of Athens to dislodge them, and the temporary relief afforded by an expedition of Chabrias,[94] they remained a menace for a considerable period.[95] So weak was Athenian sea-power at this period that the Spartan Teleutias was able to make a daring raid on the Piraeus and kidnap merchants from there in 387 BC[96] (an exploit repeated in 361 BC by Alexander of Pherae,[97] called by Xenophon[98] 'a villainous pirate'), and to sail along the coast of Attica to Sunium, seizing fishing boats and corn-carrying merchantmen. Piracy was also engaged in privately at all points of the Mediterranean at this period: an Athenian pursuing runaway slaves was seized by pirates and sold in Aegina;[99] another was attacked in the Argolic Gulf and died of wounds received in the struggle,[100] both in the period c. 370 BC. Thus the statement of Isocrates[101] made ten years earlier would seem amply justified: 'a situation . . . in which wreckers dominate the sea . . .' No effort was made to check this state of affairs. Piracy was practised in 361 BC, for a short time at any rate, by Alexander of Pherae[102] who, besides effecting the attack on Athens mentioned above, carried on operations against the Cyclades, and seized Tenos.[103] This incident may be regarded as a military operation, and such too was the attempted seizure of the Athenian corn ships by the Spartan forces in 376 BC. With the intention of cutting off the supplies of Athens (note their precarious character), the Spartans sent out a force under Pollis, which operated in the region off Aegina, Cea and Andros, and intercepted the corn ships, which had reached Cape Geraestus (south

Euboea), in the channel between Euboea and Andros (the Doro Channel). The Athenians, realizing the danger, manned their fleet, and won the battle of Naxos under the leadership of Chabrias.[104]

The configuration of the Aegean is such that the route followed by vessels from the Black Sea passed from island to island: after emerging from the narrow seas of the Bosporus, Propontis and Hellespont, the islands of Lemnos, Imbros and Scyros stretch to the south-west. We therefore find that these three islands were of such importance to Athenian trade that their possession by Athens was never contested. Imbros was colonized by Athens in 445–442 BC and offered to Athens by Sparta at the end of the Peloponnesian War;[105] all three were recognized as Athenian by the King's Peace, and by that of 338 BC with Philip. It was to the advantage of Athens to keep these islands free from pirates. Not far from Scyros, to the north-west was Halonesus in the northern Sporades, claimed as a possession by Athens. The Athenians, however, failed to do their duty, so that Philip of Macedon in 343 BC was forced to clear the island of pirates,[106] the result of which was contention with Athens. As in the fifth century,[107] the Thracian Chersonese was infested with sea robbers, who found there an ideal base for operations.[108]

Some effort was made by Athens in the days of the second Athenian League to put down piracy by fining those states which gave shelter to pirates. The 'Psephisma of Moirokles' made provision for this, and Melos was fined ten talents for the offence in 344/3 BC.[109] The Peace of Philocrates also contained measures against them.[110] But Athens, on the whole, was too weak to enforce such measures, and in about 340 BC Thasos received pirate forces with the condonation of Athens.[111] Furthermore Athens herself had made use of pirates in the Social War to harass the shipping of the revolted states: 'In the Social War the Athenians voted to carry out piracy against those of her enemies sailing the seas, even if they were merchants.'[112] Comparable are the exploits of Meidias[113] and capture of Phrynon of Rhamnus by pirates.[114]

As an alternative to a direct route across the Mediterranean to the Hellespont, vessels might follow a coast route from the Saronic Gulf via Sunium by Oropos[115] and the Euripus, Chalcis,[116] Histiaea,[117] thence to Pagasae in Thessaly,[118] and so to Macedon, Thrace and the Hellespont. Whilst the dangers incurred by taking this route were no less, since in the second half of the fourth century even Euboea was pirate-infested,[119] yet such a voyage would pay better, as not only could the long-distance cargo be carried, but also a share be taken in the coasting trade from port to port.

The existence of the pirates would alone have been quite sufficient to render hazardous the corn trade of Athens; but it was further affected by another problem peculiar to the fourth century. During the period of Athenian supremacy Athens took it upon herself to regulate the corn supplies of her subject allies, at any rate in war-time. In the fourth century, in spite of the preferential treatment accorded to Athens by the rulers of Panticapaeum, and the special agreement they made with her, there were other customers for the corn of South Russia, who dealt directly with the source. Mytilene received a special privilege from the tyrant of Panticapaeum[120] around the year 350 BC. Heraclea Pontica[121] and Clazomenae[122] drew their corn from the same source, when a local shortage existed. It may be noted that in both the latter cases the writer of the work in question emphasizes a shortage of money, so that the corn could be purchased only after extraordinary financial measures had been adopted. In a period of shortage the price of corn would rise considerably, upsetting the precarious finances of small Greek states. It seems almost certain that these instances date from the same period (c. 362 BC) as the seizure of Athenian corn vessels by Byzantium, Chalcedon and Cyzicus.[123] There is also reference to the seizure of ships by Chalcedon for a somewhat different reason. Among the vessels seized by Byzantium, Chalcedon and Cyzicus were some belonging to the Athenian banker Pasion.[124] Similar action was taken by Heraclea Pontica in 330/29 BC[125] As the local supplies of these states had failed, and they were unable to pay the increased price of imported corn, they took to seizing the supplies of Athens.

Athens therefore resorted to having warships convoy the merchant vessels, together with those of other states which requested similar protection – the convoying of a ship of Maronea is a case in point.[126] This was not difficult, as the corn-conveying ships seem to have sailed in squadrons, gathering at various points on the voyage, such as Sestos, and Cape Geraestus. Thus there is mentioned the departure of the ships 'after Arcturus' from the Pontus.[127] A parallel is the 'Sicilian convoy'.[128] These convoys brought a large part of the year's supply at one time. Apart from the official convoying of such vessels, various Athenian generals found it a lucrative practice to use Athenian warships for private convoying in return for payment, called 'benevolences' (*eunoiai*). Where they did not receive money for this, they extorted it from such states as Erythrae and Chios, in return for abstaining from seizing the ships of these states. Thus Demosthenes[129] observes:

Having purchased immunity from injustice for the merchants sailing from their ports, freedom from seizure, and the convoying of their own ships, they call such 'giving benevolences', and these exactions have this name.

Aeschines also mentions[130] the exploits of Deiares, Deipyros, Polyphontes and others. With the above series of events may be coupled the general corn shortage of 356/5 BC.[131] Demosthenes tells of 'a corn shortage occurring among all men'. This was alleviated at Athens by a gift of corn from Leucon of Pontus.

The period of rivalry between Athens and Philip of Macedon, and its sequel, showed a continuation of the trends of the earlier years of the century. Demosthenes emphasizes again and again the vital character of the corn trade for the security of Athens,[132] and the certainty of losing it as one of the results of the victory of Philip.[133] Philip himself was not slow to realize the effective character of such a course of operations as would tend to cut off the Athenian supplies. Before 351 BC he captured Athenian vessels at Cape Geraestus,[134] others off the coast of Macedonia sometime after 346 BC,[135] and in 340/39 BC a very large number of ships (Philochorus says 230, Theopompus 180) at Hieron Teichos, with great profit to himself. The Athenians retaliated by blockading the coast of Macedonia (thereby robbing Philip of his revenues[136]) and seizing and selling Macedonian merchants.[137] The battle of Chaeronea produced a first-class crisis in the corn supply. Demosthenes' appointment as corn buyer is to be noted;[138] his connection with the corn trade is mentioned elsewhere.[139] A false report of the gravity of the defeat of Athens, disseminated in Rhodes by Leocrates, caused the seizure of corn ships on their way from Egypt to Athens, and their retention at Rhodes.[140] One of the witnesses against Leocrates, a certain Phyrkinos, who farmed the five percent tax on imports and exports, suffered considerable loss from the reduction of trade.

Thus it is clear that the fourth-century corn trade was in the highest degree precarious, in view of the long-continued wars and pirate-infested seas. The uncertainties of communication were revealed by the fluctuating price of corn,[141] and the conditions of the cereal market were the surest indication of a crisis.[142] The prevailing dangers for overseas mercantile ventures were reflected in the high rates of interest charged on mercantile loans. Every effort was made to encourage those with money to lend to finance trading voyages. This was mostly done by increased legal protection.[143] On the other hand the traders themselves were an international body, over which it was difficult to exercise supervision. The interests of Athens were best served by her becoming the international emporium of Greece and the chief money market. Even so merchants often behaved with great dishonesty, in failing to carry out their obligations,[144] and diverting their cargoes elsewhere, as, for example, to Acanthus[145] and to Rhodes.[146] The principle of exploiting the markets by selling corn where it was dearest is clearly recognized,[147] and specific examples are afforded us.[148] Rumours of wars and of interruption of the corn supplies were exploited to secure higher prices.[149]

The last decades of the fourth century saw yet more changes. The dangers of the north-eastern corn-route forced upon Athens the necessity of having more than one source of food supplies. After the battle of Chaeronea (338 B C) the importance of Athens was diminished, and she was less able to protect her commerce; therefore she could not offer the Black Sea tyrants so much in the way of reciprocal advantages (note the greater dependence on individual traders). It has been pointed out that the liberalities of the tyrants always took place in times of Athens' greatness. In the authorities for the period more is now heard of Sicily,[150] and of Egypt.[151] An inscription[152] records a grant of *proxenia* ('consulship') to Theogenis, for services to Athenians coming to Naucratis (349/8 B C). Another[153] honours natives of Cyrene as *proxenoi* for their protection of visiting Athenians (353/2 B C). The victories of Alexander opened up Egypt to trade to an increased extent. He appointed Cleomenes to the governorship of Egypt in 332 B C, and the latter effected a corner in the corn export trade of that country,[154] exploiting as well the export of corn, by a well-organized system of communications, through which the grain was conveyed to those markets where it would command the highest price.[155] Such an arrangement was not to the advantage of Athens, and while this route (Athens–Egypt) was not so dangerous as that to the north-east, Rhodes had to be reckoned with as a possible enemy who would seize the passing corn ships in times of necessity.[156] Cyprus was also a source of corn at a later date, or at any rate an important centre of the corn trade.[157] Thrace was in a state of anarchy at this period. The most interesting departure from the traditional policy is marked by the founding of a base somewhere in the northern Adriatic, on the Italian coast (Hadria) in 325/4 B C[158] as a central point for commerce in the Adriatic: the relevant inscription says:

In order that there may be for the [Athenian] people for all time their own trading centres and escorting of corn [ships], and that when their own base for shipping has been established, there may be a defence against the Tyrrhenians, and Miltiades the founder and the settlers may be able to employ their own naval force, and those who sail the sea, both of the Greeks and of the barbarians, may sail with security into the Adriatic, having the Athenian naval base as an anchorage, and a means of protection against the Tyrrhenian pirates.

The activities of the latter are made clear by the titles of speeches of the period which survive: of Hyperides, *Concerning the defence against the Tyrrhenians*, and of Dinarchus, *Tyrrhenikos*. The Adriatic was always dangerous, either through natural hazards or on account of pirates.[159] Lysias[160] mentions one hundred percent gain on a trading venture to the Adriatic, showing the great risk involved. The corn from this region was probably drawn from the fertile valley of the Po, and from Epirus, the source of Corinthian corn. There is the interesting reference of Lycurgus[161] to a man who: 'dwelling in Megara . . . exported corn from Epirus, from Cleopatra, to Leucas and from there to Corinth'.

The great weakness of Athens' position in this period came clearly to light in the time of corn shortage which appears to have prevailed from about 330 to about 325 BC.[162] This was caused by (i) the failure of harvests; (ii) Alexander drawing on world supplies; (iii) the machinations of Cleomenes in Egypt; iv) a decrease in the South Russian trade (cf. the seizure of Heraclides of Salamis by Heraclea Pontica). The shortage seems to have been general in the eastern Aegean. Cyrene made gifts of 805,000 medimni, including 100,000 to Athens (325–317 BC).[163] Athens now depended to an even greater extent than before on the good will of foreign merchants for her supplies. Home supplies, as far as they went, commanded high prices, and enriched landowners.[164] There is no greater proof of the precarious state of the corn trade than the decrees in honour of various foreigners who came to her assistance with gifts of corn or supplies at low prices. Demosthenes[165] enumerates three distinct periods of such services: (i) in 336 BC, when Alexander came to Thebes, a gift of money; (ii) 'previously', when corn was 16 drs per medimnus, 10,000 medimni at 5 drs (the usual price); (iii) 327/6 BC, a gift of one talent for a purchase of corn. Among the honours conferred at this period, and preserved for us in inscriptions, are those granted to two Tyrians (probably resident in the Piraeus, since Tyre was captured by Alexander in 332/1 BC, and many of the inhabitants slain), for undertaking to import corn;[166] to a native of Miletus (?) for services to the corn trade from Cyprus to Athens;[167] the commendation of two natives for the delivery of quantities of corn and barley at low prices (4000 medimni of corn at 9 drs per medimnus, and a quantity of barley at 5 drs);[168] commendation of one Potamon and a companion (name lost) for services to the corn trade, possibly from Sinope.[169] There is also a decree of *proxenia* to Praxiades of Cos, on the testimony of Athenian merchants and the people of Samos, for services to the corn trade;[170] and honours to Philomelos, for loans of money made by him in a period of scarcity of corn.[171] The most important example is that of

Heraclides of Cypriote Salamis,[172] who imported and sold corn (probably from South Russia) at a low price (330–328 BC) and later (328/7 BC) gave a sum of money for a purchase of corn. Finally, efforts were made by Lycurgus to encourage foreign corporations of merchants, by permission given to establish at Athens centres of worship of their gods. Thus sites for a temple of Aphrodite were granted to merchants of Citium[173] and for a temple of Isis to Egyptian merchants.[174]

The passage of the seas was in these years secured at any rate in theory by the treaty between the Greeks and Alexander of Macedon (336 BC).[175] The charge was nevertheless made that Alexander himself broke it by detaining the Athenian vessels at Tenedos, and not releasing them until Athens manned a hundred triremes. This act has been ascribed to 'some subordinate's excess of zeal', as Alexander always sought to conciliate Athens. The speech *On the Treaty with Alexander* was written (331/30 BC) by the extreme radical party of Hyperides, and was therefore likely to be exaggerated.

Under the leadership of Lycurgus (339–326 BC) Athens embarked on a period of recovery and encouragement of trade which included the establishment of a large fleet. By 325 BC she owned 360 triremes, 50 quadriremes and 7 quinqueremes with an effective strength of 200. Some of these were used for convoying corn ships.[176] The pirates were still a menace, as is shown by decrees[177] conferring honours on those who secured the freedom of Athenians captured by pirates.

The Lamian War, with the double defeat and destruction of Athenian fleets at Abydos and Amorgos in 322 BC, marked the end of Athenian sea-power, and of the existence of Athens as an independent state. Another corn shortage followed this event; an inscription[178] of 320/19 BC records a reward for despatching corn from the Hellespont after the battle of Abydos. To the same period belongs another inscription[179] of 321–319 BC recording honours for services to the corn trade from Asia.

Here the period covered by this work effectively ends, when Athens ceased to exist as an independent state. During the wars of the Successors the problem of the corn supply remained a difficult one, with Athens dependent upon the good will of others. A decree[180] honours Spartocus IV of the Bosporan Kingdom (285 BC):

He gave free corn to the amount of 15,000 medimni, and he announces that for the future he will supply the need of the Athenian people as far as he is able.

Another decree[181] in honour of Audoleon says:

He gave as a gift to the people 7500 medimni of corn from Macedonia at his own expense, delivering it to the harbours of the city. He undertakes for the future also to provide for [the Athenians'] needs.

These are decrees in which effusive expressions of gratitude mark the great straits that Athens was in.

Next we must consider the privileges accorded to Athens by the Bosporan power. These privileges were embodied in agreements between Athens and the successive tyrants of Panticapaeum, and we possess literary and epigraphical evidence of them. The earliest, in Isocrates,[182] shows Satyrus I and Spartocus I, the father and grandfather of Leucon, apparently exercising some sort of preference on behalf of Athens. It is recorded by Demosthenes in his speech against Leptines, the subject of which is the proposed abolition of the honour of freedom from taxation. This privilege was held by Leucon I (393–353 BC) and his successors, in return for preferences granted to exporters of corn from the Cimmerian Bosporus to Athens. The freedom from taxation in question was probably not exemption from import duties (which would not benefit Leucon), but freedom from public duties (*leitourgiai*). The orator makes this abundantly clear by emphasizing the fact that in the case of Leucon, only a question of honorary distinction and not of material advantage would be involved, if he were deprived of his freedom from taxation. Thus the agreement was not one embodying reciprocal advantages, for Athens alone was really benefited. Of course Panticapaeum had the advantage of trading with a state able to convoy vessels, and possessing a widely-used coinage.

The decree formulating the agreement was publicly exhibited, at the Piraeus, at Panticapaeum, and in the temple of Zeus Ourios, on the Asiatic shore of the Bosporus, near the entrance of the straits as approached from the Black Sea. Athenian commanders met ships for convoy there. In 340/39 Philip of Macedon seized merchant ships at the same spot. The references of Demosthenes enable us to reconstruct the text of the treaty. It was an agreement, established by a resolution of the people of Athens, and its provisions, as given by Demosthenes[183] were: (i) the right of pre-emption; (ii) exemption from the $3\frac{1}{3}$ percent tax imposed by the tyrants of Panticapaeum on all exports of corn. The Mytilenaeans paid 1/90 plus 1/60 on their imports, thereby saving 0·55 percent. Demosthenes[184] calculates that the remission of the tax is equal to a gift of $13,333\frac{1}{3}$ medimni, i.e. 400,000/30. In return Leucon received the honour of freedom from taxation at Athens. The evidence of Demosthenes is supplemented by the inscription renewing the honour of freedom from taxation, to the sons of Leucon, Spartocus and Paerisades, on their undertaking to continue the privileges granted to Athens by Leucon (and apparently by Satyrus his predecessor also). The inscription reads:[185]

The Athenian People praises Spartocus and Paerisades since they are good men, and undertake for the Athenian People to supervise the export of corn, as their father did . . . The ambassadors are to say to them that if they do this they will be deprived of nothing on the part of the Athenian People. And when they give to the Athenians the concessions which Satyrus and Leucon gave, Spartocus and Paerisades shall have the concessions which the Athenian People gave to Satyrus and Leucon.

These privileges are called 'gifts' or 'concessions', proving that this is no ordinary trade agreement. (It is to be noted also that the tyrants of Panticapaeum are always regarded as benefactors.) There is further evidence of such privileges, granted to Paerisades, in Demosthenes' speech against Phormio.[186] Paerisades made a proclamation in Bosporus: 'Whosoever wishes to import corn to Athens into the Attic trading port, shall export it [i.e. from South Russia] free of tax.' It is also stated that it was proclaimed at Panticapaeum that anyone exporting corn to Athens was to be exempted from the export tax. As Grote points out,[187] such privileges would tend to put the whole corn trade in the hands of traders from Athens. It is easy to see that by the use of this right, in combination with the law requiring (i) that loans made at Athens on double voyages should be on such vessels as were returning to that port (not as some interpret it, that every vessel returning to Athens should carry corn), and (ii) that Athenian citizens or metics should not import corn into any port other than the Piraeus, the Athenian state sought to obtain once again control over the Black Sea corn trade.

It is only in the case of the Bosporan kingdom that such an agreement is found (the privilege was sometimes illegally used, as in the case of Lampis,[188] who, taking advantage of it, carried corn to Acanthus), and if we may believe Demosthenes,[189] more than half of the corn imported into Athens came from this region. This might have been due to the fact that the South Russian plain was such an important producing area; on the other hand, it may have proceeded from the fact that corn could be obtained from this source with greater dependability and cheapness.

Finally, a word may be said on Demosthenes' statement concerning the dimensions of Athenian imports of corn. He asserts[190] that the corn imported from Pontus was equal to that coming from all the other foreign sources. He goes on to say that 400,000 medimni was the amount obtained from the kingdom of Leucon, and that therefore 800,000 medimni represents the total sum of Athenian corn imports. Attempts have been made to calculate the population of Attica, and thus reckon the amount of corn needed for the yearly consumption.

The Eleusinian tithe inscription of 329/8 BC[191] indicates the production of Attica (with Salamis, Scyros and Imbros) for what was probably a bad year, since it occurs in the corn shortage of 330–326 BC. It affords a basis for the following figures of production: barley, 360,000 medimni; wheat, 33,600 medimni. Beloch[192] calculates that, setting aside one seventh as seed, on an average 7 medimni are required, of wheat, per year per person. Boeckh[193] reckons one *choenix* of barley as rations for an adult slave in ancient Greece, which amounts to 7·6 medimni per year of 360 days. The amount given above would suffice for 40,000–45,000 people. At a yearly ration per head of 6 medimni (since less wheat than barley would be needed) the 800,000 medimni of imported cereals (mostly wheat) would support 130,000 people. The total would therefore be sufficient for 175,000 people. Beloch, who has studied the question closely, sets the free population of Attica at 100,000, and so the residue of cereals indicates a metic and slave population of 75,000. But Beloch himself admits that his basis of facts is uncertain. Indeed another authority Jardé[194] reckons that most of the barley would be needed for feeding animals.

All the varied assessments of population appear to make the figures both of imported corn and of local production too low. This holds true even in a year of good harvests locally, though the amount of such a harvest cannot certainly be calculated, since it is not known how bad that of 329/8 BC was. It may be noted that Beloch attributes the famine of 330-326 BC not to bad harvests, but to the manoeuvres of Cleomenes, governor of Egypt, despite the fact that (Aristotle)[195] says that his plans succeeded only because of the general famine in Greece. The attempts of Gernet and Beloch to extract the truth from the varied and conflicting statements of ancient sources are rightly rejected by Jardé.[196] It is sufficient to say that there is no ground for the attack of Gernet[197] on the evidence of Demosthenes, as being exaggerated in favour of the trade with the Bosporan tyrants. In the light of the general fourth-century evidence it would be expected that a far greater proportion than one half of the corn would come from South Russia.

One further point remains to be discussed. Demosthenes mentions[198] that Leucon in 356/5 BC came to the assistance of Athens in a general corn shortage. Strabo[199] says that the same monarch sent her 2,100,000 medimni of corn. It is generally assumed that if the tradition is good, Leucon sent that quantity of corn as a gift to Athens, so that not only were her needs supplied, but the surplus was sold at a profit of fifteen talents; in the words of Demosthenes: 'Not only did he send you sufficient corn, but so much that there were fifteen talents of silver over and above, which Callisthenes administered.' But the wording of the sentence, the fact that no mention of a sale is made, the specification of the sum in silver, and the mention of the administration of Callisthenes, all make it much more likely that the sum in question was that raised for a purchase of corn, which was saved by Leucon's gift (or possibly corn exported at a lower price is meant, since the word used is 'sent' not 'gave') meeting the need without any expenditure. It is unnecessary, however, to connect Strabo's statement with that of Demosthenes. A modern writer Kocevalov[200] associates the event noticed by Strabo with Demosthenes' mention[201] of the equipment, by Leucon, of Theodosia (captured by his father's forces because it received exiles from Panticapaeum): '... establishing in addition Theodosia as a trading centre, which those who sail there say is in no wise inferior to Bosporus; and there also he has given us freedom from taxes.' Kocevalov and E. von Stern[202] believe that Strabo's figure represents the whole export of corn from Theodosia in Leucon's reign. Kocevalov also thinks that the yearly import of corn into Athens was more than 800,000 medimni, and in his opinion, Demosthenes[203] appears to say that 400,000 medimni were exported from Panticapaeum alone (since 'from himself' means from Leucon's residence, Panticapaeum). In the case of Theodosia, Kocevalov takes 'not inferior' to mean 'not inferior in export', and not 'not inferior in equipment'. Therefore Theodosia must have exported 400,000 medimni also. Demosthenes' participle 'establishing in addition' then represents a newly equipped port, in which the Athenians had hitherto not benefited from the freedom from taxes. Kocevalov therefore concludes that the equipment of Theodosia was completed in the year of Demosthenes' speech (355/4 BC). From 355/4 to 349/8 BC (the date of the death of Leucon) was a period during which corn was exported from Theodosia to Athens. The total of 2,100,000 medimni, spread over a period of five to six years, gives a yearly total of 350,000–420,000 medimni per year.

The whole idea is very original, but it is open to some serious criticisms. The phrase 'from himself' must mean 'from his kingdom', and therefore applies to the total corn export; 'not worse' must mean 'not worse equipped', since if its significance was 'equalled in export', it would not be necessary to learn this fact from seafaring merchants, but rather from the officials who administered the corn trade at Athens. In any case Demosthenes' calculation of Leucon's grant of freedom from taxation as constituting a free gift yearly of 13,000 medimni, seems to indicate that 400,000 medimni was the total export. If Theodosia exported a like amount during the last six years of Leucon's reign, this must represent a doubling of the South Russian export to Athens, unless we assume that this amount was previously shipped from a port not under Leucon's control. Hence the assumption of Kocevalov that Athens received corn through her colony Athenaion until 356/5 BC, when Leucon established Theodosia as a counterblast to this port of a foreign power, and gave the freedom from taxes in compensation. We have no hint of this from Demosthenes. It is better to conclude that 2,100,000 medimni formed the total export from Theodosia in Leucon's reign of forty years, representing a yearly average of 52,500 medimni, not so important as Panticapaeum, but relieving the congestion at that port.

Other foodstuffs imported into Athens could not vie in importance with corn. Dried fish for the lower classes at Athens, and fish pickle were imported from Byzantium and the Cimmerian Bosporus.[204] Tallow and cheese were produced in Sicily;[205] salt meat in Italy;[206] dates and fine wheaten flour came from Phoenicia;[207] almonds and chestnuts from Paphlagonia;[208] raisins and figs from Rhodes;[209] silphium from Cyrene.[210] But of all this edible merchandise only fish can have bulked largely in the total of the imports. Some regard the importation of cattle as important, but in view of the primitive and slow methods of transport, it was unlikely to have reached considerable dimensions; the essential thing was the importation of hides.

There were, of course, other imports. The construction, for instance, of large buildings required stone and timber and a host of other materials. There was importation of metals, though in the case of silver, lead, copper and iron the whole process of their manufacture could be carried out in Attica, and elsewhere in certain cases. In general, information on such things comes from epigraphical sources, such as building inscriptions, and such information is generally closely related to craftsmen or to those who dealt in the materials in question. It seems better, therefore, to consider such imports together with trades and crafts in Chapter VI.

CHAPTER FOUR

EXPORTS AND
INDUSTRIAL PRODUCTION

WHEN WE COME TO CONSIDER Athenian exports a distinction may be made, just as in the case of imports, between (i) natural products; (ii) manufactured articles; (iii) raw materials for the use of industries and the arts.

Among natural products the oil obtained from the olive berry naturally occurs first to the mind, owing to the traditional association of the city of Athens with the olive tree and fruit, the gift of Athena. Its culture, with that of the vine, seems to have expanded at the expense of corn-growing before the time of Solon. Both were suitable for stony and less fertile soils. Olive-oil alone was exempt from the general ban placed by Solon on the export of agricultural products from Attica. Athens certainly carried on a thriving trade in this commodity from probably the seventh century BC, as the so-called 'SOS' amphorae seem to indicate. It has been suggested by Seltman[1] that there was an archaic trade-route from Prasiae in east Attica via Carthaea in Cea to the wider Aegean and eastern Mediterranean (cp. the 'oil'-amphora depicted on coins of Carthaea). But the cultivation of the olive spread in Samos, Rhodes, and elsewhere. In Rhodes and Crete it may have been first introduced by the Phoenicians. For western Asia Minor we have the story of Thales cornering the oil presses. So Athens ceased to be the sole exporter of olive-oil in this direction. It was in the fifth and fourth centuries BC, when Athens became the successor of Miletus and Aegina in the Black Sea region, that she found what was undoubtedly her most profitable market; the more so because from this region she drew the bulk of her most important import – corn. The pottery industry also must have gained a continuing advantage from the opening up of this region, through the manufacture of the clay jars mentioned above and their successors. There were also the Panathenaic prize oil vases; but it is unlikely that all the oil distributed was contained in painted vases (possibly one painted vase of the traditional design went with each prize). In the West, where commerce via Corinth reigned supreme, it is uncertain whether oil from Athens penetrated at an early period to Italy and Sicily. The spread of the cultivation of the olive was slow in these regions (Pliny asserted that no olives existed in Italy in the reign of Tarquinius Priscus in the sixth century, a statement of uncertain value; it was not until the consulship of Pompey, in the first century, that the production of oil became sufficient for export), but some of the Sicilian cities, for example Acragas, exported olive-oil in Classical times.[2] At Athens the increase of population may actually have led to an increase of imported oil at certain periods. Some considerable damage was done to the olive groves of Attica by the Peloponnesian invasions and the occupation of Decelea, and by the incursions of the Boeotians.[3] Aristophanes seems to suggest[4] a possible shortage of olive-oil in 422 BC, parallel to a similar shortage of figs, usually the cheapest of food.[5] There is an indication of an oil shortage in later times,[6] but there is no suggestion that the export of olive-oil was ever forbidden.[7]

The cultivation of the vine, of religious significance owing to its association with Dionysus, extensive as it undoubtedly was, does not seem to have attained the same outstanding position in Attica as olive culture. No doubt the home demand was largely supplied by home production, and fine wines were certainly imported, as is indicated by evidence from the Athenian Agora. Whether wine figures in the exports from the Piraeus is unclear. The wine trade of Athens, whatever its dimensions, was in no danger from foreign competition in the fourth century, for otherwise money would not have been lent at Athens on a mercantile venture[8] in which Chalcidian wine was to be conveyed from Mende or Scione to the Cimmerian Bosporus. As Demosthenes points out:

I beg you, men of the jury, to think whether you ever knew or heard of any people importing wine from Pontos to Athens, and especially Coan wine. Surely it is just the reverse: wine is carried to Pontos from the places about us, from Peparethos and Cos and Thasos and Mende and from a variety of other places; and quite different things are imported here from Pontos.

Thus these are the sources of the wine imports of the region north of the Black Sea, Athens remaining unmentioned. Consequently, we shall not be far wrong in assuming that as far as wine was concerned Athens did not play a part comparable to the export of olive-oil. Wine as an export commodity was not regarded as of paramount importance. On the other hand, Thasos, whose wine trade was of the greatest significance for the prosperity of the island, possessed enactments designed to protect her position as an exporting state:[9]

A) 1. It is forbidden to purchase grape juice or wine when the fruit is on the vine [i.e. speculation by pre-emption] before the first day of Plynterion [May–June] – – – [penalty]: 2. He who purchases wine in jars, the purchase shall be lawful, if he seals the jars for himself. B) 1. A Thasian ship shall not import foreign wine to the region between Athos and Pacheie [i.e. the mainland opposite Thasos]. If he does, he shall be liable to the same penalties as for adding water to the wine – – –. 2. No one shall retail wine from amphorae, a smaller wine-jar or from a false jar.

We may compare with this the law concerning the export of olive-oil at Athens. Though the existing document dates from the reign of the Emperor Hadrian, probably something similar existed in pre-Roman times. In this enactment of the early second century AD,[10] records of production are to be kept in order that one-third (or sometimes one-eighth) may be made over to the state oil-buyers;

... if the owner of the property or the cultivator or the fruit-dealer sells the fruit. And the buyer for export shall make a declaration to the same on the quantity he is purchasing, for whom, and where his ship is anchored. The [sea-going] merchant too shall put on record what he is exporting and how much from each [dealer]. If he is detected in failing to make the declaration he shall be deprived [of his cargo] at his departure. If he sails and information is laid against him let him be charged in his own state by the Demos and for me [the Emperor].

In the Imperial period the arm of Rome was long, but even in the fifth and fourth centuries BC there was much a powerful state like Athens could do. In this inscription there are to be noted the three categories of person involved: the producer, the dealer, and the exporting merchant.[11]

Thasos, Rhodes, and Cnidus, with Paros and Chios, followed the custom of putting impressed stamps on the large clay jars, in which the native wine was exported. The discovery of such stamps among the fragments of wine jars throws valuable light on the wine trade of these states. They have been found on many sites, including Athens, on the west side of the Acropolis, and more important still, in the Agora, during the American excavations. Those found in the Agora have been carefully investigated in conjunction with the other archaeological material, with the result that the chronology has been more accurately established. The editor of the Agora jar-stamps draws the following conclusions.[12] Stamped jars containing wine were imported into Athens from Thasos from the end of the fifth century to the end of the third century BC; from Rhodes from the early third century and probably the late fourth century, until late in the second century BC; from Cnidus from early in the third century to well on in the first century BC. Of 1543 stamps published to 1934, 565 were Rhodian, 437 were Cnidian and 75 Thasian (uncertain 468); Parian 1; South Russian 1.

Among the Acropolis stamps Cnidian are in the majority (303), followed by Rhodian (93) and Thasian (11). Thus, valuable light is thrown on the wine import trade of Athens. In the Hellenistic period when Athens and her trade were at a low ebb, and presumably production suffered also, much was imported from Rhodes, corresponding to the commercial greatness of that state, as Rostovzeff points out:[13] 'The export of wine was but a trifling part of Rhodian trade, but its spread testifies to the extended voyages of the Rhodian ships, which imposed their mediocre wine on customers with whom they were in constant relations, and for whom Rhodian merchants with their money and influence were always welcome guests.' At an earlier period, however, when Athenian trade was still flourishing, we find only a relatively small number of Thasian stamps, showing in all probability that the import of wine was small. Thasian was a fine wine[14] and therefore its import was to be expected. The same is true of Chian. The Chian vase-stamp has been recognized on five fragmentary amphorae from the Athenian Agora, which can be dated to the third quarter of the fifth century. Chian wine, again, was a luxury which might be and was imported (in the characteristic *lagynai* (flasks)) in all periods.[15] Thus, we may reasonably conclude that in the fifth and fourth centuries only finer wines were imported in relatively small quantities, so that there was no need to protect the native product, as there was in the case of Thasos.

The Athenians do not appear to have stamped their wine amphorae, so we are deprived of this valuable means of checking the dimensions of the export of this commodity. It has been asserted[16] that no stamped handles have been found to indicate that Athens regulated or guaranteed her exports. None has been found in South Russia. A fragment from the Agora bearing an impressed head of Athena must have belonged rather to a standard measure used in an Agora shop, and may therefore be compared with a previously discovered clay measuring-cup with a stamped head of Athena and Owl, and an inscription *demosion*, 'public measure'.

We may now pass to the question of the nature of manufactured articles in the export trade of Athens. Raw materials – hides, timber, ruddle, copper, iron and ivory – were imported, and used for the manufacture of articles of use and ornament. The difficulty lies in deciding the magnitude of such manufactures, and the part they played in the export trade.

The articles of export from the workshops of Athens (see Pls 45–47) that are firmly rooted in the modern mind as important are pots and vases of all descriptions, made of clay; on many of these were lavished the arts of the Athenian vase-painters. Certain types of pot (plain clay jars) were in demand for the conveyance abroad of liquids, wine (possibly) and oil (certainly), from Athens; and, furthermore, for the export of fish pickle back to Athens. Other types were fashioned for use in the home, i.e. plates, amphorae, mixing-bowls, water-pots, drinking-cups for the banquet, perfume-flasks and caskets (*pyxides*) for the toilet; for funeral and marriage rites, *lekythoi* and *loutrophoroi*, and no doubt many pots were created purely for ornament. The Panathenaic amphorae used as prizes form a class by themselves.

The black-figure Athenian style (Pl. 22), developed alongside other variations of that technique, was extensively exported, replacing in the course of time the Corinthian productions of the late seventh and sixth centuries and replaced in turn by the Attic red-figure. The fact that the pottery export was widespread, and that the pottery of Athens was particularly esteemed, is proved by the painted vases found pre-eminently in Etruscan tombs as part of the tomb furniture, as well as those from the early Scythian graves. In fact they are forthcoming from the whole area of the Mediterranean world and those regions related to it. For a time, indeed, trade with Etruria declined and disappeared, and the vase exports to the Black Sea region were also suspended. This connection, however, was revived in the second half of the fifth century and in the early fourth, and ended with the final decline of Athenian vase-painting and the rise of the South Italian. The florid fourth-century style appealed to the taste of the Graeco-Scythians, and some vases were probably executed to order by Athenian craftsmen.

A great problem is that concerning the dimensions of the export trade in pottery. It may be agreed that the common everyday articles of domestic use were not exported or imported, but made on the spot where they were needed. The finer painted pots were 'luxury objects', for which there would not be a great demand; even the considerable numbers in which inferior examples have survived do not prove that the painted-pot industry was of any great dimensions, if the long period over which it is spread and the relatively indestructible character of pottery sherds are taken into account. An observation of Aristophanes[17] has been taken by Hasebroek as serious evidence for the slight character of the pottery export trade; but the passage is intended to be humorous, and pottery is here rejected as an article of export in order to bring in the Sycophant, who is packed up like a fragile pot. The historian Beloch instances the widespread nature of pottery finds to argue therefrom for the importance not only of the pottery industry but also of other manufacturing industries, producing articles more perishable or not so easily recognized as Attic. Bücher and Hasebroek, to explain the same phenomenon, produced the idea of the itinerant potter: a suggestion rightly discredited by others (Beloch and Oertel). Oertel, with some reason, ascribes the wide distribution of Attic pottery to the fairs held on the occasion of the great national games; he also points out that the Panathenaic vases, though very few in number, relatively speaking, are widely distributed. In conclusion it may be said that pottery exports comprised in the main not large clay receptacles (except with their contents), but decorated or black-glazed pottery, which, as luxury objects, must have formed a relatively small proportion of the total exports from Athens. They afford some evidence for the directions of trade from and through Athens, but nothing else, certainly not its relative intensity at particular periods.

The Scythian and semi-Greek graves of South Russia, belonging to the ruling and noble classes, indicate that a great variety of manufactured articles in bronze and ivory, furniture and weapons, engraved gems and personal ornaments in various metals, were imported,[18] and no doubt Athens had a large share in the production of such things. The shield-factories of Lysias and Pasion, the sword- and couch-factories of the father of Demosthenes (obviously engaged in producing luxury goods, in view of the materials used) must be considered as supplying evidence confirming that given rather inadequately by archaeology.

Naturally textiles have long since disappeared, though such isolated fragments as survive show a high technical skill. This industry has been regarded (e.g. by Beloch) as of importance in Athens, but there is little direct evidence for it except the domestic (?) scenes of weaving on Attic pots (Pls 31–33). Other cities were famous for various fabrics; and Megara was particularly characterized in the fifth and fourth centuries as the manufacturing centre of coarse garments suitable for slaves. Some have thought it surprising that Athens should have lagged behind; but the emphasis laid on this industry in the case of Megara shows that its development there was regarded as unique.[19] Attica was, of course, famous for its breed of wool-bearing sheep in early times (they were imported into Samos by Polycrates),[20] but it is probably incorrect to regard wool as an important export, as Hasebroek does.[21] The amount of pasture available in Attica was small, and the home demand was considerable, so it is unlikely that any was left for export. Indeed, a large quantity was probably imported.

No more precise details can be given of the Athenian export trade. Invaluable documents such as bills of lading, of the sort which have been preserved among the papyri of a later period,[22] are non-existent for the Hellenic Age, though 'ship's papers' appear to have been used in the fifth century B C.[23] So too the accounts and records of the collectors of the two percent tax (*pentekostologoi*), and those of the *sitophylakes* (corn-controllers) mentioned by Demosthenes for Athens, Syracuse and Panticapaeum[24]), would throw a flood of light on both imports and exports, if recorded in literary or epigraphical form. No doubt such details of all imports and exports were recorded temporarily by those who farmed the two percent tax, in order that they might render account to the administration, but the particulars were regarded as too ephemeral for permanent preservation.

This brings up the whole question of the dimensions of Athenian commerce. No doubt to the Greek mind anything like present-day statistics were quite foreign, while the modern student is in even worse case, since such records as were kept have long since disappeared. Public accounts of building operations and inventories of temple treasures were drawn up in detail, and even recorded permanently on stone, and they now form an invaluable category of evidence on some questions. Few of our literary authorities had the occasion to quote detailed figures in questions relating to public affairs: they would have found the research involved complicated and tiresome. The Orators generally had good reason for avoiding such details, in view of the Athenian dislike of too expert knowledge of any sort in those who undertook to advise them. It might have been expected that the writer (Xenophon) of the pamphlet *On Ways and Means* would have illustrated his argument more fully thus, but this is not so, which indicates the absence of permanent records.

In regard to fifth-century Athens there exists some difficulty in getting the position of that city in economic matters in the right perspective, since her status as head of an empire was unique. This fact was early accepted, and it was proposed to explain the economic greatness of Athens as due to her empire, regarding her population as largely supported by the tribute. This was reaffirmed more recently by Hasebroek[25] in a very modified form, which combined with it the view of the duty of the State to support its citizens without work. This view, however, required the assumption of exaggerated dimensions for the tribute (as by Bücher).[26] Otherwise it was put, in 424–413 B C, after it had been doubled, at 1300 talents, which is more or less the sum suggested by the researches of Meritt and West into the Tribute Lists. Aristides' original assessment was said to be 460 talents. Pericles names a figure of 600 talents,[27] which is irreconcilable with the Tribute

Lists; therefore all revenue from the empire must be included therein. M. N. Tod[28] points out that the number of members varied from year to year. He estimates the tribute at 369 talents 1690 drachmae in 454/3 BC (137 members); 349 talents 1140 drachmae in 443/2 BC (165 members), or the amount may be increased by 29 talents 5500 drachmae, if we read Thasioi in place of Sermēs;[29] 388 talents 390 drachmae in 433/2 BC (166 members). In 425 BC, if we double the latter figure, the tribute brought in 776 talents 780 drachmae. After 404 BC Athens lost all her subject allies. During the period of the Second Athenian Confederacy she had allies, who, however, only made war contributions, at most 200 talents. After the Social War (357–355 BC) this decreased to 60–46 talents. All disappeared after Chaeronea (338 BC). In any case in the Peloponnesian War period the tribute scarcely covered the cost of the war, and the population of Athens, as far as it was not engaged in war service, must have been supported by industry and agriculture in the regions less exposed to hostile attack and by the wealthier classes, who ultimately suffered from a number of causes from 413 BC on.[30]

The great losses from Decelea, and the other heavy charges that fell upon them, produced their financial embarrassment; and it was at this time that they imposed upon their subjects, instead of the tribute, the tax of a twentieth upon all imports and exports by sea, which they thought would bring them in more money. . . . Their expenditure was far greater . . .; but their revenues decayed.

A tax on all imports and exports in the ports of the Athenian Empire (imposed in place of the tribute) was intended to produce 1000 talents or more. As the rate of the tax was five percent this sum represented a total trade value of 20,000 talents. In view of the fact that it is considered that Athenians and possibly Athenian metics were exempt, and that the allies who were not subject, i.e. Chios (which very soon revolted) and Samos, were as well, no real certainty can be attributed to the figure. None the less it proves that even at this time (413/12 BC), in a very difficult period of the Peloponnesian War, the maritime trade of the Aegean was very substantial.

It is clear, also, that at that time the share of Athens would have been considerably higher than that indicated for the year 399/8 BC, when the imports and exports at the Piraeus represented a value of 2000 talents.[31] Though the Athenian Empire included many ports of considerable importance (the Tribute Lists provide indirect information), the commerce of Athens would certainly have been more than one-tenth of the total: one-quarter (5000 talents) would not be an overestimate, if the trade of Athenians and metics (assumed to be duty free) is included. Apparently before the occupation of Decelea, and perhaps after the end of the war, a great deal of corn was imported via Oropos[32], as Thucydides records:

Besides, the transport of provisions from Euboea, which had before been carried on so much more quickly overland by Decelea from Oropos, was now effected at great cost by sea round Cape Sunium. Everything the city required had to be imported from abroad, and instead of a city it became a fortress.

The second piece of evidence for the dimensions of Athenian trade is afforded by a passage in Andocides' speech *De Mysteriis*.[33] He there states that in 400/399 BC Agyrrhius and an association of capitalists purchased the contract for the farming of the two percent tax on all imports and exports.[34] There are other references to this tax.[35] The contract was purchased for 30 talents, and made a profit of three talents. Taking into account the cost of collection the tax probably produced 35 talents. The next year (399/8 BC) Andocides outbid the same people and purchased the contract for 36 talents. Consequently we may assume that in 399/8 BC the revenue from the tax amounted to 40 talents, representing commerce of the value of 2000 talents, an advance of 200 talents in comparison with the previous year. The rivals of Andocides proposed by collusion to obtain the contract again for 30 talents, and so make an even greater profit; the wording of the passage[36] shows that they expected to encounter more opposition on the second occasion, by reason of the greater profit available. The advance in the total value of Athenian commerce no doubt represents the rapid recovery of Athens after the Peloponnesian War. If we consider the circumstances of the time we shall see that this increase was not occasioned by increased imports of food-stuffs (indeed corn imports probably decreased slightly as Attica once more came under the cultivation which had been interrupted by the occupation of Decelea and the earlier yearly invasions), but by increased importation of raw materials for the industries of Athens and Attica, and the corresponding export of manufactured articles. Attempts to convert the value of Athenian exports and imports into modern figures rest on too many arbitrary assumptions to be of any real value.

Some account of the evidence for Athenian industrial development must now be given. The first item in point of time, of which we have any considerable information, is the shield-factory of Cephalus, a metic at Athens, and father of Lysias and Polemarchus, who jointly carried on the undertaking after their father's death.[37] The establishment contained 120 slaves.[38] In the list given by Lysias of the plunder carried off by the emissaries of the 'Thirty Tyrants', in the Oligarchic

Revolution at the end of the great Peloponnesian War, he clearly enumerates the contents of the factory and of the houses of himself and his brother. Seven hundred shields are mentioned, undoubtedly the stock-in-hand; in the case of the 120 slaves, the 'Thirty' took the best (those with the highest technical training?) and handed the rest over to the Treasury.

Concerning Pasion's shield-factory (see above, p. 98 and below, p. 121), Demosthenes says that it produced a yearly income of one talent.[39] From this datum it has been calculated by Beloch[40] that the factory contained about eighty workers. This deduction is rightly rejected by Hasebroek[41] on the ground that there are too many individual considerations to permit any such conclusion. He instances the bronze-workers of Leocrates,[42] sold for 35 minae, in which case too it is impossible to calculate their number. Nevertheless the number of workers must have been considerable. Demosthenes gives more precise information about the two factories owned by his father, referred to earlier: (i) a couch-factory, employing 20 slaves, taken over by him as security for a mortgage; (ii) a sword-factory, in which 32–33 slaves were engaged in productive work.

The Orator uses the term *ergasterion* in reference to these factories. He describes them as 'each of no small dimensions'.[43] In view of these expressions it has been considered that they are over the average in size; the normal dimensions, it is thought, are represented by the shoemaking factory of Timarchus,[44] which employed nine or ten workers under the direction of a 'leader of the factory'. It is to be noted that in this case there were not only the shoemakers, but also a female weaver of fine fabrics (*amorgina*), and a man embroiderer. Further evidence for 'factories' at Athens is afforded by the flute-makers owned by the father of Isocrates, from whom the former drew his income.[45] In view of the fact that his son received an excellent education, the income must have been a large one; flutes were in greater demand in ancient times than at present. Several instances of similar undertakings of smaller size are provided by Xenophon, and by Demosthenes (in the case of Conon).[46]

Whatever view we may adopt of the industrial development of Athens, the evidence of Thucydides,[47] that twenty-thousand slaves or 'craftsmen' fled to Decelea during its occupation by the Spartans, must be borne in mind, besides the fact that metics and citizens were also engaged in such occupations. No argument about the dimensions of Attic industry can be drawn from the fact that we have evidence of personal participation: undoubtedly many small craftsmen purchased a few slaves to assist them.[48] Yet even those who carried on industry on a larger scale would need practical experience, in order to administer their undertakings efficiently. Mention may be made of Cleon's father,[49] and of Anytus and his son.[50] Anytus, who has been regarded as a simple craftsman by Bücher, must have been fairly well off, since his son had the time and opportunity to frequent Socrates' company. Cleon's father Cleaenetus was a wealthy man, almost certainly the Cleaenetus of the *phyle Pandionos* mentioned in an inscription.[51] It has been argued that Cleon would not have been attacked for embezzling public funds, if he had been wealthy; this is proved incorrect by the case of Pericles. Hyperbolus, who studied under Gorgias,[52] was not just a simple lamp-maker.[53] He must in addition have possessed a metal-foundry.

In relation to this question of 'industrial establishments'[54] there is the matter of the numbers of slaves employed. A considerable number worked in the silver mines of Laurium (for mining slaves, see below pp. 176, 180). Apart from Nicias and other owners of mining slaves who seem to have impressed the ancient tradition, there was Mnason. He owned one thousand slaves,[55] who were employed (as the Greek phrase suggests) as household servants in agriculture and handicrafts. Undoubtedly members of a household exercised their skill for the market but it is unlikely that Mnason had a thousand slaves to begin with. No doubt the figure represents the gradual development of industry in close connection with the household. There were many others who worked, relatively independently, on the *apophora* system. Despite what has been said above, it could be argued that industrial establishments worthy of the name did exist. It should be noted that even in cases where the industry was pursued purely as an investment, it must be assumed that the owner exercised some supervision over the undertaking, since the *apeleutheros* of Demosthenes, and the *hegemon ergasteriou* of Timarchus were only foremen.

There was, of necessity, a limit imposed on the division of labour in the *ergasteria* of ancient Athens, on account of the non-existence of machinery. It has also been pointed out that slaves, unlike machines, are not capable of improvement in technical skill beyond a certain point. There are some interesting comments on the ancient division of labour: so Plato:[56]

Among human beings hardly any person is adequate to follow skilfully two professions or crafts ... no one who is a bronze-worker should also be a carpenter, nor yet should a carpenter be supervisor of others, such as bronze-workers, other than his own craft. It can be urged that one supervising many household slaves in his own service is rightly concerned with them by reason of the income coming to him from them, which is the greater by reason of his expertise.

So also Diodorus:[57] 'Among the Egyptians, if one of the craftsmen possesses citizenship or pursues more crafts than one, he is liable to great penalties.'

And Xenophon:[58]

the other crafts too are in detailed fashion pursued in the great cities ... So if in small communities the same craftsman makes a bed, a door, a plough and a table, and often this same man is also a house-builder, then he is satisfied if thus he has sufficient clients to maintain himself. It is impossible for a man engaged in many arts to pursue them all well. In the great cities by reason of the fact that many people have need of individual items, each craft suffices for the livelihood of one individual. And often not even one entire craft. For one man makes men's shoes, and another women's. And in some cases in shoemaking one craftsman makes a living sewing, another cutting, and another trimming the uppers, and yet another doing no more than assembling the pieces. Therefore, the craftsman who exercises his function in the most restricted sphere must of necessity do it best.

There is a point, in such conditions, at which further development ceases to be profitable. Probably personally superintended factories of small dimensions were both better supervised and cost less in supervision. Likewise the dimensions of an industrial undertaking were limited by the difficulty of getting together enough capital to effect development on a large scale. There was also the absence of what might be called an 'industrializing mentality'. The Greek (in effect Athenian) banks had not embarked on the function of gathering together capital and making it available for industry (see below, Chapter VI). Consequently, we find that establishments were built up in no methodical fashion, as can be seen in the case of those owned by the father of Demosthenes. There were other factors which militated against the success of the banks in amassing capital. There were the constant economic difficulties of the fourth century: war taxes and liturgies made capital expensive and scarce. Banks and private individuals preferred to lend money on mercantile ventures, where there were quick and high returns, and a concealment of investment. Thus (Xenophon) says that the interest from the loan of capital for silver mining would equal mercantile interest (twenty percent). Hasebroek and Oertel are probably correct in assuming that the average factory contained twenty to thirty workers. One of them (Oertel) regards *ergasteria* as *Grosswerkstätte* as far as numbers are concerned, but characterizes their product and way of working as *Handwerk*. The term *ergasterion* could be applied to slaves,[59] but in inscriptions the term *ergasterion* represents both the establishment and the slaves.[60] The fact that slave labour and not that of free men was employed in them had its advantages and disadvantages. Slave labour was characterized by permanence and continuity (not interrupted, as often was the case of free men, by political duties), and better work at a cheaper rate, through fear of punishment or hope of freedom. On the other hand, there was the disadvantage that capital invested in the purchase of slaves was hazarded by sickness and death; their training was costly, and they might adopt a course of passive resistance. But large gains were obtained by their employment in industry[61] and consequently the success or failure of an industrial undertaking depended largely on the degree of availability of a supply of cheap slaves, and also, of course, on cheap raw materials. The grandiose scheme of (Xenophon) for the founding of a loan fund and its use in acquiring slaves to be owned by the State and employed in the silver mines has been shown to be impracticable. There is reason for believing that even in this industry where large numbers of slaves were employed, the individual undertaking, or that pursued by a partnership of two or more, was relatively small (see Chapter IX).

It is interesting at this juncture to consider the influence exerted by a large body of slaves on the economic relations of the classes at Athens. This subject is fully entered into by Pöhlmann[62] in support of his thesis of the opposition of Capital and Labour in Ancient Athens. The principles expressed by him are true, whatever view is taken of Athenian industry, given the existence of slave labour. The use of slaves increased the share of their owners, the Athenian wealthy class, in the national wealth, and diminished the share of the poor free population displaced from trade and industry by the slaves. As a consequence the demand for industrial products at home, conditioned by the wealth (i.e. purchasing power) of the various classes, would be diminished. Therefore, large quantities of industrial products must have been disposed of to foreign consumers in return for foodstuffs and raw materials. In such conditions there was a particular need for cheap corn, and the relative poverty of a large section of the populace made fluctuations in its price all the more disturbing.

The problem was not so serious in the fifth century, for in cases where citizens could not earn a whole living in industrial pursuits, they could be partially supported without too much difficulty by the State, thanks to the existence of the revenue from the empire. At the end of the Peloponnesian War the tribute disappeared with the empire, and the use of slaves again concentrated wealth in relatively few hands, while the ordinary citizens were very badly off. Those who came from the country to the city, abandoning agricultural pursuits, found themselves without work, as did those who returned from war service. Idle land required capital to recommence its cultivation, so large estates were formed by capitalists, on which free men, little better than slaves, might find employment. The efforts of the State to support the poor after the fashion of the fifth century were doomed to failure, if no attempt was made to distribute wealth more equitably. This end was apparently secured by the numerous *eisphorai* (war-taxes) of the fourth century, to which metics made an even greater contribution than citizens, and by the financial contributions (*leitourgiai*) designed to secure for the poorer citizens a share in the advantages of the wealth they could not earn themselves. The ultimate effect, however, was to hamper the growth of industry on a capitalistic basis.

The slight evidence we possess of the dimensions of Athenian industry supplements and confirms to some extent the view expressed above. The import trade in both the fifth and fourth centuries was very important, but considerable uncertainty exists concerning the export trade. Certainly on the establishment in the latter part of the Peloponnesian War of the Spartan garrison at Decelea the industries of Attica and the silver mines received a severe blow from which they did not recover for some years after the war ended (the Corinthian War struck another though less severe blow at Athenian industry, through its export trade). The period 400–398 BC was certainly one in which imports were but little reduced, if at all, while on the other hand the export trade will have been much diminished, firstly by the harm done to industry through the defection of the slaves and increased financial difficulties (thus Athens had to resort to striking tetradrachms of bronze in 406 BC, which were not withdrawn until 394 BC[63]), and no less by the loss of markets.[64]

The fourth century, therefore, must have seen an adverse balance of trade for a few years, but Athens made a speedy recovery, though possessing no advantages over other industrial states. The expenses of public administration, and a view of the State as a sort of provident fund, developed when Athens possessed her empire, rendered it difficult to balance the State budget, which was unable to bear the burden of extraordinary charges, i.e. military and naval expenses. The tax on capital, the *eisphora*, of which the purpose has already been considered, undoubtedly tended to drive investments from real property and industry, which were easy of assessment, to mercantile loans, in which the capital became *ousia aphanēs* and more easily concealed; thus only fifty-three percent of the fortune of Demosthenes' father was invested in industry.[65] This phenomenon probably developed slowly in the fourth century, but after the war with her allies of the Second Athenian Confederacy (the Social War of 357–355 BC), Athens may have found her industries seriously reduced, while the increased competition for the corn of the Cimmerian Bosporus region meant a corresponding competition in supplying that region with the necessary objects of return trade.

It was in these circumstances that (Xenophon) composed his short treatise *On Ways and Means*,[66] supporting the policy of Eubulus, who wished to prevent Athens engaging in war, and to build up the Theoric Fund for the benefit of the citizens. The author makes specific proposals: besides the encouragement of aliens to settle in Athens and the extension of the practical and legal facilities for commerce there, he advocates the extensive development of the silver mines, which he regarded as inexhaustible. Though his proposals for a 'Loan Fund', for the formation of a body of State-owned slaves, are somewhat nebulous and his calculations dubious in the extreme, his emphasis on the importance of silver (e.g. its value as a 'return cargo') indicates that he relied on this metal to redress the adverse balance of trade, which is shown, for instance, by the money owing to Leucon and his sons at Athens.[67]

Much the same view may be taken of his proposals to form a fleet of State-owned merchant ships. By hiring them to suitable persons, he believed, a substantial profit might be made for the State – a parallel, had the suggestion materialized, to the 'invisible exports' of modern times, which help largely to diminish the British adverse trade balance. At the same time the State would have available a fleet of vessels for the conveyance of essential commodities, such as corn, thereby rendering itself less dependent on the good will of the *emporoi*, in whose hands the Athenian corn trade almost entirely rested at this period.

The tendencies and conditions prompting such proposals are more important than the proposals themselves. The general trend of economic affairs in the second half of the fourth century, combined with the troubled course of events, were no doubt contributory causes of the famine years which we find occurring.

CHAPTER FIVE

STATE ATTITUDES
TO TRADE AND TRADERS

IN MODERN TIMES, and particularly in the last fifty years, since the principle of free trade has been abandoned, the idea of the encouragement of commerce by the State is naturally conceived under two heads. First, the advancement of home industry, and the restriction as far as possible of foreign goods by means of tariffs, and second, the development of export trade, and securing of new markets by competition or commercial treaties. Greater attention has been concentrated on the export trade, as the outlet for the products of the nation's industrial undertakings.

In recent years, however, the adverse balance of trade which has arisen between the exports and imports of Great Britain, has shown with increasing insistency that the primary and original function of the export trade is to pay for the essential commodities which have to be imported. A secondary function is the building-up of capital abroad.

This view of international trade is the one which we find prevailing in the Athens of Classical times. Her economic policy was governed by two aims on the part of the State: the desire to augment the revenues by the tax on imported and exported goods, an end as much served by the increase of imports as of exports, but more particularly by the ever present preoccupation to secure the corn supply from overseas. This supply, which became increasingly precarious after Athens lost the command of the seas, was much competed for by other states, and the whole trade depended on the good will of the traders, who were aliens in almost every case. The fact that no national mercantile marine existed led (Xenophon)[1] to propose the creation of a State-owned merchant fleet, with the additional aim of augmenting the revenues. The lack of such a fleet rendered it imperative that merchants should be encouraged to make Athens the destination of their voyages, and this was not easy.

As far as legal protection was concerned, the efforts of the Athenian State took two directions: (i) legal facilities for the settlement of mercantile disputes at Athens, for citizens, resident aliens, and foreigners temporarily visiting the port; (ii) arrangements to secure the rights, in legal matters, of Athenians and those trading from Athens, in other states.

It was rare, to judge from the literary sources, for an Athenian citizen to engage in trade (i.e. overseas commerce).[2] The absence over long periods, which was necessary in such a calling, rendered it impossible for one who followed it to fulfil his duties as a good citizen; while at the same time the sea-going merchant (*emporos*) would share in the contempt generally felt for all middlemen, in some measure at least, though less than the retailer. Poverty or the sentence of exile were the only likely reasons, it might be argued, for an Athenian adopting the life of a merchant. In such circumstances we find Andocides (the orator) leading a wandering life.[3] In the extant speeches which deal with mercantile cases, we find no instance of an Athenian engaged directly as a sea-going merchant. On the other hand, in the inscriptions relating to *proxenia*, etc., there are numerous references to Athenians engaged abroad, some at least of whom must have been concerned in trade. But while Athenian citizens did not themselves do so directly, they furthered the development of trade by lending capital on mercantile undertakings. This was a favourite method of investment, which if not as safe as real property, yet produced a high return. Such loans would represent *ousia aphanēs*, (unseen) capital, and as such would not be exposed to the same degree as *ousia phanera* (manifest or real property) to assessment for the war tax or the vexatious comparison of one fortune with another. We have abundant evidence in the Orators of large sums disposed in this way. It was to the advantage of the Athenian State to encourage such speculation in order that the corn trade in particular might benefit thereby. The lenders, therefore, were afforded protection and redress against fraudulent merchants by the institution of the mercantile suits. Taking the widest definition of this term, *emporikai dikai* were disputes arising out of contracts made in Athens at the Athenian *emporion*. These were settled more rapidly than others under the direction of the magistrates named *thesmothetai*. They were instituted primarily for the benefit of the *emporoi*, in order that traders ·might be delayed as little as possible, yet their existence benefited the lenders by the same fact of their speedy decision, and the advantage of a special court.[4] Thus it could be said: 'In the laws there are many and advantageous aids to those who lend money.' Emphasis is constantly being laid in the extant speeches on the importance of conciliating the lenders by a decision favourable to them, and of encouraging others to similar speculations.

It was, however, the large number of foreigners, the *xenoi metoikoi*,[5] resident permanently or temporarily in the city, who were responsible for the active furtherance of overseas trade. This foreign population was divided into two classes, the *metoikoi* (metics) or resident aliens, and the *xenoi parepidemountes*, or visiting foreigners. Athens, or any other state, could deal with them either by the institution of a special group of laws, and a special board of magistrates, comprising together the one means of legal redress for such aliens, or else make various inter-state judicial agreements, which secured for members of the contracting states resident for a period in either one of them legal rights in the other. Such agreements, as we shall see, existed between Athens and other states, and in certain instances foreigners had suits (*dikai apo symbolōn*) decided at Athens according to these agreements (*symbola*).[6]

Generally, the first method was adopted for metics and the second for temporarily resident *xenoi*, but the two were sometimes in a way connected, in that the inter-state agreement appointed magistrates to judge cases concerning *xenoi* who already had competence over those involving metics. Thus, in the case of the city of Phaselis[7], disputes in Athens in which a Phaselite was concerned were to be tried by the *polemarch*, who also exercised a general competence over the legal disputes of resident aliens. However, in the fourth century at Athens *dikai apo symbolōn* were in the charge of the *thesmothetai*.[8] It is uncertain whether it was so in the fifth century. Finally, that resident aliens enjoyed the privileges of *symbola*, if such existed between Athens and their native state seems unlikely. They were probably wholly amenable to the laws made at Athens regarding them.

Though the class of *emporikai dikai* interests us mainly, since the aim of its establishment was the encouragement of trade, it will be well to outline the procedure followed when a metic was involved in a suit which fell outside that category. It appears from Aristotle[9] that the *polemarch* exercised preliminary judgment in private suits of *metoikoi*, *isoteleis* and *proxenoi* (the latter two being the privileged class of foreigners given special rights by the Athenian State). This is shown by the phrase often occurring in honorary inscriptions: 'Approach shall be available to the *polemarch* as for the other *proxenoi*.' He then passed them on to one of the ten groups of four *dikastai* (? judges), whose function it was to introduce private actions concerning members of each tribe. Metics were not members of a tribe, so the private suits involving them were divided by lot among the ten groups of four tribal judges. They in turn transferred the cases to the public arbitrators; if the latter failed to reach a settlement, the tribal judges brought the case before a Heliastic court based on citizen jurymen, at which they presided.[10] Generally speaking the *polemarch* in cases of all categories (except mercantile suits) stood in the same relationship to a metic as did the *archon basileus* to a citizen.[11] It was a lengthy and cumbersome process.

The whole question of the judicial position of metics and the significance of the office of *prostates* (representative), has been investigated by Clerc.[12] There is no mention of a *prostates* in the literature of the fifth century, says Clerc, but Aristophanes refers[13] to Cleon as *prostates*, though here it may mean 'champion' as Clerc takes it to do in another passage.[14] There are several references in fourth-century literature: (i) in Aristotle,[15] in connection with certain privileges granted to metics: 'but they must have a *prostates*'; (ii) in Demosthenes:[16] 'Call the *prostates* of Zobia'; (iii) again in the same Orator;[17] (iv) in Hyperides;[18] (v) in Isocrates.[19] Hesychius,[20] it is worth noting, mentions the *dike aprostasiou* (action for failure to have a *prostates*) in a reference to the *Laws* of the fifth-century comic playwright Cratinus, but the actual reference is only to the *polemarch*, who had charge of such actions in the fourth century[21] The office of *prostates* also existed at Megara,[22] Oropos,[23] and no doubt elsewhere. There is, therefore, some evidence for the existence of the office of *prostates* in the fourth century if not in the fifth. The question remains how important his intervention was in the affairs of a metic. The *Suda* states that the metic paid the metic tax through the *prostates*, in addition to having all his other affairs supervised by him.[24] Where the metic tax was concerned, despite what the *Suda* says, the metic himself seems to have been responsible for its payment, as he was liable to be sold in the event of non-payment. In private suits there is no reference to a *prostates*.[25] In any event such resort to a representative for the execution of all legal business would be extremely burdensome. In public actions (*graphai*) there is also no mention of the office, except in the instances of Zobia and Aristagora, who, being women, required a *kyrios* (protector); this applied equally to foreigners and citizens. In Lysias' speech for Callias[26] the citizen who aids Callias is a friend. In Isaeus' speech for the banker Eumathes the discourse is pronounced by a citizen to whom Eumathes had rendered service. In the speech of Lysias against the corn-dealers (xxii) there is no reference to *prostatai*. The evidence of the lexicographers may well be discredited, but that of the fourth-century texts cannot be ignored.[27] They show that the office of *prostates* was of little importance (three of the fourth-century examples refer to women),[28] though it was required as a guarantee.[29]

When the defendant in a case was a metic it is to be expected that the case would be referred to the judges of the tribe of the plaintiff, if the latter was a citizen. But if it be assumed that *dikai hai tois metoikois gignomenai* means 'cases brought against metics', then we learn from Aristotle[30] that the *polemarch* had charge of these, and referred them by lot to the tribal judges. Where a metic was plaintiff (if we adopt the view that the *polemarch* did not function in this instance too), his *prostates* may have introduced him to the official tribal judges of his own tribe.

Clerc holds[31] that the most reasonable course would be for the person cited to determine the competent judge. Thus if a metic was defendant, the *polemarch* would be in charge of the case (this view is confirmed by the case against Pancleon,[32] and the action of Pasion against the son of Sopaios).[33] According to this arrangement, therefore, if a citizen was defendant, the tribal judges of his tribe would introduce the case. Clerc's own opinion, however, is that the Aristotle text refers to all cases, i.e. whether the metic was defendant or plaintiff, the suit was introduced by the *polemarch*. Be that as it may, the difference was purely formal since the subsequent procedure was the same in either event.

With regard to public actions, which might concern a metic if he attempted to raise a loan on a cargo already pledged, the ordinary magistrates were competent in all cases concerning metics, who generally appeared only as defendants in such actions.[34] Thus (i) in Aeschines, Diophantos (an orphan) cites a foreigner for debt before the *archon eponymos*;[35] (ii) in Demosthenes,[36] Apainetos of Andros brings a charge of unlawful imprisonment against a citizen Stephanos; (iii) cases of illegal lending on mercantile ventures[37] were universally cited before the officials in charge of the port. (The place of Athenian metics outside Athens, is discussed by Clerc,[38] and the supervision of their interests is illustrated by the example of Heraclides of Salamis,[39] which is a special case since the person concerned was engaged in the corn trade.)

Turning to the *xenoi* in the narrower sense, we find that they faced three possible situations. If they were implicated in *emporikai dikai*, such cases, which always had a commercial basis, were tried by the *thesmothetai*.[40] Obviously this class was the largest of those in which *xenoi* were involved. When disputes outside the above category arose, involving non-resident aliens, the case was tried according to the provisions of an inter-state judicial agreement (*symbola*), if such existed between Athens and the state of the alien in question. Generally, the *thesmothetai* had charge of it.[41] If no agreement existed, the ordinary laws and courts of Athens decided the case. Non-resident aliens obviously could not have a *prostates*, but it is probable that the official *proxenos* of their state at Athens afforded them his assistance.

1 Sub-Mycenaean and Protogeometric pottery from the Athens Kerameikos

2 Geometric bronze tripod-cauldron from Olympia, Greece

3 Geometric bronze tripod-cauldron leg from Olympia, Greece

4 Cauldron with conical support from Praeneste, Italy

5 Phoenician silver bowl from Etruria

6 Incised ivory depicting a man attacked by griffon and lion, from Carmona, near Seville, Spain

8 Attic Geometric fragment with naval battle (?)

7 Attic Geometric amphora of the
Dipylon Group

9 Attic Geometric jug depicting
shipwrecked sailor on his upturned ship

10 The Argive panoply from Argos, Greece

11 Corinthian globular *aryballos*

12 Corinthian Geometric mixing-bowl with warship (*pentekonter*)

13 Protoattic amphora with Herakles and Nessos, *c.* 675–650 BC

14 Corinthian Transitional jug (*olpe*), *c.* 625 BC

15 Early Corinthian amphora, *c.* 625–600 BC

16 The Crowe corselet. Drawing, source unknown, made before its recovery

17 Early Greek coins: a, b, earliest East Greek electrum; c, earliest electrum of Phocaea; d, early stater of Aegina; e, early stater of Corinth

18 Early Attic black-figure amphora with Herakles and Nessos, c. 620 BC

19 Attic bowl in Corinthian style, *c.* 610 BC

20 The early Attic black-figure Gorgon *Dinos, c.* 600–590 BC

21 (*above right*) The Laconian-style Arkesilas Cup, *c.* 565 BC

22 Attic black-figure amphora by Exekias with the Dioscuri and their parents, *c.* 530–525 BC

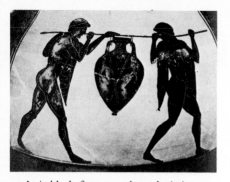

23 Attic black-figure amphora depicting men carrying a pointed storage vessel, *c.* 500 BC

24 Attic black-figure amphora depicting man carrying two tunny fish, *c.* 500 BC

25 Fourth-century red-figure Italiote (Campanian) bell-krater depicting bargaining at the fishmonger over a tunny fish

26 Attic black-figure *pelike* depicting a sale of oil

27 Attic red-figure *pelike* depicting a sale of perfume. Near Altamura Painter

28 Attic black-figure cup depicting farm operations

29 Attic black-figure neck-amphora depicting olive gathering. By the Antimenes Painter, late sixth century

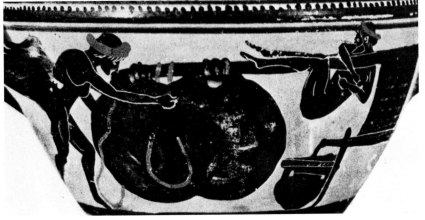

30 Attic black-figure *skyphos* depicting an olive press

31 Attic black-figure *lekythos* depicting women at the warp-weighted loom, and women spinning; *c.* 540 BC

32 The same. Women folding finished fabrics and spinning with distaff and spindle

33 Attic red-figure *skyphos* portraying Penelope at her tapestry-weaving. By the Penelope Painter

34 Attic red-figure cup depicting a carpenter shaping wood with an adze. By the Carpenter Painter

35 Attic red-figure *hydria* depicting the making of the Chest of Danaë; a carpenter using a bow drill. By the Gallatin Painter

36 Attic black-figure *pelike* depicting a shoemaker cutting a last for a small boy

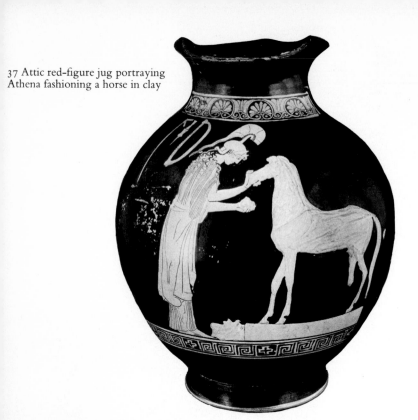

37 Attic red-figure jug portraying Athena fashioning a horse in clay

38 Fragments of a terracotta mould, *c.* 70 cm high, for the lower part of a statue; late sixth century

39 Casting pit on the West Slope of the Areopagus, Athens

40 Attic black-figure amphora depicting a blacksmith's forge; end of sixth century

41 Attic red-figure cup depicting a bronze foundry. By the Foundry Painter

42 The same. Completion of large statue

43 Attic trefoil-mouth black-figure jug depicting a man with tongs, and youth holding a hammer

44 Marble relief, dedication of a potter. A tithe, carved by Endoios (?) and dedicated perhaps by Pamphaios; last decade of sixth century

45 Attic black-figure cup, interior, showing a potter and his wheel

46 Attic black-figure *hydria* depicting a pottery and its activities; end of sixth century

47 Attic red-figure cup fragment showing a pot-painter drawing a relief line

48 A large mine shaft at Laurium, Attica

49 A cistern in the mining area, Laurium, Attica

50 A washing table, Laurium,
Attica

51 A Hellenistic fortification
wall, of the fourth century BC at
Messene, showing standard
block dimensions, and sockets
giving sizes of beams

A good deal of the above discussion might seem somewhat irrelevant to the immediate theme, but it emphasizes the difficulties under which foreigners, both resident and visiting, might have to conduct their business activities, and this would influence their attitude of potential benevolence to Athens. Athens might be indifferent to this in the great days of the empire, but she could not be so in the fourth century. Hence the impulse to facilitation, for obvious reasons, more to benefit visitors than resident aliens.

The efforts made by the Athenian State to protect its citizens and those trading to and from Athens, when in another state, are to be regarded as no less important than the judicial arrangements existing in Athens itself. Such efforts can be summarized under two heads: the appointment of *proxenoi* in foreign states, and the institution of inter-state agreements for the decision of private suits.

It is customary to compare the office of *proxenos* with the position of a consul in modern times, the difference being that the latter is mostly a citizen of the state he represents, while the *proxenos* was a citizen of the state in which he lived and performed his duties.[42] Further-more, he received only a semi-official recognition in his own state as the representative of another. The office was developed from that of the private guest-friend, and is regarded by Hasebroek,[43] with good reason, as being older than the institution of *symbola* (*Rechtshilfverträge*). In fact, in its earlier stages, the office of *proxenos* would no doubt be contempor-ary with the practice of seizure (*syle*), to which all foreigners in a state were exposed. When foreign traders suffered the seizure of their goods or person, the support of the *proxenos* was particularly necessary. Later the right of *syle* was replaced by judicial proceedings on the basis of an inter-state agreement.[44] Hasebroek[45], however, is almost certainly wrong in assuming a decline in the office of *proxenos*, when the insti-tution of inter-state judicial agreements developed (if granted to metics, of course, it became purely honorary).[46] It seems unlikely that *symbola* were developed to any great extent, especially by states at some distance from each other, or by those unconnected by alliance. As will be seen later, the rule seems rather to have been that resident foreigners were amenable to the laws of the state in which they were located, while it was the duty of the *proxenos* of their state to afford them any protection of which they might stand in need. The best examples of *proxenoi* are provided by those cases in which the office was held by famous public men: Pindar (*proxenos* of Athens at Thebes); Cimon, Alcibiades and Callias (of Sparta at Athens); Nicias (of Syracuse), and Demosthenes (of Thebes). If this assumption of the continuing importance of *proxenoi* is not accepted, it is difficult to explain the almost complete lack of evidence for *symbola* between Athens and other great mercantile and industrial cities, such as Corinth, Syracuse and Megara.

An examination of the large number of Athenian decrees granting or renewing the honour of *proxenos* reveals that they may be divided into three classes. Firstly, this honour was granted to those who had given public political service to the Athenian State.[47] There exists a large class also of decrees in which the services rendered are not specified.[48] In both classes the grant of *proxenia* is often accompanied by the privilege of acquisition of land,[49] *isoteleia* (financial equality with citizens),[50] or *ateleia* (freedom from taxes). Where the latter is granted, it is sometimes more expressly specified as *ateleia metoikiou*;[51] in other cases it undoubtedly means immunity from public financial burdens (*leitourgiai*) at Athens, and not *ateleia hapantōn* (including import and export duties) which the Athenian state rarely gave. The third class, in which the office of *proxenos* was granted for services to commerce or trade, was clearly more practical in its aim than the other two classes, though in the latter too there was probably some thought of utilizing the potential services of friends of Athens.

The third class of decree is well represented outside Athens. In most cases the grant of *proxenia* was coupled with the privilege of freedom from tax, and other rights summed up in the phrase 'the right of sailing in and sailing out in war and peace with immunity and without a treaty agreement'. It may fairly be argued that the granting of such rights marks out the recipients as being engaged in commerce – though there are exceptions: as from the Erythraeans to Conon (394 BC): 'freedom from all payments both on imports and exports, and *proxenia*';[52] from the Erythraeans to Mausollus of Caria (357/6 BC):[53] '*proxenia* and freedom from all taxes; passage into the harbour and out, in war and peace, with immunity, and without a treaty'. Of interest is a grant made by Oropos to Macedonian nobles.[54] But these were all public figures, and the privileges to Mausollus might apply to all trading from his kingdom. As for Conon we may bear in mind that freedom from export tax was sometimes granted for private exports;[55] and we may compare the phrases 'for his personal household', 'for his personal acquisition'.[56] Such men were particularly suited to represent the state appointing them, and to protect its merchants: thus the Boeotians honour Nuba of Carthage (364/3 BC, the year of the creation of the Boeotian navy), with 'freedom from taxes and immunity both by land and sea.[57] Cnidus honoured Iphiades of Abydos (360 BC) with *proxenia*, the right of sailing into Cnidus and out with immunity, and without a treaty, in peace and in war.[58] The Rhodians of Lindos honoured thus an Aeginetan of Naucratis,[59] and the Olbiopolitans Chaerigenes of Mesembria.[60] Similar privileges were granted by Paerisades to a citizen of Euxine Piraeus.[61]

Where Athens is concerned, there exist abundant examples of the granting of *proxenia* to those engaged in trade, or alternatively the 'commendation' or 'decoration' (grant of a wreath) as we would call it today, of those who already held this office. Apart from an indeterminate class[62] and instances where honours were given for past or promised services to the corn trade,[63] examples occur where it is expressly stated that those who are receiving or have received the honour of *proxenia*, exercise protection over Athenian citizens visiting their state. Thus, honours are given to natives of Cyrene (353/2 BC): 'concerning *proxenoi*, that there may be those who will care at Cyrene for the Athenians coming there ... commendation to be given to [these] men of Cyrene since they have been good men in respect of the Athenians coming there';[64] similarly to Theagenes of Naucratis (349/8 BC): 'he is a good man in relation to the people of Athens and does what good he can privately and publicly for those who come [to Naucratis]';[65] honours also are given to a Corinthian (341/40 BC) 'since he has continued to concern himself with the needs of Athenians in Corinth'.[66] There are other similarly worded decrees: *proxenia* for two Chians (mid-fourth century);[67] for Lycus of Pydna (333/2 BC);[68] for Apollonides of Sidon (332/1 BC) on the testimony of merchants and shipmen;[69] for an inhabitant of Asia, a grant of citizenship (c. 320/19 BC);[70] for Eurylochus of Cydonia (320/19 BC);[71] for the son of Metrodorus of Cyzicus (321–319 BC);[72] for Praxiades of Cos, 'the merchants of Athens and the people of Samos, the other Athenians present, and the rest declare that Praxiades of Cos concerns himself with the merchants and shipmen, so that corn comes into the port for the Athenian people as abundantly as possible'.[73] In some cases those receiving the honour had already previously afforded protection to merchants coming to their state from Athens, no doubt with a view to securing the office which they afterwards received, and its valuable privileges at Athens.

It may be noted that at Athens, unlike the practice of the other states mentioned above, the privileges of *asylia* and *ateleia hapantōn* were but rarely coupled with the grant of *proxenia*.[74] The tax on imports and exports was too important as revenue for exemption to be frequently granted.[75] The fact that the office of *proxenos* was often renewed from father to son goes to prove that it marked an important connection rather than a mere honour.[76]

A *proxenos* also had duties in the state of which he was a member. Though the office developed from the private guest-friend, the official *proxenos* was an important person, and exercised considerable influence. This fact is made clear by Demosthenes' speech against Callippus,[77] whose statement that he was *proxenos* of the Heracleots, was sufficient to gain for him the right to examine the business accounts of the banker Pasion. The action was against Apollodorus, after he had taken over the banking establishment from his father, Pasion. A certain Lycon of Heraclea had deposited with Pasion the sum of 1640 drachmae, instructing him to pay it to his partner, Cephisiades of Scyros, when the latter came to Athens. After the vessel in which Lycon was sailing to Libya had been seized by pirates and he himself had died of wounds at Argos, Callippus, the *proxenos* of Heraclea, demanded to examine Pasion's accounts, but did nothing further. After the money had been paid to Cephisiades – it may have been a loan raised as insurance – Callippus sought to persuade Pasion to frighten Cephisiades into returning the money. This attempt failed and three years afterwards Callippus brought an action against Pasion for the wrongful payment of the money to Cephisiades. When Pasion died, the case was renewed against his son.

The same speech suggests that the official *proxenos* of a state exercised a general supervision over its members visiting his own city.[78] No doubt the same conditions obtained in other states, as the agreement shows between Oianthea and Chaleum,[79] where a fine is laid down for misconduct of *proxenoi*.

A *proxenos* also obtained audience for visitors, with the magistrates, council or assembly.[80] When suits were tried in the country of the defendant (*dikai apo symbolōn*) the plaintiffs coming from abroad were presented to the court by the *proxenos* of their state. He sometimes received money on deposit,[81] or if a foreigner wished to raise a loan, he would be the most likely to stand surety. Similarly, he probably identified persons due to receive money from bankers, placed on deposit for them by people absent from Athens.[82] If we may believe the evidence of the grammarian Pollux,[83] the *proxenos* sometimes acted as an agent for a foreign merchant, since he was better acquainted than the latter with the local market; thus he acted as a *proprator* and disposed of the cargo imported by the foreign merchant, and secured a return freight.[84] This duty was of particular importance if the return cargo was corn. Two honorary inscriptions record services of this character; the recipients of honours are not specified as *proxenoi*, but it seems fairly certain that they held this office.[85] It will thus be seen that it was the duty of the *proxenos* to perform extensive duties. Still further services might be required of him by the state which had appointed him: thus it is said of one, 'he became *proxenos* and takes charge of all the matters enjoined on him by the Athenian people both private and public.'[86]

Theoretically, there could be only one official *proxenos* of one state in another, but in practice there was often more than one. Probably the number varied according to the magnitude of the intercourse between the states. Thus it appears that there was only one official *proxenos* of the Heracleots at Athens, and one also of the same state at Argos.[87] On the other hand, there appear to have been several representatives of Corcyra at Corinth.[88] There are extant a number of lists of *proxenoi*, mostly of late date, drawn up by several Greek states. One of the most complete of these, belonging to Histiaea,[89] and dating from the end of the third century, shows that a state was sometimes represented by more than one *proxenos*, though such states were not necessarily the most important or most closely connected with Histiaea.

CHAPTER SIX

FINANCE AND BANKING

THE GREEK CLASSICAL STATES could not dispense with various financial procedures,[1] though some moral theorists might have wished this.[2] In consequence, many transactions are recorded particularly in the Orators, though the term 'banking' in the modern sense can be used only with caution and in a limited way.

Financial operations started in a modest fashion with money-changing. Hence the name for a banker, *trapezites*, from the table (*trapeza*) of the money-changer, which appears on the coins of the Black Sea city of Trapezus.[3] In the late sixth and fifth centuries BC the multiplicity of state currencies in Greek lands (not in practical terms quite as numerous as is sometimes thought) made the function of money-changer necessary. A part of his function was to check the fineness and genuineness of coinage since there were not only private forgers[4] but also states such as Phocaea which issued poor-quality coinage.[5] It was probably this function that suggested the idea of a (State?) money-changing monopoly.[6] We have evidence of official testers of Attic coinage in Athens in the fourth century BC, partly for the protection of merchants.[7] In that century with the development of major currencies, the electrum of Cyzicus and Phocaea, the Athenian silver tetradrachm and latterly the gold and silver of Philip II of Macedon and then of Alexander the Great, the money-changing function may not have been so prominent,[8] and the *trapezites* acquired other functions – he may have done so earlier. He had deposited with him tangible assets (bullion, plate and the like) and also received in charge, as sureties for loans, craft establishments, including slaves,[9] and other property, and took charge of documents.[10] This was in some measure a bridge between the earlier simple functions and true deposit banking and the accumulation of capital for (potentially) the development of economic projects.[11] The complete transition to modern capitalistic concepts was never effected.

In general terms the Athenian bankers (in the Classical period the only ones really known)[12] were accumulators of deposits which were for various reasons committed to them. These they used certainly for emergency loans. If, for instance, an Athenian general, such as Apollodorus, required money to pay troops or naval crews—and this in the chaotic financial conditions of the fourth century was quite possible— he could be advanced money by a banker.[13] On a much lower level, in an emergency where someone was faced with an official entertainment, for example, a banker might lend plate and the like.[14] It is not clear that bankers employed an accumulation of capital for the development of industrial or, indeed, agricultural undertakings; but it cannot be disproved.[15] It must, however, be pointed out that the former was inhibited by problems of the control of slaves (hence the *apophora* system[16]) and the lack of technical devices; the latter, by the limitations on land (and the competition of special investment, as in mining or foreign trade) and fluctuations in the price of foreign corn.[17] Investment, at any rate in land, outside Attica, was checked by the regulations of the Second Athenian League.[18] There was also the nature of the source from which deposits came – individuals who might require these back at any time. Any kind of investment system based on transferable 'shares' was lacking.

Before the Hellenistic (post-Alexander) period the only literary source on banking is the collection of forensic speeches, in effect exclusively Athenian. It has already been pointed out[19] how limited our knowledge is. The most extensive source, in a haphazard way, is the body of speeches which goes under the name of 'Demosthenes', but not all authentically his. There is also an important speech of Isocrates, the *Trapeziticus*,[20] which makes clear the overseas ramifications of Athenian banking. Small bits and pieces of information can be extracted, directly or indirectly, from other orators.

In these speeches a very considerable amount of unsystematic information is given – there is always the preoccupation whether it is tendentious, and whether it represents the norm or the exception – on many aspects of banking. There are the names: Pasion,[21] father of Apollodorus who engaged himself in public life and acquired a reputation for litigatiousness;[22] both appear frequently in the Demosthenic *corpus*[23] and notably in speech xxxvi (see below). There are others: Phormio, ex-slave of Pasion,[24] Socles,[25] Aristolochus;[26] Socrates and Strymodorus.[27] Pasion himself was the ex-slave of Archestratus, associate in banking of Antisthenes;[28] Pylades and Demomeles are others named as holding deposits from the father of Demosthenes.[29] (See also n. 79 below.)

The greatest of Athenian bankers was Pasion. In the murky world of fourth-century 'finance' and commerce the name of Pasion is only once impugned (unlike that of his son). (See n. 71 below.) In the tire-

some issue of Demosthenes' speech XXXVI, involving Pasion's sons
Apollodorus and Pasicles and his freedman Phormio, details are given
of Pasion's bank and private fortune.[30] The following statement
reveals the complexities in the issue, some of which might be common,
others exceptional.

You must hear and understand in what way Pasion came to owe the eleven
talents[31] to the bank. He owed that sum not on account of poverty but on
account of his industry in business. For the landed property of Pasion was about
twenty talents, and in addition to that he had money of his own lent at interest,
amounting to more than fifty talents. With these fifty talents there were eleven
talents from the deposits of the bank profitably invested.[32] When Phormio,
therefore, became lessee of the bank business and received the deposits, seeing
that, as long as he did not enjoy the rights of Athenian citizenship, he should not
be able to get in the monies that Pasion had lent on land and lodging houses,
he chose that Pasion himself should owe him those sums rather than the other
debtors to whom he [Pasion] had lent them. And so, on this account, Pasion
was set down [as debtor] in the lease as owing eleven talents . . .

There should be noted here the disadvantage suffered by a slave or
freedman-metic, namely that non-citizens as bankers (or other non-
citizens) could not take over real estate pledged to cover loans. How
much of the eleven talents was thus engaged we are not told, but we
must suppose it was the whole sum and that these loans were made
after Pasion became a citizen. It must also be supposed that the shield-
factory leased to Phormio and subsequently inherited by Apollodorus
was in a separate category.

The amount of wealth possessed by Pasion is striking. As already
mentioned, his landed property came to twenty talents (re-investment
after he became a citizen?). Unfortunately we do not know in detail
how Pasion's fortune other than in landed property was disposed. It can
only be guessed that it was invested in similar fashion to the eleven
talents.

Occasionally we get more detail, as in the case of the father of Demosthenes, particulars of whose fortune are given in a speech delivered by
his son, the future Orator, and directed against his guardians who
sought to defraud him after his father's death. The list is given thus[33] (it
demonstrates a diversity of interests which cannot have been unique):

(a)   A sword-factory with 32–33 slaves, yielding an annual income of
      30 minae.[34]
(b)   A couch-factory with 20 slaves, pledged to Demosthenes' father
      for a debt (loan?) of 40 minae, producing an annual income of
      12 minae. Note in this case the high return of 30 percent in con-

trast to the approximate 16 percent on the sword-factory, or at most 17·4 percent.[35]

(c) One talent cash, lent at 12 percent interest, producing 7 minae per year; strictly it should be 7·2 percent.

(d) Stocks of factory materials, of 80 minae value.

(e) House, furniture, plate, jewels, valued at 100 minae – the bulk of this would be represented by the house.

(f) 80 minae cash in the house.

(g) 70 minae maritime loan.

(h) Bank deposits, 24 minae with Pasion; 6 with Pylades; 6 with Demomeles.

(i) 'Friendly loans' (= without interest, security or witnesses?) of one talent.

The grand total is given at 14 talents.[36]

In Pasion's arrangement (if, in effect, there was an arrangement) there was an elaborate interrelation of personalities. It has been seen that Pasion himself at the beginning of his career was a slave of Archestratus, associate in banking of Antisthenes,[37] and that subsequently he became first freedman and then citizen, acquired two sons and a faithful slave, later freedman, Phormio. There then followed complications, made apparent in the Demosthenic speech on behalf of Phormio, defending him against Apollodorus the son of the now deceased Pasion.[38] The following will make clear the circumstances and the complications:[39]

Phormio was slave of Pasion, whose business he managed for a long time. When Pasion died he left a widow [Archippe], to be married to Phormio, and two sons Apollodorus and Pasicles [the latter a minor]. The bulk of Pasion's property was divided between the two sons by the guardian of Pasicles. There was the bank and a shield-factory. These Pasion had leased to Phormio, who paid rent for them until Pasicles came of age, when Apollodorus took the shield-factory and Pasicles the bank, Phormio being discharged from his obligation. On the death of Archippe, the wife of Pasion subsequently married to Phormio, Apollodorus made claims on Phormio for certain property alleged to be in his possession. There was a compromise by arbitration and Phormio was given release from these demands.

Eighteen years after Pasion's death Apollodorus put forward the claim which is the theme of Demosthenes xxxvi. The claim by Apollodorus was that Phormio had converted to his own use a sum of bank stock alleged to have been left by Pasion in the bank. The explanation or ostensible explanation of all this has been set out earlier, in so far as it is possible to explain anything on the basis of ancient Greek assertions in court.

There are various interesting features in this particular legal exercise. The stress on 'papers'[40] should be noted, just as 'ship's papers' are stressed in connection with maritime loans. There is the interesting point concerning the two properties: the different return, from the bank of a hundred minae, and from the factory of one talent (sixty minae). Further the observation is made: 'the plaintiff [Apollodorus] acted wisely in choosing the shield manufactory; for that is a property *without risk*, whereas the bank is a business yielding a precarious revenue from other people's money.'[41] This is, indeed, a partisan argument in a court of law, but it carries a certain conviction. Again there is the question of the 'transfer' of the bank. It is stated[42] that Phormio 'let' the bank to Xenon, Euphraeus, Euphron and Callistratus, and that they also had no private banking stock delivered to them, but took a lease only of the deposits (which implies a series of records) and of the profits arising from them. What of the confidence and good will?

There emerges, in terms of finance, a picture at once curiously simple in some matters, but complicated in others. Banking matters ramified from Athens to other parts of Greece, and as far as South Russia across the Black Sea.[43] Among the bequests to Archippe, widow of Pasion, there is 'a talent in Peparethus', whatever that may mean.[44] In the complicated issue of the ship of Polycles, and the problem, which trierarchs faced, of paying their crews in foreign parts, there is the interesting description, as given by Apollodorus,[45] of the problem of raising money for this purpose:

Accordingly I obtained a loan from Kleanax and Eperatus, two friends of my father in Tenedos . . . for through being Pasion's son and his being on terms of friendship with many foreigners and having great credit in Greece, I had no difficulty in borrowing money where I wanted it.

The career of Pasion is striking, though there must have been others, but hardly with such a grandiose fortune: first he was a slave,[46] then a freedman metic (*c.* 394–391 BC) and finally a citizen[47] of the deme of Acharnae,[48] though he was resident in Piraeus.[49] His illness and death[50] set in train the events relating to his two sons and his ex-slave.

It is natural to compare Pasion with the other traditionally wealthy men known to Classical Greek writers,[51] the basis of whose fortunes rested in some cases on slave-owning and almost certainly on agriculture. We are quite ignorant of the sources of Alcibiades' fortune; that of Xenophon's prototypal 'gentleman' Ischomachus was agriculture.[52] As pointed out already, 'the landed property of Pasion was about twenty talents, and in addition to that he had money of his own lent at interest, amounting to more than fifty talents.'[53] It is hard to see how such great assets were built up, especially in the difficult times at the end of the fifth century and in the fourth, with the multiplication of public financial burdens[54] laid on the wealthy (Pasion served as trierarch), and the vexatious institution of the *antidosis* (the challenge to an exchange of properties in relation to the discharge of these public financial obligations). There were natural dangers such as drought,[55] which could affect bankers, certainly indirectly, and the debtor who might have to default through one of many causes. Further, though Apollodorus received very considerable sums from what had originally been his father's fortune,[56] he had to bear, as he himself claimed, extensive public financial burdens.[57]

Some special pleading may be suspected here. This introduces us to another interesting aspect of the same Athenian forensic practice, producing the same uncertainty concerning the interpretation of the sources, this time in relation to the integrity of those engaged in banking. The speaker in defence of Phormio explains that the latter won golden opinions from Pasion for his diligence, as did Pasion previously from *his* masters.[58] Here a striking statement is made:

Pasion while he was with his masters Antisthenes and Archestratus, the bankers, gave proof that he was honest and just in his dealings and won their confidence. In the commercial world and the money market it is thought a wonderful thing when the same person shows himself honest and diligent.

The implication is of rampant dishonesty. Hence the stress on written records,[59] for loans and for payments by book transfer, in which a sum was deposited by an individual with a banker and payments were made at his instruction to another. Or it could be that two such might make deposits in the same bank. This is the so-called giro-banking, a term long used by German scholars (*Giroverkehr*) and now familiar in Britain for the payment of accounts.[60]

The special pleading in the speech in defence of Phormio is that Pasion and he were exceptionally honest and competent bankers at a time when banking was a risky business.[61] This may be so, but the great sums involved are hard to explain, and the risks could not all be overcome either by honesty or diligence. There was the competition of agriculture[62] and other forms of investment; the risks of anything to do with mercantile affairs[63] and trade loans,[64] while war, the depredations of other states and of pirates all affected capital engaged in this sphere.

The banker's functions covered a wide spectrum of activities, from lending not only money but also material objects (coverlets (*stromata*), outer garments (*himatia*) and silver cups),[65] and the acceptance, as pledges, of cups and a gold crown for a loan[66] – all rather reminiscent of the pawnshop. More in keeping with modern ideas of banking is first and foremost the process of giro-banking,[67] mentioned above, which must have been of great importance in the discharge of business. There was also the payment of freight charges, as, for example, on a cargo of timber.[68] Such a function, with mercantile loans, would have played a considerable part in the promotion of trade. There was also the acceptance of deposits.[69]

Moreover a network of foreign connections on a basis of personal acquaintance clearly existed. One case has already been quoted.[70] There is another example:[71] Lycon of Heraclea uses Pasion's bank 'like the other merchants' (? Heracleots). We may also mention Pasion's connection with South Russia.[72] In such sometimes distant inter-state connections a nice point arises: were such transactions simply on the basis of book transfers,[73] or was there a depositing or conveying of sums of cash over long distances, to match giro-banking within one city-state?[74]

Although the gods might engage in banking through the temple treasuries,[75] it appears that it was not an activity befitting a citizen born free. Thus it emerges from another passage in the speech in defence of Phormio:[76]

For, although to you, men of Athens, who are citizens by birth, it would be disgraceful to prefer wealth, however great, to honourable descent, yet these persons who have obtained citizenship as a gift either from you or from others, and who owed that honour originally to their good fortune, to their having prospered in business and ma⌐ ᵣ ᵢore money than their neighbours, are obliged to preserve these advantages.

Yet Demosthenes' father does not appear to have objected, nor yet earlier did wealthy men such as Nicias (so another piece of special pleading?). In any case, after a fashion, rich citizens could engage in business through the bankers as intermediaries, just as Roman senators did through the Equites.

The failure to use capital more extensively for economic expansion is somewhat puzzling. When the writer of the pamphlet *On Ways and Means* suggests such expansion in shipping and mining, which would not, like workshop development, be inhibited by a lack of technological skill, it is the State, the writer suggests, which is to provide the capital.[77]

One curious phenomenon should be pointed out also, which may underline the fragmentary and incomplete nature of the sources. It is to be noted that Pasion, Apollodorus, Pasicles and Phormio appear in a striking number[78] of speeches in the Demosthenic *corpus*. Elsewhere, to judge from the index to the *corpus* of Attic Orators,[79] Pasion appears only in Demosthenes and Isocrates XVII; Apollodorus in Aeschines (once), Pasicles in Hyperides (once), Phormio in Dinarchus (once) and in Aeschines (once). Outside the 'House of Pasion', of those bankers named in Demosthenes' speeches, Archestratus appears once in Isocrates XVII, and Demomeles twice in Aeschines. Others are hard to find in any number.[80] Some of those described as 'lenders' in Demosthenic speeches[81] may have been bankers. It is to be suspected much has been lost. There are many speeches represented only by quotations or references in the lexicographers (thus Isaeus, fr. 16, mentions 'a metic among those functioning as bankers at Athens'). The prominence of the Pasion family is not easy to explain except by the comment of Dinarchus stressing Demosthenes' great activity as a forensic orator. But then there is the problem of authenticity!

CHAPTER SEVEN

TRADES AND CRAFTS

THERE IS A CLEAR CONNECTION between traders, and trades and crafts, and between craft establishments and those who provided materials for the work carried out in them. The craft organization and the working establishments vary in size from the very small to those State undertakings in Athens and elsewhere concerned with the construction of large public buildings involving elaborate arrangements of work-flow, heavy transport and large masses of material, for which the public account inscriptions give fuller information than is available in other spheres of craft or industry, fuller even, in some respects, than for mining. Apart from the building inscriptions and the light they throw on men, methods and materials, and on prices and wages, in contemporary and later (less reliable) literature there are scattered references to general principles. In the private speeches of the Orators, where questions of property arise, some examples of what may be called 'industrial' establishments occur, and examples also of the employment of individual slaves or small groups of slaves on the *apophora* system. Something has already been said about these, as matters of general principle, and also on the attitude at least of some Greeks to such activities. Here certain matters of detail need to be considered and mention made of further sources which bring us more closely into contact with the individual: the scattered references to craftsmen, and especially the dedications they set up to the gods, particularly Athena. There are also the lease and mortgage inscriptions. In a class somewhat apart are the mining inscriptions relating to the silver mines at Laurium, which will be dealt with in Chapter IX. For the material equipment, the tools and the establishments in which the pursuit of arts and crafts took place, there is the evidence of archaeology, including pictorial representations: the excavations in the region of the Athenian marketplace, and elsewhere within and without the walls of Athens, and in the country. With the exception of the pamphlet under the name of Xenophon, *On Ways and Means*, which is in any case concerned with revenues rather than directly with trade and industry, there is little direct comment on trade, industry, crafts and so on, except where, in the philosophers, these impinge on personal or community well-being from the moral standpoint.

The household was the cradle of much craft activity, and this to some extent remained true even when there was a very considerable elaboration of crafts, when Xenophon[1] could comment on the division of labour in manufacture in large cities. The same author, in his *Memorabilia*, caused his subject, Socrates, to make certain observations on domestic industry, not unconnected with the circumstances of the times, i.e. the period immediately after the Peloponnesian War. The war had impoverished many of the middle and upper classes, through the occupation of Decelea, the defeat of Athens, and the depredations of the Thirty Tyrants. Those who still possessed slaves put them to work to produce not only for the household but also for the market[2] and various forms of production which could reasonably be carried out in the household are associated with specific names: Nausicydes and the preparation of meal (*alphitopoiia*), Cyrebus and bread-making (*artopoiia*), Demeas and Menon with the making of simple garments (*chlamydourgia*; *chlamidopoiia*).[3] Indeed Socrates is made to suggest that the economic difficulties of his acquaintance Aristarchus should be relieved by setting his female relatives to work at what they know, namely the domestic industry of weaving (Pls 31–33). Even if this is a fictitious example, there is no reason to believe that such house industry, at any rate for free women, did not exist.[4] Here Xenophon seems to make Socrates stress the value of useful knowledge, and its application in productive work[5] as against the suggested idleness of free people (*eleutheroi*), which was the Athenian and Greek ideal, at any rate for men. Socrates himself was a sculptor; a close friend, Simon, was a shoemaker. Independent work, as in these cases, was just possible though, in the eyes of many, undesirable; work under a master was intolerable to an Athenian (at any rate as we meet him in the *Memorabilia*). He might do casual agricultural work under pressure of necessity; he could not think of working at the beck and call of another as a steward, suited as his talents might be to the job. It is difficult to judge how much this is just high-toned philosophical stuff. It is true that there were men who stood for hire at Kolonos Agoraios in Athens: some were no doubt slaves who had been sent out to work by their masters. Some may have been free men.[6] Many or most might find mercenary military service more attractive.

The most natural form of domestic 'industry' was concerned with food, textiles and the like. Since it was domestic it was of necessity the province of either women or slaves. Once given the principle, it could be extended to cover other fields of craft activity followed by slaves; metics would not engage themselves to another if they could help it. Starting from slaves already in the household it was possible to go on to purchase slaves expert at some crafts as an investment. An extension of this, in a way, was the business of those, Nicias among them, who acquired large numbers of mining slaves, and hired them out through a manager. A modest application of the same principle, whereby someone engaged in craft or business purchased a slave expert at the same calling, or trained him for it, to act as a prop for old age or physical disability, seems to lie behind the arrangements of the 'disabled person' who is the subject of a speech of Lysias.[7] There was no critical size to such an undertaking; a modest shed (*klision*) attached to an equally modest dwelling could house one slave and his owner: the *ergasterion* often mentioned in leases as attached to low-value houses. This would be the parallel to the single slave employed in the mines.[8] A slave establishment might be acquired on mortgage as a security; it might be inherited. In both cases its operation would not presuppose the complete technical expertise of the owner. A more expert slave would function as manager, and thus act as the link between the master and the rest, having perhaps been purchased for this purpose, as Nicias' 'mining-slave manager' was.

Of this type of industry we have a certain number of examples given in the literary sources: that they are so well known, and that they have been discussed in great detail and *ad nauseam* is an indication of the paucity of the information available. There was the shield-factory of the metic orator Lysias and his brother (it owed its existence to some extent, at any rate, to the needs of the Peloponnesian War). It is the largest recorded of these establishments. At a later date there was the shield-factory of the freedman banker Pasion,[9] which brought him in an income of one talent.[10] It seems to have been a side-show to his banking business. Perhaps best known, because it set Demosthenes on the path of oratory, was the property of his father, which after the latter's death was maladministered by Demosthenes' guardians. The property included what is called variously a sword-factory or a cutlery-factory, and a couch-factory: the one employed thirty-two to thirty-three slaves, the other twenty slaves. To some extent the products were luxury objects (of the sort that sometimes figure as dedications to the gods in temple treasuries), since we hear of ivory among the stock of raw materials.[11] These are the only 'large' establishments to which reference is made. They are not, in reality, large.

Some mining and ore-preparation establishments were probably larger, but not much so: the problem was one of the organization of labour and of supervision. While a considerable degree of specialization and division of labour might and did exist among individual workers, the cost of the supervision of slaves would be considerable and very soon involve diminishing returns. There were few non-human sources of energy, only animal- and water-power and these limited in use.

Indeed the Athenian attitude to such industrial activity was a curious one. First, while there are instances of the use of loans to acquire such undertakings (and to their kind some at least, of the many surviving, mortgage stones must refer), there is no evidence for the accumulation and use of capital to develop or extend 'factories' in any way parallel to modern practice. Unless we are grossly misled by the sources, such manufacturing industry was not regarded as a usual sphere of employment of large-scale capital, even in the Classical Athenian sense of 'large scale'. Furthermore, there is a certain indication that establishments were not particularly efficient, and that their owners had no particular expertise or understanding of the activities involved. It is also clear that on occasions the acquisition of such concerns was a matter of chance, as in the case of one of the two owned by the father of Demosthenes, which had been acquired as a pledge for a loan. This rather haphazard, unconvinced and not particularly efficient manifestation of 'factory' production fits in with the character of Athens' major industry, namely mining. Here again, in addition to the characteristics of speculations and irregular activity, there was much subdivision and use of small labour forces. This was made possible by the existence of purveyors of labour for hire, such as Nicias. So too, just as an individual's stake in the Laurium mines might amount to no more than one slave, so the participation in manufacturing industry might be, and generally was, little more: an extension of the individual *apophora* system, or what might be called the oriental bazaar system, but sometimes located in a private house rather than in the market, though many were separate establishments in a suitable quarter of Athens where one skilled slave exercised his craft. Thus we hear of small manufactures: of makers of hair-nets(?) (*sakkhyphantai*),[12] and colour- or drug-makers (*pharmakotribai*). In one of his speeches Aeschines[13] mentions

a house behind the Acropolis, a hill-side farm at Sphettos and another plot at Alopeke; *apart from these*, nine or ten house-slaves [*oiketai*], craftsmen in leatherwork [shoemaking], of whom each one paid two obols *apophora* each day to their master, while the man in charge of the establishment [*ergasterion*] paid three obols.

In addition to these there was a woman (? slave) skilled in weaving fine diaphanous fabrics (*amorgina*), and disposing of these in the market, and a man skilled in embroidery. The latter, it is clear, operated separately from the shoemakers. These craftsmen, it should be noted, formed part of a diversified fortune of which the basis was real estate. It may be suggested that there were many such, and that the industry of Athens did consist of hundreds or indeed thousands of such tiny organizations. The collection from them of cargoes for export involved a very considerable service of middlemen.

Similar again were the bronze-workers owned by Leocrates in the later fourth century.[14] How many they were we do not know. Earlier in the same speech, by Lycurgus, are mentioned a house and slaves sold for one talent;[15] later the slaves were sold for 3500 drachmae, a price which would indicate that they ranged in number between fifteen and twenty-five—an establishment on the large side for Athens. The bronze-workers[16] are called *chalkotypoi*. They might, therefore, be bronze-casters (Pls 37, 42, 43), and establishments which housed the activities of such are represented in some numbers in the industrial, but also residential, district of Melite, on the fringe of the Agora and hard by the temple of Athena and Hephaestus, patrons of the arts and crafts. In that region have been found their casting-pits and the broken fragments of moulds (Pls 38, 39). Not very far away is modern Hephaistos Street, with the open-fronted shops of the metalworkers and repairers hung about with fantastic collections of metallic junk. They must have been the same in Antiquity, except that the primitive forge was not then supplemented by Hephaestus' greatest gift to man – oxy-acetylene welding! Such a bronze-worker's shop, it seems from the Orator Andocides,[17] saw some of the intrigues which attended the departure of the Sicilian Expedition in 415 BC, and in such a milieu we gather that Euphemus the smith acted as a go-between among persons of very different social status.

This reminds us also that not all craftsmen were slaves, whatever the prejudices of the philosophers, though it is as difficult to decide whether a man called a smith actually followed the craft, as it is to assess the exact position of a free 'miner' at Laurium, or of the man who claimed to be free and an Athenian who was employed in a fuller's shop (*gnapheion*).[18] This was another type of industrial establishment probably represented among those found on the fringes of the Athenian Agora – an essential industry of Athens since wool was the predominant material for cloth.[19] Others found in the Agora are the workshops of the terracotta-makers (*koroplastai*), a simple industry involving relatively little in the way of technical equipment. Inside and outside the walls of Athens away beyond the Agora, where began the processional way which led up to the Acropolis, was the Potters' Quarter, the Kerameikos. For the most part these potteries, where the celebrated Attic pottery with first black- and then red-figure decoration was manufactured, have disappeared except for the 'wasters'. What went on in them appears in vase-paintings, as does the work of the foundry. Indeed one vase-painter is actually called the Foundry Painter. Another vase may represent a scene in a shop where vases were sold: the purchaser stands with purse in hand viewing the wares. From such a retail potter's shop came the mass of pottery dumped in a well in the Agora. The shop had been destroyed in the Persian sack of Athens in 480/79 BC.

Factories or workshops and shops alike were often small and unpretentious structures. They were very often so unpretentious that no traces of them have survived. Sufficient has been preserved in the form of foundations, which have contrived to survive the repeated making-over of the industrial region of Athens, to show that the picture given by mortgage inscriptions is a true one. Despite the great compression, sometimes, of buildings, and the narrow streets between them, in the industrial area small plots were associated with houses, themselves frequently of relatively low value, and so permitted the construction of shanties in which industrial activity could be carried out. So, in inscriptions,[20] appear an *ergasterion*; a house and *ergasterion*; a curious combination of *ergasterion*, garden and fountain; another *ergasterion*; a furnace (*kaminos*) and plots of land; an *ergasterion* and house actually recorded as in Melite, that is, in the region close to the temple of Hephaestus and Athena and the Agora. In several instances such *ergasteria* are recorded as mortgaged together with the slaves who presumably were employed in them.[21] One example, oddly, mentions slaves and a garden. The American excavations in the region of the Agora, and the German excavations in that of the Kerameikos reveal the remains of such houses-with-workshops, which confirm the impression of the prevalent character of industry given by the written sources. In the region west and north of the Areopagus there have been found:[22] (i) a casting pit; (ii) remains of kilns, and evidence of clay-working; (iii) a curious establishment with an elaborate system of shallow drains and basins, perhaps a fuller's shop. Demosthenes mentions a fuller in Melite.[23] A bronze foundry and mould fragments (Pls 38, 39) have been found in the region of the temple of Hephaestus.[24] In the Kerameikos also some rather obscure establishments may be industrial (fullery?), if not public baths. Other industrial undertakings have been found elsewhere, even outside the walls in the vicinity of the Olympieion. But the tradition which connected crafts and industry with the region of the Agora was a strong one and survived the organization of this area with public amenities, though at all times splendid public buildings and industrial hovels must have existed in close proximity, and large private houses. For instance in the south Stoa there are traces of iron-working which seem to belong to the first century BC, and the sludge of marble-working.[25]

Craftsman and trader, freeman, freedman and slave are not always easy to distinguish. The latter two classes, with that of resident aliens, were always important, and especially so, if we may believe the pamphlet-writer of the later fifth century called the Old Oligarch, during the period of the Athenian naval empire. They were important also during the Peloponnesian War, and in the fourth century, as becomes apparent when all the many activities are borne in mind to which a citizen might be called, and especially military service, despite the increased use of mercenaries.

There was a recognized division between masculine and feminine trades.[26] It was also felt that certain trades and callings were more to be despised than others: lodging-house keeper, tax-collector, auctioneer, cook-house keeper (*mageiros*). The editor of Theophrastus' *Characters*, Sir Richard Jebb, appears to hold that *mageireuein*[27] means 'to follow the trade of cook'. He may be correct, but the low cook-house was a place of ill-repute, and the man who is credited with being engaged in this calling (The Reckless Man) is free not slave, so that Jebb's quotation of Livy[28] on the incoming of Asiatic luxury to Rome, is hardly apposite: 'Then it was that the cook, esteemed and treated by the ancients as the vilest of slaves, began to be prized.' It is to be noted that Jebb can adduce no definite evidence for the Classical period on the 'crier' or 'auctioneer', any more than he can on the cook either free or slave. In connection with the tax-collector (whom he calls 'tax-farmer') he quotes, from Andocides,[29] a celebrated passage:

Agyrrhius became chief-farmer of the two percent tax two years ago, buying it for thirty talents, and had for his partners the whole set who muster under the white poplar. *You know what they are like.*

Such speculators, who were disliked as many of the others who are seen from the records of the *poletai* to engage in collecting one particular tax, were men of some standing and property; they had to be, for financial reasons. Theophrastus has in mind rather the petty tax-collector whose sordid calling is not even relieved by the magnitude of his undertakings. On the inn-keeper Jebb comes nearer to the point, though he fails to see that the objection to these callings, in addition to the temptations of petty gain, is that they placed those who followed them at the beck and call of others: and thus they were fit only for slaves. 'The unpopularity of inn-keepers arose partly, no doubt, from the general feeling in ancient Greece against taking money for hospitality; but they were also infamous, as a class, for extortion.' There is a curious passage in Plato's *Laws*:[30]

On this account [eagerness for gain] all the lines of life connected with retail trade, commerce, inn-keeping, have fallen under suspicion and become utterly disreputable . . . A man opens lodgings, for the sake of trade, in a lonely place, a long way from anywhere. He receives bewildered travellers in barely tolerable quarters, or affords warmth, quiet, and rest in his close rooms to people driven in by angry storms. And then, after receiving them as friends, he does not provide them with hospitable entertainment in accordance with that reception, but *holds them to ransom* – like captive enemies whom he has got into his clutches, – on the most exorbitant, unjust, rascally terms. It is these offences, and others like them, shamefully common in all such callings, which have brought discredit upon such ministration to men's need.

'But', adds Jebb, commenting on this passage, 'though it was discreditable to keep, it was not so to frequent an inn. The Athenian ambassadors to Philip stay at inns[31] and Dionysus in the *Frogs*[32] inquires which are the best inns on the road to Hades.' And, it may be added, the one he gets to (formerly frequented by Herakles) is no impressive specimen of its kind!

Another calling, that of nurse (*titthos*, basically, perhaps, a wet-nurse, but used in general of the attendant on small children), was also not in theory highly regarded. It is called a 'lowly thing' by Demosthenes;[33] the pursuit of it might be a reproach,[34] though there is a suggestion that in times of economic stress many followed it, not only slaves. If this is true, it is a curious contrast to those innumerable epitaphs of 'good nurses' which seem to mark the gratitude of their charges, in a heart-warming way, for their services to them as children. It must be remembered, however, that a slave might be a good slave, and his calling an essential one, faithfully performed. It was, none the less, a slave's calling, and unworthy of a free man. So in general, the ancient class of *demiourgoi*, of those who once served the community by the exercise of their crafts, became debased. The word *demiourgos* was still used for 'artisan' in the fourth century BC,[35] but its status was depressed by the combined influence of slavery and democracy.

Two sources show us the multiplicity of trades and callings: epitaphs and dedications. Both bring us closer to the artisan and other types of worker than the rare and brief references in the literary sources. Some examples may be given.[36] There are the bread-makers: we are reminded of (Boeotian) terracotta representations of women at work kneading dough in what is obviously a bakery not a private house, though bread-making might be a domestic industry, and enjoying music from a flute-player while they work. Like Lycidas the miller (*mylothros*) in Demosthenes,[37] and the bakers who went, or were drafted, from the bakeries of Athens to serve on the Sicilian Expedition, they make clear that the provision of flour and bread in Athens was a trade probably of some magnitude. Then there is a slipper-maker (*persikopoios*) in the same collection;[38] also a bath-man and a washerman, a vine-tender, a silver-worker, a salt-seller and a potter. How many were slaves it is difficult to tell. Some, the *demosios* who served the state administration, and the *paidagogos* or children's attendant, certainly were.[39]

The same variety appears even in early dedications, on the Acropolis, to Athena Parthenos and Polias, elsewhere to Athena Ergane, the patroness of all crafts and callings, to whom the dedications of success-ful manufacturers and other workers were made. These dedications frequently represented a tithe (*aparche*) of gains:[40] so, fullers, ship-wrights, a bread-seller (female), a washerwoman, a lyre-player, a crier, a tanner, a carpenter and the ubiquitous potters (Pl. 44) appear. Some of their names, appearing in these tithe-dedications, are known to us also from the works which they signed, as Nearchus and Euphronius; and there are dedications of Peithon and Smikros (?)[41] from the North Slope of the Acropolis. Many were obviously well-to-do. Just as Nicias might have set up a dedication from the profits of the employ-ment of his slaves in the silver mines, so actually did Diocles of Pithos; his dedication[42] of the first half of the fourth century says:

Diocles of Pithos, son of Antichares, dedicated me to Athena, tithing the fruit of his own skill.

His 'skill' was almost certainly that of mining, as a member of a family well known from the mining inscriptions. The dedicators were not always wealthy. This seems to be indicated not only by the callings (cf. the bread-seller), but also by a touching dedication, clearly of a mother forced to rear her children by the pursuit of a craft, in the later fourth century:[43]

Melinna has dedicated to thee, Goddess of crafts, this memorial, having reared a generation of children by the skill of her hands [in spinning or wreath-making?] and by just enterprise, honouring thy grace by a tithe of the earnings she won by her labour.

The activity which paid for the dedication was not always so respectable, witness the example[44] which is probably the offering of a prostitute (*hetaira*). Nor was it always plain gratitude, but sometimes hope of favours to come:[45] 'Maiden Goddess, in the Acropolis Telesinus, the son of Ketis, set up this statue; taking pleasure in this offering, mayest thou grant him to set up another.'

The rivalry of craftsman with craftsman, which is commented on as early as Hesiod[46] ('Potter is at variance with potter and carpenter with carpenter'), appears on the very vases which materialized their rivalry, as on the Munich red-figure amphora of Euthymides: 'Euphronius never did anything like this!' It has its reflection in the dedications and epitaphs of craftsmen. For example a potter again,[47] Bacchius of the Kerameikos, in the later fourth century says:

All Hellas has judged Bacchius as by nature bearing away the first prize of those craftsmen who by their craft bring together earth and water and fire. And in those skills in which this city has established contests, he has won the crowns, all of them.

This seems to indicate a pride in craft which we would not guess from the philosophers. And indeed the sons of this man, sometime before 321 BC, received a grant of citizenship from the city of Ephesus. In the nature of things the status of those who appear in such inscriptions is difficult to assess, but while many were undoubtedly free citizens, many others were either slaves or freedmen, or resident aliens. There is an interesting combination of names of foreigners or slaves (cf. the names of vase-painters and potters such as Kolchos and Lydos) in a dedication of washermen to the Nymphs in the mid-fourth century.[48]

The lively and immediate picture given by these inscriptions is but little supplemented in literature, even in the Old, Middle and New Comedy, where political life and domestic life, rather than the life of the craftsman is the centre of interest – perhaps following the aristocratic and indeed democratic prejudice. There are casual references; among them, naturally, to armament-makers when the question of peace or war is at issue. Otherwise crafts are very little mentioned. Aristophanes[49] cites jewellers and shoemakers in a comic context. Shoemakers in particular had their peculiarities: the revolutionary women in the *Ecclesiazusae*[50] are mistaken for 'pale-faced shoemakers'. As at other times and places they were regarded as suffering both from cramped bodies and subversive ideas: in Lucian's *Voyage to the Underworld*[51] the dead cobbler, who was an egalitarian, greets with satisfaction the prospect of 'equal rights for all, and no man better than his neighbour' in the World of the Dead. One of the friends of Socrates was the shoemaker Simon, and a house with a great quantity of shoe-nails, found in the vicinity of the Agora, may have been his.

In view of contemporary prejudices little is directly recorded on techniques in the period under consideration. There are, indeed, in literature, indirect references: appearing, for instance, in metaphor or description, such as the celebrated comparison, in the *Bacchae* of Euripides, of the Maenads drawing down the pine tree in order to kill Pentheus, with the working of a lathe.[52] There are other isolated references, such as to the burning-glass.[53], which could also function as a magnifying glass, and was an indispensable instrument of the gem- and die-engraver; and yet almost nothing is said of an instrument with such great potentialities. There are, in inscriptions,[54] abundant references to tools and equipment. Some have survived, especially agricultural tools, even from the sixth century B C. There are iron tools, sickle, mattock, etc., from the North Slope of the Acropolis.[55] Vase-paintings (Pls 34–36, 40–42) and dedicatory plaques show simple tools and the workshops of potters and bronze-casters, with furnaces, ovens, wheels, and the rest of the relatively simple equipment. Furthermore, mythological scenes sometimes show the use of tools, such as the bow-drill in a scene of the preparation of the Chest of Danaë (Pl. 35). The processes of spinning and of weaving (with representation of a loom) are a common decoration on vases (Pls 31–33). In some cases, however, as in the literary references, the exact detail of the use of tools or of the carrying-out of technical processes is not clear from such representations; there is, for example, the problem of the exact way in which the celebrated 'relief lines' of Attic red-figure pottery were produced (Pl. 47).

To a very considerable extent it is clear that basic processes, in the quarrying (with wooden wedges)[56] and preparation of stone, in the working of metal (bronze-casting rather than iron-working), in the conversion of natural fibres (flax, wool, hemp, cotton, silk(?)) into thread and cloth, and in the working of wood and clay, have varied little from Classical Greek times to the present day in communities of a comparable state of development. Basic tools, in much the same form as in Roman and modern times, were possessed by the Classical Greeks and indeed by those of the Bronze Age. There was one fundamental difference from later times: whereas the Middle Ages saw the use not only of animal-power but also of water-power for the smelting and working of iron, while the Romans used animal-power and water-power (*and* the human tread-mill) for corn-grinding – there was a late Roman water-mill with overshot wheel in the Athenian Agora – the

Classical Greeks, including the Athenians, give little evidence of using animal- or water-power for any process, and seem to have been limited to the simplest applications of human energy, lacking even those systems of pulleys which serve to augment directly applied human force. Thus they were confined to the use of hand bellows (Pl. 41), and to the melting of some metals only, not iron, which they were forced to work by hammering (Pl. 40). Similarly they appear to have lacked the Roman skill in glass-working, and while they possessed and worked substances which are technically glass, they seem not to have produced large glass vessels.

On the other hand a high degree of technical skill is demonstrated in the manufacture of wooden vessels, which indicates the use of a simple lathe, as well as by the splendid Greek pottery, from the Mycenaean, through the innovations of Protogeometric, the monumental quality of late Geometric amphorae, the colourful and elaborate Protoattic, to black- (Pl. 22) and red-figure vases of the great period of the late sixth and fifth centuries, and the less attractive later pottery of the fourth century. There was also the well-shaped black-glazed ware, of commoner use, and the later common 'West Slope' ware, as well as the storage and export amphorae for bulk commodities. They all show a high degree of skill in the preparation of the clay and glazes, which can to some degree be followed out and reproduced, as recent experiment has shown. It is clear from the wasters and from the use of indicators (pieces of clay covered with glaze in which changes of colour served to test kiln temperatures) that the baking of the pottery was a skilled and hazardous business, and the evil eye a matter of some preoccupation for potters. The same high degree of skill is apparent also in sheet-metal work (gold, silver, bronze), and in casting: both the solid casting of small objects, and hollow-casting, sometimes by the *cire-perdue* process, of larger ones (Pls 37, 39). The finest bronze-work, cast and chased, and the hammering-out of precious metals in a mould, which combined with ivory-carving reached its height in the great gold and ivory statues of Zeus and Athena by Phidias, have for the most part been lost, but the many surviving minor bronzes, produced in the manifold schools of Greece, including Athens, the few extant major bronzes, and the clay impressions which have survived of fine relief metalwork of the fifth century BC[57] show what Greek craftsmen were capable of. Admittedly the coins of Athens do not exactly do credit to Athenian die-engravers; for the finest one has to go elsewhere. On the other hand seal-stones, as far as they can be identified as Athenian, show their capacity for fine work on a small scale, as do also the fine engraving of metal surfaces, and the detail of incision or relief-line on Attic black- and red-figure pottery. The excavation of the Agora district in Athens has demonstrated the magnitude of the terracotta industry. The *koroplastes*, with his large market for cheap and simple dedications, and the producer of common everyday pottery, provide the closest approximation in Greek antiquity to mass-production, though the producing unit could be and probably always was very small. But the charm of many terracottas, the observation apparent in representations of everyday life, show that here too craftsmanship of a high order, even artistry, was sometimes present.

The natural conditions of Greece in general have not been conducive to the preservation of organic matter. Thus textiles are very rarely forthcoming. However, specimens of textiles of the Geometric period (at Argos),[58] and of Classical Athens are known. There are also impressions on other (mainly metal) objects that were wrapped in fabrics which have long since disappeared. They confirm the high technical skill of professional weaving with the warp-weighted loom (Pl. 31). The domestic product, like that of country Greece today, was a great deal coarser. Objects of leather, such as harness, shoes, etc., have also disappeared. So, too, with rare exceptions such as the wooden vases found at Brauron, have objects of wood: as, for example, the great variety of objects and ornaments, sometimes gilded, which appear in the inventories of temple treasuries, with indications also of the former existence of superb furniture.[59] Consequently we are thrown back on representations, particularly in vase-painting, but also to some degree in sculpture, for the styles of clothes and shoes and other articles of dress; and where furniture is concerned, both for its forms (chairs, couches, tables, chests) and decoration, though often metal attachments survive where the wood does not. The vase-paintings show a great elaboration of decorative detail here, as they do in the representation of cushions and fabrics. We are a great deal less well informed, on the other hand, on the processes involved: dyeing, weaving, especially pattern-weaving, embroidery, leather-working, carpentry and cabinet-making, since the objects have not survived. We are much better placed in the case of metalworking, where we have the objects to examine, and in stonework. There are the tools – punch and plain chisel, claw chisel and bouchard, drill and saw, and the use of abrasive sand and corundum from Naxos – which have often left their traces on unfinished or concealed work. Much of the evidence is, however, hotly debated.

Whatever our ignorance of technical detail, the high degree of skill of the Attic craftsman is clear if, in fact, in the fifth/fourth centuries

'Attic' or any other local designation is relevant in view of artists' mobility. We have seen indications that the craftsman was proud of his skill: how it was advertised we do not know. There is evidence for the putting of makers' names on ships' equipment.[60] Potters and vase-painters signed their works by name, or by their characteristic style; so did die- and gem-engravers. Sculptors, of course, set their names on dedication bases; or were well known as the makers of famous works of art. Most craftsmen, undoubtedly, were advertised by the local esteem which the quality of their products won for them.

It must be borne in mind that the expression 'Greek craftsman' or 'Attic craftsman' is an ambiguous one. It means in effect Greek or foreigner, slave or free. Moreover the foreign element, which at all times was strong, frequently moved from one city-state to another. This proceeding is particularly clear in sculptors and bronze-workers, among the great exponents of the graphic arts, and is also apparent among minor artists such as coin-die engravers. Thus there was a con-siderable transmission of expertise and ideas from one city-state to another, supplemented by the import also, by way of trade or war, of manufactured objects made elsewhere, even outside the Greek area. We know for instance of an ivory sword-hilt with gold inlay,[61] and of temple treasuries which, among the masses of bric-à-brac assembled there over the years and laboriously recorded, contained also objects of foreign manufacture: a sword with an ivory sheath dedicated by the *Boule* in 407/6 BC;[62] a Persian scimitar (*akinakes*) of iron, with gold handle and ivory sheath;[63] *sidera Keltika*;[64] a 'barbaric gold phiale, dedicated by Cleon;[65] and some objects of ivory, probably described (the inscription is here defective) as 'having an inscription in Phoenician letters'.[66]

Of the technical skill of the Greek craftsman there is little indication in literature. It is true that a passage in Thucydides[67], relating the man-oeuvres with various technical 'devices' in the Great Harbour at Syra-cuse during the Syracusan Expedition, seems to indicate that the ancient Athenians possessed the same skill in improvisation that characterizes the modern Greeks, but little brings us particularly close to them, and the same is true of all the questions involving the manner of work, and use and origins of raw materials. There are a few brief references,[68] but little relevant information is contained even in the works of authors such as Aristotle and Theophrastus, who might be expected to consider such aspects of human activity. Fortunately, there survive in some volume the public documents, mainly accounts, which relate to State building activity in the fifth and fourth centuries BC and to the construction of great works of art such as the Athena Parthenos of Phidias. These documents, fragmentary as they are, provide a great deal of information on craftsmen, wages, materials and prices. They represent also an important aspect of ancient public life and administration, as Plato makes clear in his comment in the *Laws*[69] on regulations relating to contracts and control of contractors.

A good deal of light is thrown by these inscriptions on conditions of labour: they illustrate the importance of the public works, especially of the Periclean period, in Athens, as a source of employment.[70] They also illustrate the specialization and division of labour on which Xenophon comments,[71] and the relationship of citizen and foreigner, slave and free.[72]

On these great public works and on the detailed processes connected with their erection Athenian citizens, metic residents in Attica (not always easy to distinguish by their description from citizens), and slaves worked side by side. There is no indication that slaves were paid less than free men, or that their existence depressed the standards of wages: indeed, it could hardly be so, since there is no reason to believe that there were vast supplies of skilled slaves, or that their owners, anxious to make as much as possible either directly or through the *apophora* system, had any incentive to undercut free labour. In any case the slave workers seem often to have been owned in ones or twos by free craftsmen who worked side by side with them on the site or in the workshop.

It is important to note the predominance of piece-work, which was more economical from the standpoint of the State. It did not pay for idleness, and while a good deal of checking of finished work was necessary, it was probably no more than would have been necessary for time-workers, of whom examples occur,[73] in the accounts of the curators of the Erechtheum: 'sawyers working on day rates', side by side in the same inscription,[74] with other sawyers who, on piece-work, received two obols per 'cut'. How long such a 'cut' might be, and an indication that such workers, though they might take their time within reason, none the less worked hard for their money, emerges from the entry:[75] (paid) 'to a [sawyer] sawing through a beam twenty-four feet long: five cuts; each cut, one drachma'. Piece-work was the basis of the whole of industry and petty craftsmanship, and it was an essential condition of Athenian private life, which pre-supposed that the citizen had leisure for other pursuits than earning his living, for instance the performance of his public duties as a citizen. It was also assumed that he had the opportunity to take time off, without the loss of a 'job' in the modern sense. These ancient piece-work rates and the simple contract that we find in the State building inscriptions were inevitable in the absence of the *entrepreneur*, the organizer of and contractor for labour, such as we know in modern times, between the artisan and the consumer. Ancient piece-work, in fact, represented an entirely different relationship between craftsman and employer from modern factory piece-work, where the rates represent solely a means of assessing the value of labour. The ancient system gave a freedom and sense of independence which offset some at any rate of the disadvantages arising from its primitive and haphazard character, which must have included much futile standing around of craftsmen, and slaves, at the labour exchange of the Kolonos Agoraios.

As instances of piece-work there are contracts for the fine surface polishing of architectural detail (*enkausis*), for example, of a *kymation*:[76] 113 feet at five obols per foot. This rate, which appears again,[77] seems to be a standard one. The same is true of gilding. In one case the contractor (*misthotes*) is a Dionysodorus of Melite, who may be a metic resident in the industrial district of Athens. Such contractors, as is apparent in this example, had to produce a guarantor. These types of craftsmanship belong to the same category as stonemasons' and carpenters' jobs. On the other hand, there are the contracts also for what might, in the modern view, seem to be the work of artists. So:[78] (payment) 'to the clay modellers who make the models of the bronzes for the covering tiles, eight drachmae'. This might sound like repetitive work in the reproduction of clay models for casting purposes (one *akanthou paradeigma* costs eight drachmae, therefore representing some days' skilled work). The man here concerned, a bronze-caster in Melite, appears twice,[79] but not all those so employed are resident in this industrial quarter, nor do all produce the same number of bronzes (*khalkai*). Another entry,[80] relating to a model or prototype which was made and paid for, but not used on the Erechtheum, reading: (paid) 'to Stasianax [?] [resident] in Kollytos, who made the model *akanthos* for the roof, *which we did not use*', seems to indicate original work – on the borders between higher craftsmanship and true artistry, certainly something creative. Such an approach, which groups minor artists with journeymen, an attitude which is there, even if it be argued that Athenian State accounts tended to lump together all sorts of disparate matters, appears again and again, with piece-work contracts for sculptors and painters, and prices set out for the items of their work.[81] These prices naturally vary (some seem to be in units of 60, 120, 240 drachmae, the average around 60). Indeed all rates, while being within certain general limits, vary slightly, as if subject to bargaining. It is noteworthy also, that where the artist-craftsmen are converting into stone the models or sketches of the superintendent artist, the work is divided in a fashion obviously intended to provide units of about equal size; so, in the Erechtheum frieze: 'the chariot without the mules'.[82] Such division of labour is apparent everywhere. One example[83] gives a division of labour between (i) the provider of timber; (ii) the transporter of it to Eleusis; (iii) the sawyer; all accounted for separately.

The same detailed picture, in fact, emerges in reference to the materials used. One source of such information is provided by the accounts of the Commissioners for the statue of Athena Promachus,[84] with prices of materials, including tin and *anthrakes* (i.e. charcoal for the melting of metal). Various building inscriptions of the fifth and fourth centuries BC record the purchase and cost of materials for building and artistic purposes, and the sources from which they were obtained. All of these show, with a certain uniformity of prices at the different periods, the small-scale purchasing, hand-to-mouth buying, and multiplicity of sources. From which it can be concluded that just as the small craftsmen could participate in and benefit from the State undertakings without loss of their independence, so could the small traders, who, in large numbers and with simple organization, made up a widespread import-export network in which there are what appear to be standard prices:[85] tin 230 drs per talent; lead at 5 drs per talent from a dealer in Melite. For lead there appears to have been a unit called *krateutes*, 'block' or 'pig'. Olive wood is priced (oddly by weight)[86] at 1 drachma 2 obols per talent, the purveyor's name being sometimes given, as, e.g. 'from Heraclides from the Theseum'. What might be called subsidiary materials are *miltos*, at 3 or $3\frac{1}{2}$ obols per stater (weight), pitch (*pitte*) in clay containers at 6 drs the jar; *melanteria* at 8 drs the medimnus, and a curious substance called *kekis*.[87] These are all mixed up with other matters of public administration,[88] from caps for public slaves, imported from Thessaly, to glue, and, more specifically, bull's glue. The record also sheds some interesting light on the units used.

There is a great variety of other interesting details as on metals: of 'gold bought [for gilding] the bronze [ornaments], 166 leaves, each leaf at 1 drachma, from Adonis living in Melite',[89] which implies a goldbeater's trade. In connection with the same metal the Parthenon accounts mention[90] 110 or more staters of Croesus – which must have been used as a source of gold. Again, in the accounts for the Eleusinian portico,[91] there is a specification for the composition of bronze, and a reference to 'Cypriote' bronze. There are useful indications of price:

pairs of Laconian tiles at 4 drs a pair,[92] and bricks at 13,[93] 12[94] and 15[95] drs per 1000. These figures suggest interesting differences in labour costs. Stone was obtained from a wide local area, which seems to demonstrate relatively good facilities for transport. To judge from the sources indicated this transport was both by land and by sea: [96], [97] in Attica from Pentelikon, Agryle, Steiria and Eleusis, and from Aegina and Megara (see below).

A great many more very heterogeneous details on materials, sources and persons engaged in trade can be extracted from these building accounts. Rather striking points of administrative procedure appear from time to time: for example, it seems to have rested[98] with the Athenian Assembly whether a *thyroma* (door?) was to be of bronze or of gold and ivory. It is difficult to think of a Full Assembly debating such an issue, unless it had the mentality of a parish council!

There are other cases of a contradiction of the principle *de minimis*. In the supply of stone at Eleusis (446/5 BC) separate payments are itemized for (a) the quarrying of the stone in Attica and Aegina; (b) the transport in 'stone-carrying' ships; and (c) the preparation of the stone by stonemasons.[99] Here and elsewhere a great deal of book-keeping must have been involved. There are references to silver bullion for decorative metalwork (*eis poikilian*),[100] to a substance of uncertain nature, *kyanos* (blue enamel?)[101] and to bronze at 35 drs per talent.[102] An intriguing mention is the purchase of two *chartai*, which may be sheets of writing material for accounts or drawings, at 2 drs 4 obols, and *sanides*, boards, which could be drawing-boards, at 4 drs.[103] In the repair records of the walls of Athens and the Piraeus in 307/6 BC, in relation to 'the doors and the roof of the towers and of the passage', there is mention of 'pitch and *miltos* [ruddle] and *miltopittos* as each is fitting'.[104] These are evidently waterproofing materials. Again, for Philo's arsenal, in 347/6 BC, there is stone from Acte (such as is referred to frequently elsewhere), iron nails and Corinthian tiling (not, apparently, a type of tile but a reference to the source from which they were imported).[105] At Eleusis, *c.* 330 BC, iron and lead are mentioned for the clamps of stone blocks,[106] and again at Eleusis a variety of commodities are listed with the names of those who provided them, and with prices: *miltos*, *pittos*, *melanteria* (black paint?) and *kekis* (glue?). It is to be noted that all these commodities could be supplied by one man.[107] Again there are tiles from Corinth, 100 in number costing 100 drs, while the conveyance of them to Eleusis appears at 40 drs. Another 200 tiles from Corinth cost 5 obols each.[108]

Of special interest is the concern of the state organization for the equipment of the public slaves involved in these building operations: 'Cloaks [*himatia*] for the public slaves, for 17 men, for each man 18 drs 3 obols; the total from Antigenes the Megarian, 314 drs 3 obols.'[109] They were rather expensive garments from the well-known source of slaves' clothing. Further, 'Skins [or hides (*diphtherai*) for waterproof clothing?] for the public slaves, for 17 men, the *diphthera* 4 drs 3 obols; from Attos the merchant [*emporos*], total 76 drs 3 obols'; [110] 'shoes for 17 men, 6 drs per man, from Apollophanes, the son of Tyrmeides, total 102 drs'.[111] Clothing, it might be suggested, was not exactly cheap, even slaves' clothing.

Every detail was noted down of commodities and services, no doubt by the public slaves: 'Faggots, 60, at 2 for an obol, price 5 drs; the conveyance of these to the sea, to the hired man, the freight of these to Eleusis, to Melanthios the ferryman, 7 drs 3 obols';[112] 'cedar beams [*xyla*] from Simios the merchant';[113] 'elm boards from Agius of Corinth';[114] to the hired man who conveyed them down to the sea and placed them in the boat, 10 drs; the freight of all these beams to Keon the ferryman, 56 drs.'[115] Again in connection with Eleusis there is mention of tunics for State slaves, from Megara, in two cases obtained from Megarians – the prices are 7 drs 3½ obols, 7 drs 4 obols and 7 drs 1 obol[116] of *c*. 327/6 BC.

The categories of wood used in building are given, and sometimes places of origin: cypress, cedar, elm, ash and oak; to give specific examples: 4 cypress logs, 50 drs the log, the total, from Sophocles of Cnidus, 200 drs;[117] *xyla tetragona* (= squared) *tōn Makedonikōn*[118] (cf. *xyla tetragona Thouriaka* (from Thurii in South Italy)) – some wood, therefore, was brought from a distance.

These inscriptions demonstrate that a complicated trade organization existed, of which we know almost nothing from literary sources, dealing in a wide variety of commodities and involving transport, in some cases over considerable distances. Stone and wood presented the problem of the carriage sometimes of awkward and heavy weights: timber from the forest by land and sea; stone from the quarry to the site by the same means. The detail given above makes clear the use of the sea and of special ships. There were involved crafts and organization which at times of considerable building activity were of major dimensions.

Quarrying might be described as a large-scale industry of Ancient Greece. There were numerous sources of high grade stone. Pre-eminent were the marbles from Pentelikon and Hymettus in Attica[119], and the fine crystalline marbles of Naxos, Paros and Chios. There were also, from Attica, the hard Kara limestone, and Eleusinian black stone used as the background to the Erechtheum frieze; from other sources, such as Tenos, various coloured marbles, though, unlike the Romans, the Classical Greeks were not given to the use of them. The quarrying technique was simpler than that of mining, except the underground quarrying in Paros, though some of the tools would be the same. The exploitation of strata formations is apparent in ancient quarries,[120] with the use of wedges to break off blocks. At any rate in Hellenistic fortification wall construction there was probably a standard size of block which it is reasonable to suppose was determined by relative ease of handling and transport. In quarrying material for the production of major sculpture the block was sometimes trimmed and roughly shaped even before its detachment from the quarry. It may be added that the colossal unfinished statue at Apollona on Naxos[121] raises the problem of its transport down a relatively steep hill-side to the sea which is not far distant. It is obvious that some form of sledge was used for such heavy weights, and not a wheeled vehicle. These observations which may be made on the ground are not supplemented from other sources on matters of ownership and business organization, but it is to be suspected that such quarries as those on Pentelikon were state-operated if not state-owned, and the same would apply elsewhere especially when stone was needed for fortifications.

Large timbers were essential for the construction of major public buildings, as the details from the building inscriptions indicate. Something can also be determined by a study of Greek buildings such as have been left standing, or where any portions of them survive. The relationship of timbering to stonework can be established by the surviving cuttings for the former in the latter.[122] It would seem that even in the largest temples, for example, the Parthenon, the wooden beams could in effect be of manageable length and section, though from time to time an uncertainty must be felt how ridge beams, purlins and transverse roof beams, even when supported at intervals, were joined or used in sections.

Given the dimensions of blocks and timbers, vehicular transport is not too difficult to envisage.[123] For both stone and timber, from the quarry or the mountain side, in the first stage of transport, some form of sledge must be assumed, and a track cleared of the worst obstacles. Obviously sea transport was used wherever possible, as the inscriptions show. Lifting would present no greater problems at this stage than at the building site. As far as other land transport is concerned the use of wheeled vehicles required roads or tracks on which it was to operate, and the means of traction.[124] For timber such roads were likely to be temporary; more permanent in the case of quarries.[125] Who constructed them: the quarry contractors or some local authority? In modern times quarry or forest owners can construct roads to join a local or national system. But none of these existed in Ancient Greece, particularly in the remoter areas. Indeed the whole question of the road system of Classical Greece is badly in need of investigation.

Finally, the transport of heavy weights has been the subject of study in terms of the tractive power involved, of oxen rather than horses.[126] The ultimate question was not one of harnessing the animals involved but their availability. Given the solution of the problem of multiple harnessing, how were sufficient numbers assembled? It must be assumed that there were organizers of animal labour,[127] but of what numbers at any one time? They could be used in relays, particularly at a time of year when they were not needed for more conventional purposes – though there would be problems of assembly, of small groups of animals from a great many centres at some distance from each other, and the weather would render tracks and roads difficult at times when agricultural operations were not taking place. In all, there are large areas of uncertainty, largely due to the Greek lack of interest in matters banausic.

CHAPTER EIGHT

LAND, AGRICULTURE AND OTHER CULTIVATION

WHEN ALL IS SAID AND DONE, and despite the great aggregates of population in Athens and the Piraeus, with the many trades and callings which such communities engendered, the countryside and the country communities, and the activities of the country left the deepest mark on Athenian thought and life. Or so it seems: since it must be borne in mind that so many of the sources are in fact profoundly influenced by the idea, outlined earlier, that the cultivation of the soil, or at any rate the supervision of its cultivation, was the proper calling for a free citizen. And it may be stressed, that whatever the preoccupation with foreign trade, the objective was not lost sight of, that trade in exports was intended to pay for imports, and that imports were intended as a supplement to home production, the next best thing to self-sufficiency (*autarkeia*) which was best of all. Therefore it may confidently be assumed that the soil was exploited as far as possible to produce cereals, wine, olives, fruit, and to support domesticated animals. Cultivation was the natural life from the standpoint of the Greek, and this may in general terms be asserted despite certain conditions that should be mentioned, which were of temporary rather than permanent incidence.

In regard to Athens in particular, and as a generalization, the so-called Old Oligarch, as befits one of his political temper, stresses the connection of the Athenian Demos with the sea, and the advantages of sea-power: (*a*) in general terms;[1] (*b*) in addition,[2] the great advantage of the control of essential commodities by the naval power of Athens; (*c*) the enjoyment by Athens of unique benefits:[3]

Whatever is pleasant in Sicily, or in Italy or in Cyprus, or in Egypt, or in Lydia, or in the Pontus, or in the Peloponnese, or anywhere else, all these things are gathered together into one through [Athens'] rule of the sea.

(*d*) the advantage of sea-power in times of shortage:[4]

Then, diseases of the crops, which are sent by Zeus, those who are very powerful by land endure with difficulty [*or:* 'are upset by them'], those who have the advantage by sea, endure them with ease. For the whole earth is not simultaneously afflicted, so that to those who rule the sea there comes from the abundance of a flourishing region what the afflicted one needs.

The Old Oligarch forgets, however, that there is a little matter of payment involved. In all the foregoing the writer, as in much of his pamphlet, gives a correct impression of detail, but possibly a misleading interpretation over-all. In commenting on the fortifications of Athens and the Piraeus and the linking walls between them, which make Athens, but not Attica, like an island,[5] he comments:

Now the cultivators and the rich of the Athenians take a less intransigent attitude to the enemies, while the Demos, since it knows well that the enemies will burn nothing of theirs, nor lay it waste, lives without fear, taking no account of them.

Such a division between the interests of Attica, and the interests of Athens and the Piraeus, did arise when, at the beginning of the Peloponnesian War, the inhabitants of Attica were withdrawn within the walls as a matter of strategy, and a divided attitude to the war seemed to arise. Pericles too speaks of the port of Athens in much the same terms as the Old Oligarch.[6] This viewpoint is also reflected in Aristophanes, though the stress in some plays on the countryman and country interests acts as a useful corrective. It would probably be wrong to accept too readily the idea of such a clear division, one to a considerable degree based on political ideas. That the rich would draw their wealth from the land was traditional, but not wholly true, as in the case of Nicias. We are, on the other hand, directly informed by Thucydides,[7] at the beginning of his account of the Peloponnesian War, that the Athenians were essentially a country folk, and that the bulk of them lived in the country. By the 'country', however, need not be meant the remote countryside, but the whole area outside the walls of Athens, immediately beyond the developed and to some degree built-up city fringe (*proasteion*).

It is possible that in the fourth century, at any rate, foreign trade, as a sphere of investment, and mining, as not liable to public financial burdens, did compete with land-owning as a means of using capital, and that such capital might be switched to land when corn was scarce and dear, though the rapid changes in prices that could take place would hardly allow quick changes of investment, but the basic importance of land and its cultivation is evident. It can be seen from the details of estates mentioned in the Orators. Just how far we can accept certain indications that land-holding was a necessary qualification for the tenure of some offices is unclear. For instance, how far are we to accept as real the traditional interrogation, concerning their land-holding, of candidates for the chief magistracies? There is also the question which arises in Themistocles' decree from Troezen,[8] whether the warship captains of 480 BC had to have landed property or just property to a certain sum? Similarly there is the statement in Dinarchus[9] that those who are in effect 'champions of the people' must possess land 'within boundaries'.

There are some indications that Athenians held landed property abroad, that is, outside Attica. Certain regulations relating to the Second Athenian League of the fourth century BC (forbidding the holding of land by an Athenian in an allied state)[10] seem to indicate an earlier abuse during the existence of the Delian League in the preceding century, which became the Athenian Empire. Land-holding in an allied state led to legal difficulties and abuses, quite apart from the land-lot (cleruchy) system, where the Athenian land-holders were either present or else absent, as perhaps were those to whom land was allotted in Lesbos in 427 BC. There is the interesting and curious passage of the Old Oligarch:[11]

Since therefore they [the Athenians] did not chance from the beginning to inhabit an island, they now do this. They commit their property to the islands, trusting in their rule on the sea, and they suffer the Attic land to be laid waste.

The interpretation of this passage will depend on the date given to this work. In part, undoubtedly, the reference is to steps taken by the Athenians when the war started and Attica became liable to invasion, but the practice may have been followed before, with the war in view. So, among the confiscations of property as a sequel to the Mutilation of the Hermae, there is the mention of farms abroad,[12] e.g. in Thasos. In Thucydides[13] it is said that the Athenian oligarchs at Samos raised funds from their own resources (ek tōn idiōn oikōn). They were, to a considerable degree, cut off from Athens. They may have raised loans, but it is just possible that they or some of them owned property in Samos. Plato[14] refers to the property of an Athenian in Naxos, worked by a pelates (dependent) as a hired labourer. Such arrangements may have arisen from inheritance, or from precautions against what actually happened in the Peloponnesian War. Indeed in the renewed war (413–405 BC) land-owners may well have suffered not only from the occupation by the Peloponnesians of Decelea, but also from the revolts of allied states, especially in such areas as Euboea, in which they held property.

Leaving these special considerations aside, there can be no doubt of the importance of land cultivation both in the rather 'aristocratic' view of some Athenian writers (though it should be noted that the lovers of the countryside in Aristophanes are not rich men), and as a practical matter. Thus according to the Xenophontic Socrates:[15] 'the most noble and necessary pursuits are those of husbandry and war'. So, too, it is said:[16]

Further, agriculture is natural; for by nature all derive their sustenance from their mother, and so men derive it from the earth. In addition to this it also conduces greatly to bravery; for it does not make men's bodies unserviceable, as do the illiberal arts . . .

As distinct from the theory, the practice seems to have been well developed certainly in Attica. The Oxyrrhynchus Historian[17] points out that the Boeotians, as the northern neighbours and enemies of the Athenians, benefited from the establishment of the Spartan post at Decelea and the plundering of the Attic countryside:

They obtained the slaves [i.e. the runaway slaves also mentioned by Thucydides][18] and all the rest of the plunder taken in the war for a small sum, and as near neighbours they conveyed to themselves all the equipment of the Attic countryside, beginning with the woodwork and tiling of the houses. For the Athenian countryside was at that time the most elaborately equipped in Greece.

Again the same authority explains[19] that the Attic land had not suffered greatly in the previous incursions of the enemy in the Archidamian War (431–421 BC):

It had suffered little ill in the previous invasions by the Lacedaemonians, and it had been so developed and highly cultivated in a surpassing manner, that it seemed there was no deficiency to be found among them, and the dwellings were more finely built than among the other Greeks.

The text is somewhat restored, but the general meaning is clear. There was, then, no neglect of the Attic countryside, despite the opportunities for import from elsewhere during the period of Athenian sea-domination. On the other hand the countryside did suffer in the renewed Peloponnesian War. There was the ravaging of farmhouses; the burning of crops, the carrying away of cattle; above all, the sort of destruction which was not easily restored, namely the cutting down of vines and olive trees. There may have been at first a convention whereby the burning or reaping of standing cereal crops, which could be planted again another year, was regarded as a legitimate act of war, whereas it was felt, in small inter-state hostilities, that trees, which took some years to reach maturity, should not be harmed. But such conventions would soon disappear in a long and bitter war. Thus Aristophanes[20] comments on the destruction of vines and figs in war-time.[21] So too Lysias[22] mentions the uprooting of olive trees in the later stages of the Peloponnesian War.

The literature of the fourth century makes it quite clear that the condition of Attica declined, not only through enemy depredations, but also through neglect. The cultivation of Attica from the sixth century onwards involved an advance up the hill-sides and the terracing of these – the remains of terrace walls can still be seen. They were particularly vulnerable to heavy rain, especially as deforestation progressed. This is evident from Demosthenes,[23] even in relation to a period of peace. Still more was it so in war-time. It is apparent[24] that the danger existed for houses as well as for land. To this period of depredation and neglect is to be ascribed the poverty of farmers in the early fourth century, to which Aristophanes seems to refer.[25] There was also the danger that some low-lying areas would, if neglected, become a marsh such as 'the Phaleric marsh' with its wet soil, contrasted with the dry area around Lykabettus.[26] In the earlier fourth century we have indications of the re-development of neglected estates and farms,[27] and the re-sale of such, which could be a form of speculation.[28] Thus there appears to have been a rapid change of owners and cultivators.[29] The fourth century saw the restoration of farming, and its prime importance: the cultivation line was still pushed up the hill-sides as it appears from a lexicographer[30] who defines *eschatia* as a delimitation of property either on a mountain boundary or on the sea (a 'border farm' at Sphettos is also mentioned). This was true despite the fact that there were other ways of employing capital. Even in peace-time farming in Greece required close attention. Thus the rather thin poor soil of Attica (though it is doubtful whether it was as bad in Antiquity as it is now on the lower hill-sides) did not provide an easy or generous life; barley for the most part could be cultivated, not wheat.

There was a continual struggle to conserve the soil, check erosion[31] and control watercourses; also to maintain water-channels for the positive purpose of water supply as well as for the negative aspect of drainage. In this connection the walls which seem often to enclose properties are interesting. In a speech of Demosthenes[32] there is mention of a wall around a 'plot' (*chōrion*). The reason given for its construction[33] is illuminating in a number of respects:

And further, men of the jury, when a downpour of rain took place, it happened that the water broke into this plot. My father did not yet own it at that time. It was owned by a man who altogether disliked the country and was more a townsman; and being neglected the water bursting in twice or three times damaged the land and made more of a way through. So, my father seeing this, as I hear from those who know, and the neighbours encroaching and making a path through the property, he built this dry stone wall around it.

It was true that the stony soil of Greece provided unlimited material for such walls, but their maintenance was none the less laborious. They did not necessarily exclude the depredations of the goat, the main enemy of all growing trees.[34] They did help against the intrusion of neighbours, who also had to be unremittingly watched. The same speech of Demosthenes[35] refers to the neighbours encroaching on the road which lay between two farms, 'moving out the stone wall', and dumping rubbish into the road. This road was a boundary (hence the speaker's objection to encroachment on it) and at the same time a watercourse, as were many Greek country lanes, which with their stony surface were and are hard to distinguish from a stream bed. In fact, they become one in heavy rain. In this particular case there was the problem of the storm water. If a neighbour was careless, incompetent or ill-disposed, he could divert it through another's land.

The cultivator's life was in general, or could be, a life of incident: not every man's ideal. The theory was that it made good soldiers. It also certainly would, in the majority of cases, inculcate consideration for neighbours, who were often very close. There were remote and lonely regions in Greece; but with a considerable population, as in Attica, the cultivable areas could be fairly thickly populated. Here the difficulty arises of deciding whether the bulk of the cultivators lived together in country towns and villages, or scattered in the countryside. There were probably some of the latter, but the greater number (as in Attica today) lived in communities and went out into the country to work. However this might be, there was a considerable suburban area around Athens, where farms were close (in the sense of the habitations) to each other. A speech of Demosthenes[36] refers to a farm near the 'hippodrome' (a race-course) in Athens, where the speaker had lived since his boyhood; the house was close to others, and there is a reference to passers-by. One is reminded of those curious fragments of *rus in urbe* which in Athens today exist mixed up with the suburbs, and even the industrial suburbs (they are, for example, found on the line of the ancient Long Walls, between Athens and the Piraeus, not far from the electric railway and the main road to the Piraeus). There was no clear or profound dividing line between townsman and countryman, non-cultivator and cultivator, even in spirit and interest. It is worth mentioning the curious observation which Xenophon makes,[37] in discussing the question of judging the fertility of land from its appearance. He speaks of fishermen (!) as experts:

And furthermore, I said, I recalled the point about fishermen, that being engaged in a livelihood on the sea, and neither halting to look nor walking quietly, but while scudding along past the fields, when they see the crops on land, they none the less do not hesitate to indicate the land such as is good or bad, for they criticize the one and praise the other.

An odd point to mention, and, whatever its particular relevance, implies basically that there is nothing odd in fishermen, or, indeed men of other callings, having ideas on such a subject. So too in 372 BC at Corcyra, the Athenian commander Iphicrates,[38] partly no doubt because of shortage of funds, but partly also because there was no current military employment for his soldiers, hired them out as cultivators (no doubt for some special seasonal labour) to the Corcyreans. Many were mercenaries, but they must from their origins (like the Roman legionary soldier) have had some acquaintance with farming operations. There was not, in fact, so great a division between townsman or sea-goer and countryman as is sometimes inferred.

The prosperity of the cultivator and land-owner varied no doubt with his skill, the weather and the prices his product would fetch. Many cultivators, as we have seen, may have depended on their country farms for much of the food which fed their households; or a *chorion* may have provided one commodity such as wine, oil or fruit. Most small farmers must have been subsistence-farmers. The mixed character of property may indicate that some of the more well-to-do were also. Others, undoubtedly, were cash-crop-producers, as of olives. Some, like Pericles, found it more convenient to sell their farm produce, and buy in Athens the necessities of life with the money. Of this, and of the question who produced such natural products as fruit, wine, oil and honey in bulk, little is known, and the same is true of the middle-man organization between producer and exporter. Some farmers at any rate fared pretty well. Among those who made dedications to Athena on the Acropolis at Athens figure a few farmers or owners of land cultivated by others. It would probably be unjust and incorrect to suggest that artisans, craftsmen and traders showed more gratitude to the goddess. It is likely that a far greater number of these named their calling, than did farmers, since farming was, as it were, the normal employment. One such dedication[39] mentions 'the tithe of land and money' i.e. farming and other investment, more probably a tithe of income than of capital. Another speaks of 'a tithe of land for the vow of his son'.[40] In the fourth century BC at Athens, and indeed in the fifth century in the last years of the Peloponnesian War, land, like other 'visible property', was liable to war-tax, and above a certain capital amount rendered its owner liable to the 'liturgies' (financial obligations to the State). The system, sometimes entailing the pledging of property to raise emergency money, cannot have made for the efficiency of Athenian farming. In addition the potentialities of the light soil of Attica were not great. Other areas, such as Thessaly, were more fortunate.

The details of farming practice come from a multitude of small references and from some lengthier observations on it, contained in the literature of Athens. It is the best known economic activity, but that is not saying very much. A good deal more comes from epigraphical evidence relating to Athens, Attica, and certain other regions. All information that can be gleaned on communities outside Athens is relevant. There is important material on farm-houses, relating to the temple estates of Delos, Rheneia and Myconos[41] and on farm-houses and towers near Sunium.[42] A good deal is available (especially in the inscriptions concerned with the Mutilators of the Hermae) in reference to crops (grapes, olives, wine), stores, furniture, slaves, prices and measures.[43] Relatively little comes from sources outside Attica. There is some epigraphical material such as that relating to the wine trade of Thasos. For the equipment and technical aspects there are vase-paintings (Pls 28, 29).

A major problem, one aspect of a much larger one, is the question of the employment of slaves on farms. They were certainly to be found on Attic farms. That is clear from the lists of the State officials (*poletai*) relating to the confiscation of the property of the Mutilators.[44] But these were wealthy men, and the question is, did the poorer farmer also possess slaves? It is a much disputed point. How many of those slaves, mainly as Thucydides calls them[45] 'craftsmen', who fled from their masters to the Spartans at Decelea between 413 and 405 BC, were employed on the land? In the circumstances of the times, perhaps, not very many, since cultivation ground to a standstill; but so did other activities. The small farmer in Aristophanes, Dikaiopolis for instance in the *Acharnians*, has two slaves, but it is difficult to decide the value of such 'evidence'. How far could a farmer do the work of his farm, which had better be called a small-holding, and his citizen duties as well, with the aid only of his wife, his children, some neighbourly help at times, and a little hired labour at certain seasons? It is not very easy to say; and opinion divides pretty distinctly into two schools of thought. On the whole the Greek tradition from Hesiod on justifies the belief that if a man could get a slave or two, he would. One feels that sometimes it might be more for prestige reasons than for anything else. Working animals would surely come first. There is a certain stress on the use of slaves in farming in another play of Aristophanes,[46] but the position is again very obscure.

On the other hand as an alternative to slave labour we hear in Aristophanes[47] of casual and seasonal labour, of olive-pickers for example (Pl. 29). For some forms of seasonal labour, and for the tending of goats and other animals, children were available, but the poor cultivator would be wise not to acquire too many children, male or female. So there was a place for the hired free labourer. In Theophrastus, the Boor 'tells the hired labourers who work with him in the field all the news from the Assembly'. Jebb,[48] in his commentary, points out that there is other evidence for hired labourers: 'poor men, chiefly foreigners, found employment as artisans, farm labourers or domestics', and instances the shrine of Eurysaces in the market place, mentioned by Pollux as the place at which 'those who ply for hire used to congregate'. It is, however, unclear how valuable a source Theophrastus is in the *Characters*. The New Comedy provides some evidence for slaves, in the country at any rate, but little for hired labourers, and those who worked for hire in Athens and elsewhere were for the most part either artisan slaves, or what might be called casual domestic labour, also slave. There is some slight evidence for free men labouring in the fields of others under the stress of necessity or as a sort of favour, though disliking the idea of being in the service of another, e.g. as a steward.[49] In times of stress some were no doubt driven to such work, but would get out of it as soon as possible. Others could be turned off when there was no work and so were cheaper than slaves. Again, as with farm slaves, the position of these men is uncertain in the Classical period, though the *thes*, who was originally a landless hired man, survived officially as a notional income class. A curious position was that of the serf or *pelates* in Naxos, whose death introduces Plato's dialogue the *Euthyphro*. The story[50] is worth quoting (can it be wholly fictitious?). The speaker gives the following account:

The man who died was a serf of mine, and when we were farming in Naxos, he served as a hired labourer [*ethēteuen*] there with us. Being drunk and becoming angry with one of our household slaves [*oiketēs*] he killed him. So my father, tying his hands and his feet, threw him into a ditch, and sent a man to Athens to enquire of the Interpreters of the Sacred Law what should be done. In the meantime he took little account of the captive and neglected him as being a murderer and no matter if he died; and he did die. For through hunger and cold and his bonds he died before the messenger came from the Interpreters.

We need not preoccupy ourselves with the moral and religious niceties which worried Euthyphro. Here the point is the status of the man, to some extent indicated by his treatment and by the term *pelates*, who clearly stood between free man and slave, serving as a hired labourer.

Of agricultural operations and the products of farming we are tolerably well informed only in the case of Attica. To literary, epigraphical and archaeological sources, including some important vase-paintings (cf. Pls 28, 29), can be added what is observed in the more primitive parts of Greece today. The cereals cultivated were wheat and barley, mainly the shallow-rooting barley rather than the deep-rooting wheat (but horned wheat appears in modern times). As in modern Greece there must have been that combination of cereals and olives, and of vines and cereals in what seem to us pitifully small patches. Indeed the division of family property, when it was divided, as in inheritance and dowries, and the character of the soil (as in modern Aegina) made for small fields which can hardly have been ploughed in the conventional sense. But the primitive plough, not greatly different from the prehistoric *ard*, which is seen on some Attic black-figure vases (Pl. 28), and can still be seen in Greece today, was used to scratch the surface of the generally shallow soil. It was not wholly inefficient: adequate for the light soil of Attica, and with its wooden plough-share less liable to be clogged up by heavy soil than an iron share, and suitable for contour ploughing.

The gentleman farmer Xenophon sets out[51] the techniques of cereal and fruit-tree cultivation in his *Oeconomicus*, in the form of a dialogue between a teacher, Ischomachus and a learner, Socrates. The underlying principle is that of the Socratic method, the bringing out from the learner the knowledge which he was unaware he possessed. The discussion covers a considerable amount of detail, declaring the aim of the cultivator as 'the production of the greatest possible quantity of barley and wheat'. The stress is therefore on cereals. A systematic consideration is given to the successive processes starting from the preparation of the fallow: the ploughing, not in winter wet or in summer heat, but in spring, using the weeds, before they seed, as green manure; later, in high summer the soil is turned over to bake in the sun, so killing the weed roots. There is to follow the sowing at the autumn rain, at varying points in this period; connected with the sowing is the question of the amount of seed to be used for rich and poor soils, and the hoeing which is to take place in winter. Finally, there is the harvest, with advice on reaping, threshing and winnowing, and the burning of the standing straw to enrich the ground.

The discussion then moves on to fruit-bearing trees, vines, figs and olives in particular: the right way to plant them in trenches, at the right depth and position, and firmly. There is further discussion on the making of green manure and the removal of salt from the soil, followed by

interesting comment on the restoration of neglected land as a speculation, giving the father of Ischomachus as an example.

In all this there is a strong moral tone, and a significant stress on the
latent expertise which exists in the learner. In other words, as a Greek,
whether countryman or townsman, he is naturally if subconsciously
identified with the soil. The whole is a useful commentary on the leases
to be discussed below.

One point is particularly noteworthy: that animal husbandry is not
included in the term *georgein*, and that no effort is made to discover
Socrates' stores of hidden knowledge on this subject, though it would
equally well fit into the theme of the *Oeconomicus*. Nowhere in
Classical Greek literature is there any practical discussion of the breed-
ing of domesticated animals and their tendance, though the Greeks must
have acquired some body of experience on the subject, and references
to genetics, in the matter of mixing good and bad breeds, as in the
observations of Theognis, and the training of animals, in very general
terms, are something of a commonplace in literature. This seems to
indicate that this form of activity was little developed in Attica, which
is to be expected since there was only very limited grazing, certainly
for larger animals. Yet the Athenians were inordinately interested in
horses, as their art shows, and something might have been expected on
the horses of Macedonia, Thessaly and Argos. There must also have
been those who raised large cattle for traction and sacrifice, quite apart
from the pair of oxen which were the farmer's 'best friends'.

There were the smaller domesticated animals. Sheep could not, in
Attica, have been numerous; some were better wool-producers than
others. Goats were, in some respects, the real asset, producing hair,
skins, milk and meat, but there seems to have been no systematic
development of goat-breeding or any rules for their maintenance and
exploitation. The Greek goat was, after all, a semi-wild animal – and
the same appears to have been true of the pig, which must also have
been common as a source of sacrifices and meat. Both animals were
foragers, and on the whole the countryside of Greece could support
only this type, and principally the goat, since oak and beech forests for
pigs existed only in remote areas. Possibly small animals, such as sheep
and lambs were imported to the larger cities from islands and areas
where there was more pasturage, as the Paschal lambs are into Athens
to this day.

The other Greek sources provide a picture which resembles and
sometimes supplements that of Xenophon. In the prose writers,
especially the Orators, such details as we are given tend to be from the

property or production aspect. A farm produces grapes and figs;[52] more than a thousand olive trees are numbered on the farm of Hagnias.[53] From such sources also come the technical aspects.[54] There are plants and trees which, it is claimed, were the objects of a rival's malicious damage: the high-grade (*gennaia*) fruit trees, the vines that can be trained on trees (*anadendrades*), the plantations of olives set out in rows, and, in this particular case, most interesting 'the growing rose-bed', perhaps for the provision of flowers for sacrificial and convivial garlands rather than for decoration. Of this the speaker goes on to tell of a curious action of his opponents:

In addition to this after daybreak they sent in a small boy, who was a citizen, since they were neighbours and the land was contiguous with theirs, instructing him to strip the growing rose-garden, in order that if I caught him I might bind or imprison him as a slave, and so they could bring against me an action for public violence.

The rose-garden is one of those colourful details which are all too few. The generality of observations are pedestrian enough, both as regards theory, as in the ideas of the philosophers on cultivation, and estate management, only on occasions enlivened by curious detail such as the regulations concerning the consumption of fruit by way-farers,[55] and practice. The Orators naturally confine themselves to the barest details of description: enumerating the categories of property: buildings (*synoikiai*), land (*agroi*), slaves and equipment (*skeue*), which[56] may include the wooden (and removable) doors of buildings, and, less movable, the wine-vat (*lakkos*), like the *pithaknai* ('storage tanks' (?)) of another speech of Demosthenes.[57] Frequently, as befits a legal action, details of dimensions and quantities are given. So[58] Demosthenes gives the following account, of the sort which is largely the basis of our knowledge of the economics of Athens and Attica. Incidentally, with its reference to the summoning of friends as witnesses and the business trips to the country, it illustrates that busy going to and fro, and that close interest and participation in the affairs of friends and acquaintances, which appear to have been the staple entertainment both of the rich and of the *petite bourgeoisie*. The speaker says:

Then after I had challenged him [i.e. to an *antidosis* or exchange of property] I took some of my kinsmen and friends and went off to Kytherron to his hill [or border] farm, and first of all taking them around the farm, which is more than forty stadia in circuit, I showed them and called them to witness in the presence of Phainippus that there was no mortgage stone on the property. If he asserted that there was, I told him to declare it now and point it out, in order that a debt obligation on the property might not subsequently be revealed. Then I sealed up the farm buildings [*oikemata*] for myself, and instructed him to come to my property. After this I asked where the grain was that had been threshed? For there were, men of the jury, by all the gods and goddesses, two threshing floors on the spot, a little less than a hundred feet in diameter. He answered me that some had been sold.

Later[59] the speaker claims:

. . . you are a rich man, as is not surprising, selling, as you now do, barley from your farm at eighteen drachmae the medimnus, and wine at twelve [the measure], and producing more than a thousand medimni of grain, and over eight hundred measures of wine; the rest was stored in the barns. Finally, in order that I may not make too long a story of it, I set watchers in the storage barns, and also, by Heaven, forbade and prevented the ass drivers from carrying away the wood from the farm. For I should explain that Phainippus, in addition to his other property, has this large source of income also. Six asses are engaged throughout the year in conveying wood, and he receives more than twelve drachmae a day from this source. As I say, forbidding them to touch the wood, and solemnly summoning Phainippus to meet me according to the law, I went away back to town.

Such detailed and colourful episodes as this business outing in the country are rare. There is a certain interest in the fact that this same speech really rests on the rivalry of the cultivator and the industrialist. The speaker is himself engaged in mining activity. He has made money in the past, at the cost of hard labour,[60] and has lost it, for times are bad.[61] On the other hand the farmers are doing well, and getting high prices:[62] '. . . Those engaged in the mines have been unfortunate, but you farmers are doing better than is right.' So much so that the speaker is willing to exchange all his property, including his mining interests, for the other man's farm,[63] or so he says.

As in the case of building activity,[64] the more reliable if pedestrian detail comes from inscriptions,[65] and from such information as the renting of an estate or plot called Raria (? Rharia), by Hyperides the Orator,[66] from whom the Eleusinian authorities received for a period of four years the amount of 2732 medimni of barley. From the standpoint of land cultivation considerable importance attaches not only to the public inscriptions which give some indications of prices, commodities produced, and quantities, but also to the inscriptions, most frequently leases, recorded between public bodies, such as demes, clans, *phratriai*, *orgeones*, and private individuals. These show the conditions under which land could be exploited. It seems likely that the conditions as between a public corporate body and an individual were easier than between individuals, though the same general conditions would prevail. Unfortunately, since private contracts between individuals have not survived, as they were not written on stone but on more perishable materials, we are much in ignorance of their character. From the public-private contracts the ways emerge in which it was felt that land could best be developed, the character of its planting and the obligations of the lessee in this respect; and, finally, the manner in which the financial obligations to the corporate body, which were imposed on the land, were to be met.

The great majority of these leases belong to the fourth century or later, but there is no reason to believe that the fifth century, or even the sixth, was different except in the matter of the considerable expansion, as time went by, of olive cultivation. There is nothing to suggest that the cultivation of cereals decreased when importation increased: the latter took place undoubtedly to meet a need which could not be satisfied by home production. The great difference between the earlier fifth century, after recovery from the Persian invasion, and the early fourth was the damage done, both economic and physical, by the Peloponnesian occupation of Decelea and the depression following the war: a recorded example is of a plot which incurred damage, remained unsold for three years, and suffered in the general cutting down of olives.[67]

The relevant details from a number of these leases are worthy of consideration, and from them will emerge clearly the preoccupations of property owners, the main tasks of cultivators, and something of the general practice in farming, including the prevention of soil loss and the use of green manure in a region where animal manure was scarce. The inscriptions involved may be itemized as follows:

(a) A defective inscription of the middle of the fourth century.[68] It shows the frequent concern with supplies of water and its conveyance to where it was needed. The lease is granted

on condition that the water supply [?] from the whole area of the land shall belong to them [i.e. the property owners], and they shall be permitted to lay [agein] water pipes [hyponomoi] through the property, as many and of what kind they desire, and at such depth as they may wish.

(b) A lease (date 346/5 BC?) of the deme of Aixone at the southern end of Hymettus,[69] of what sounds like neglected property.

On these conditions the members of the deme of Aixone lease the Phelleis [a proper name related to phelleus (a stony patch)?] to Autokles the son of Anteas and to Anteas the son of Autokles for forty years at 152 drachmae per year, on condition of their planting it and cultivating it in whatsoever way they wish. They are to pay the rent in the month of Hekatombaion [July–August], and if they do not pay it the demesmen of Aixone are to have the right of distraint on the crops of the property and on all the other goods of the defaulters. The demesmen of Aixone are not permitted either to sell it or to rent it to anyone else, until the forty years have expired. If the enemies of the state cut off access or inflict damage, the demesmen of Aixone shall receive the half of the crops of the property. When the forty years are expired, the lessees are to hand over the half of the land in fallow [or 'clear', *cherron*] and the trees [= including vines?] as many as are in the property. The demesmen of Aixone shall introduce a vine-dresser in the last five years.

The inscription continues:

It is not permitted that earth from trenching operations be carried by any one to any other place than the property; . . . since the lessees of the Phelleis, Autokles and Anteas, come to an agreement with the demesmen of Aixone to cut down the olive trees, they shall choose men who with the demarch, the stewards and the lessees shall sell the olive trees to whomsoever offers the most. . . . He who purchases the olive trees is to cut them down when Anteas gathers the fruit in the year after the archonship of Archias [346/5 BC] before the ploughing. And he is to leave the stumps not less than a palm high in the trenches, in order that the olives may be as fine and as large as possible in these years [?]

Here cutting down the olive trees means removing the ancient wood, but leaving the stumps to shoot again.

(c) This is the lease of a sacred property in Sunium.[70] Certain of the procedures mentioned are paralleled elsewhere and seem to be the general practice in land cultivation. It has been somewhat restored.

On these conditions the demesmen . . . lease the sacred domain which is *en Hermei*, which Hierocles previously cultivated. . . . He who leases the plot will plough it crosswise [? *enallax* = both ways].[71] The half of it[72] he will sow with corn and barley; of the other half he will plant the fallow [?] with beans;[73] the rest of the land he will not sow, leaving it uncultivated.

There follows a rather obscure passage, complicated by an otherwise unknown technical term:

Twice in the year and at first yearly [?] he will make heaps [*korthilas*, an unknown word which may have the same meaning as *korthys*, which seems to mean a heap.[74] The reference would then be to some form of digging, either trenching or earthing up] on the land; he will dig about the figs on the land, and about the other cultivated trees in the same manner, and he will set up stakes [?] so that the new [vines] may grow up them. . . . When he quits the property . . . he shall leave all that has grown on the property, the dung and the stakes . . . and the rows of plants; and if the figs fail [i.e. die][75] – elsewhere a fixed number of figs is named to be planted each year[76] – he shall plant figs not less than ten in each year . . .

(d) Another inscription[77] of much the same period (?) is a lease of the sacred property of Apollo Lyceius at Sunium. The Laurium-Sunium region is relatively barren in modern times, and part of it, at least, was in ancient times affected by the smelting of argentiferous lead ore. Possibly special efforts had to be made to bring it under cultivation. Some considerable stress seems to be laid here again on water supply whether for irrigation or for other purposes. Others (neighbours?) are not to be impeded in obtaining water. The inscription is too defective to be valuable, but the following is worth quoting:

He will keep the trees in a good state, olives, figs and other fruit trees. If not, he must immediately plant new ones from the old [?], and prune [*kolouein*] the old ones sufficiently. In the *temenos* he must neither plough nor cut down the cultivated trees, nor any other tree at all, nor pasture animals nor carry manure [*kopreuein*][78]

'Manure' here might mean green manure or humus made from weeds, of the sort mentioned in Xenophon's *Oeconomicus*, but it could be one of the rare references to animal manure.

And if the lessee leaves the *temenos*, he shall plant the half of the garden ... with cabbage [?, rape (?) = *raphanos*] and leave half unplanted.

It is not without interest to notice the purpose to which the rent was put, to provide the sacrifice of two oxen each year.

(*e*) This inscription (of 321 BC)[79] deals with the lease of a number of *temene*. Apart from the general provisions for the payment of rent, there are some interesting details.

Mud [*ilus*] and earth it is not permitted to the lessees to take away, either from the Theseion or from the other sacred properties. Nor is it permitted to take away the vegetable matter [*hyle*, here clearly meaning the weeds and other vegetation so important in the formation of green manure and humus] to any other place than the plot itself. The lessees shall cultivate it thus: for nine years as they wish. In the tenth year they shall plough the half only and not more, in order that the next lessee shall be able to carry out his ploughing from the sixth to the tenth of Anthesterion [February–March]. If they plough more than the half, the excess of produce shall belong to the demesmen. The lessee, taking over the house in Halmyris watertight [i.e. roofed] and standing, shall hand it back in the same state ...

The reference here to house property going with the land serves to make a link with three leases of some interest in that, as some of the above must be connected with the restoration of neglected land, so these appear to deal with dilapidated building property.[80–81] It is to be noted that the first and third, which relate to shrines of small private cults maintained by members of a *thiasos* (religious association) might indicate that the general circumstances of the late fourth century meant that such associations became impoverished and were forced to get their maintenance done for them by lessees who supervised the property, and maintained the buildings in a fit state for the ceremonial to be carried out in them.

To what has been said above on water rights may be added some further details. There are fragmentary references to an *ochetos*, a water-pipe or channel, and to a cistern (*phrear*), and in an *apotimema* (pledge) boundary inscription the mention of water-rights again.

Thus the lease inscriptions provide a great deal in the way of indications on cultivation, and on the problems connected with it which beset the Greeks. Not only water was precious, but also soil (which was the raw material, it must not be forgotten, for the predominantly mud-brick building construction) and vegetation, even in the form of weeds, which carefully cut, as in present-day Greece, formed food for animals, or, dug in, provided the essential humus, the 'manure' which the paucity of large domesticated animals could not provide. Here it may be noticed that apart from general references to pasturage little is said of domesticated farm animals in the leases, and little in literature generally. A mention of 'soft-woolled' sheep,[82] and another to the spring shearing of sheep[83] are the most interesting among the few that occur. This is curious. These animals existed, but somehow they failed, except in a very secondary way, to make their appearance in the records.

The working day was determined by the essentially agricultural life of a large proportion of the population. It was also, in part, determined by the inadequacy of sources of artificial light, a fact which precluded profitable activity after dark, and many activities of leisure such as reading, which the Greeks replaced not wholly by sleeping but also by simple games which could be played even in an inadequate light, and conversation; not, it may be suggested, by drinking except on special occasions. 'I am accustomed', says Xenophon's Ischomachus,[84] 'to rise up from bed at an hour when I am likely to find still at home anyone whom I might chance to need to see ...' A practice, one feels, liable to lead to progressively more serious problems if imitated by others, and in any case likely to occasion the unpopularity of Xenophon's hero. Even now in Greece people are astir early in both large towns and remote villages where artificial light is still sometimes inadequate. The main factor is the approach of dawn, though people are up and about well before. So too in ancient Athens. It must be recalled that a man could set out on foot to walk from Athens to Laurium, starting in the middle of the night, and that to collect a few drachmae!

CHAPTER NINE

MINING

THE EXTRACTION OF MINERAL RESOURCES from the earth was of great importance in the economy of Greece. A number of substances were mined: precious metals, electrum, silver and gold, in that order of use for coinage, and in the case of silver associated with lead in the mineral galena. Iron ore is widespread in Greece (see Chapter I for its use in Early Greece) and its exploitation attracted no particular comment in ancient sources. Copper was less common,[1] and is always associated by name, rightly or wrongly, with Chalcis in Euboea. Tin is not clearly native to Greece. Imported, it was used by itself, as in the tin-coating of pottery vases, and with copper for the making of bronze. In this connection, be it noted, it was not essential: there was also a native association of arsenic with copper to produce arsenical bronze.[2] Non-metallic substances which should be mentioned are emery abrasive, for marble-working, in Naxos, *miltos* (ruddle or red ochre) from Cea,[3] Melian earth[4] and earth from Cimolus used in soap-making.[5] Realgar (red sulphate of arsenic) may also be added to the list – it came from the Black Sea coast, and, like *miltos*, was used for waterproofing ships' timbers. A form of mining is represented by the underground quarrying of marble called *lychnites* (mined by artificial light) on the island of Paros. It should be recalled that *metallon* 'mine' could also be used for a quarry. Singularly little appears on these aspects of mining in Antiquity, even in the *De Lapidibus* of Theophrastus. There are, indeed, Athenian efforts to regulate the trade in *miltos* because of its use in shipbuilding (see above, p. 60), but that is about all. The literary and epigraphical evidence is concerned with the mining of precious metals and particularly the interests of Athens. The areas involved in such mining were North Greece, Macedonia and Thrace, and the island of Thasos off the coast of the latter; in the Aegean, almost exclusively the island of Siphnos, and the Laurium mines in south-east Attica. There is some evidence for Cean silver-working.

Thasos

The island of Thasos, rich in other natural resources (see Chapter X), early attracted the attention of the Greeks, especially the Parians. It is not clear that mining was the first objective, but Herodotus[6] writes thus: 'I myself saw these mines, and by far the most remarkable of them were those which were found by the Phoenicians.' They were located in Thasos between the regions called Ainyra and Koinyra[7] – both, seemingly, names of Phoenician origin – where, Herodotus says, 'there is a great mountain ransacked in the quest'. The mention of the Phoenicians here may be added to what is said on their activities in Chapter I. The place is probably to be located[8] south-east of the village of Potamia, north-west of the Bay of Koinyra. The area is difficult of access and ill-explored, but there appear to be indications of mining, as also in the west of the island around the Bay of Limenaria.[9]

Macedonia–Thrace

Thasos was always closely connected with the mainland opposite, the tribal regions of Macedonia (to the west of the Struma (anc. Strymon)) and of Thrace to the east. Along the seaboard from the Gulf of Thermae to the Hellespont were numerous Greek colonies, especially in the three-pronged peninsula of Chalcidice. The whole area, and particularly Thrace, was very fertile, rich in timber (so that fuel was in good supply), and like Thasos, rich in both silver and gold. The wealth of the area is demonstrated, in the Archaic period and later, by the issues of coins.[10] Thus the mining area of Damastium (located in the Paeonian region of eastern Macedonia) had coins bearing representations of ingots and miners' picks.[11] A number of other tribal areas issued coins,[12] some of them of exceptional size (octodrachms), clearly intended as a means of exporting silver bullion, which is confirmed by their appearance in Egyptian hoards, and hoards from other East Mediterranean areas, as, for instance, Ras Shamra in northern Syria.[13] The Greek colonists of the coast (like the Thasians) cast envious eyes on these riches, and from time to time sought to penetrate into the interior, encountering a hostile reception from the savage natives. Some of these Greek colonies also issued important series of coins, though it is not always clear how they obtained their supplies of precious metal. Particularly impressive are the coins of Acanthus, and of some other Chalcidic colonies. Some Thracian cities issuing noble coin series, Abdera, Maronea and Aenus owed their wealth to trade with the interior.

The whole region played a considerable part in Greek history. First came the incursion of Megabazus, lieutenant of Darius, into Macedonia, his preoccupation with two scoundrel leaders of the Eastern Greeks, Histiaeus and Aristagoras, and their ambitions to establish themselves at Myrcinus on the Strymon,[14] in a region which Herodotus describes as possessing limitless shipbuilding timber, 'many oars' and silver mines.[15] At the time of the Persian wars there was the appearance of Miltiades the Younger,[16] who was tyrant of the Thracian Chersonese and married Hegesipyle, the daughter of the Thracian ruler Olorus.[17] He and his family, of the Philidae, may thus have acquired an interest in northern mining. Finally, there was the invasion, by land as well as by sea, of Xerxes in 481/80 B C. How exactly these northern mines were controlled and administered is unclear. Herodotus, in commenting on Xerxes' advance, and describing Thrace and its lakes,[18] mentions Mount Pangaeus and its gold and silver mines, which, he says, were worked (nemontai) by the Pieres, Odomantoi and Satrae (the warlike Thracians). In all this he makes no mention of Athenian interests.

Athens in fact took a particular interest in the North, from the beginning of the sixth century. The real connection began with Pisistratus, who, at his second displacement from the tyranny, went off with his sons to North Greece: 'And first he settled in the region of the Thermaic Gulf in a place called Rhaecelus, and thence he passed into the regions about Pangaeus, whence he returned having made money for himself [or, 'engaged in business'] and hired soldiers.'[19]

Herodotus[20] says nothing of this region in connection with the second exile of Pisistratus, but states that 'he based [rooted] his tyranny on many mercenaries and revenues, some from Attica [autothen] and others from the river Strymon'. As this is a description of his tyranny, not just of his return, it sounds as if there were some permanent connection with the Strymon region until the advance of the Persians. It would be surprising if the Philidae, Miltiades the Younger in particular, did not have a similar connection.[21]

The outstanding event of the fifth century in this area, after the reduction of the Persian garrisons in the North, was the Athenian clash with Thasos.[22] Some time after the battles of the Eurymedon, c. 469 B C, the Thasians defected from the Delian League, because of disagreements about the 'marts' on the coast of Thrace opposite (the colonies of Thasos on the mainland were Galepsus and Oesime), and about 'the mine' in their possession. Sailing to Thasos, the Athenians defeated them at sea and effected a landing on the island. About the same time they sent ten thousand of their own citizens and allies to settle the place then called Ennea Hodoi or 'Nine Ways', afterwards Amphipolis. They succeeded in gaining possession of Ennea Hodoi from the Edonians, but on advancing into the interior of Thrace they were cut off in Drabescus (in the interior behind Crenides, either Drama or a village, Zdravik, eight miles north of Amphipolis), a town of the Edonians, by the assembled Thracians, who regarded the settlement of Ennea Hodoi as an act of hostility.[23] Then

... The Thasians in the third year of the siege obtained terms from the Athenians by razing their walls, delivering up their ships, and arranging to pay the monies demanded at once, and tribute in future; *giving up their possessions on the mainland together with the mine.*[24]

Thereafter, as indeed before, the Athenians persevered in attempts to settle in Thrace on the Strymon. Finally, they succeeded in 437 BC in founding Amphipolis, where the Strymon could be bridged, in effect on the frontier between the Macedonians and the Thracians. Thucydides, who gives the history of the site from the time of Aristagoras,[25] comments on its importance for ship-timber and revenues (from mining?).[26] The loss of Amphipolis to Brasidas in the Peloponnesian War was a great blow, both in terms of political influence and revenues.[27]

An outstanding example of a personal interest in Thrace, and a connection with mines, is provided by Thucydides (the historian) himself, who possessed the right of working gold mines in Thrace, and who operated as a commander there against Brasidas in 424 BC.[28] These gold mines were said to be the property of Thucydides as the dowry of his wife, a Thracian. Was Thucydides already connected with Thrace through his father Olorus? It is worth noting the name of Miltiades' father-in-law, Olorus, again (see above, p. 166) and the connection of Thucydides with Miltiades and Cimon of the Philidae. It is suggested that these mines were at Skaptēsylē, a Hellenized Thracian place-name, probably more correct than the plausible Skapte Hyle. The site of the source of gold (as seems apparent from the description of Stephanus: 'A small city of Thrace opposite Thasos') was probably south of Mount Pangaeus on the sea coast. According to Herodotus[29] it produced eighty talents (? annually) and was richer than Thasos. Temple accounts[30] mention 'ingots of gold of Skaptēsylē', which, it is suggested, were offerings of the historian, and the coins inscribed 'Thasiōn Ēpeiro' may have been struck from gold from this source. The gold probably came from placer deposits,[31] not from mines, i.e. pockets of broken-down auriferous quartz, which may therefore have been relatively soon exhausted (see below).

The end of the Archidamian War (421 BC) saw the loss to the Athenians of these North Greek assets. In theory they were in part recoverable on the basis of the Peace of Nicias. In fact they were not. Some attempts were made to regain a foothold in North Greece, but everything was gone after the defeat of Athens, except the strong interest in 'Tom Tiddler's ground'. Athens was, for the future, interested in North Greece for three principal reasons: the question of the rise of Olynthus and the Chalcidic League; the hope of the recovery of at least influence at Amphipolis; and the protection of the corn route to the Black Sea. So both as a state and as individuals (the marriage of the Athenian commander Iphicrates to the daughter of the Thracian King Cotys is one instance of this) the Athenians sought to establish a renewed foothold in Thrace. Ultimately, however, Philip II of Macedon triumphed over both Olynthus and Athens, with the resulting control of the resources of precious metals in the whole of this area.

In particular, it appears that there were mines in the region east of Mount Pangaeus somewhere in the vicinity of the road from Kavalla to Drama. There are various literary references to the mines of Crenides (surely meaning 'the place of fountains' and not derived from a personal name), distinct from those of Mount Pangaeus. Appian[32] mentions a ridge (lophos) with gold mines called Ta Asyla. These mines to the East (?) of the site of (later) Philippi were developed by Philip II. Diodorus Siculus[33] gives the product of these (gold) mines under Philip as 'more than a thousand talents'. It will be recalled that the coins of gold, inscribed Thasiōn Ēpeiro[34] could be from gold from this area. It appears also (from Stephanus of Byzantium) that Philip II came to the aid of the inhabitants of Crenides, under attack by the Thracians, and took over the region, calling its centre Philippi. These sources of gold at Crenides were probably placer deposits, and there may have been only a temporary boom in this area.[35] Crenides was originally a colony of Thasos, later known as Datos or Daton. Strabo[36] describes the area as one of 'fertile plains, a marshy lake and rivers, having gold mines and profitable shipyards, from which region comes the proverb "a Daton of advantages" '. An epineion (sea-port) of the Datinoi was Antisara (= Kavalla = Neapolis of the Tribute Lists, and Crenides = Daton = Philippi).[37] The development of the mines of Crenides/Philippi provided the gold and silver for the issues of gold staters and silver tetradrachms of Philip II.[38] With the conquests of his son Alexander III (the Great), and the capture of the Persian treasures, these North Greek sources, like those of Attica, became of relatively small importance, but they continued to be exploited when the Romans took charge of them.

What has been said so far is based on literary sources frequently inadequate or obscure. The material evidence on the ground is totally inadequate. As far as the origins of the gold are concerned there are three sources to be taken into account: reef gold (*chrysorycheia*) which is mined, 'placer gold' (*chrysolysia*)[39] and alluvial gold, as that of the Hebrus,[40] the River Echeidorus east of the River Axius (Vardar),[41] and the upper Strymon.

It is striking that there has been a good deal of interest directed to North Greece (to city sites in particular), but singularly little systematic investigation of possible traces of ancient mining, though these must exist. Whatever the source of the gold, galena, the mineral from which came argentiferous lead, *must* have been mined. From his book (see Bibliography) it would appear that Casson covered most of the ground. Yet the most important areas in the ancient records, the massif of Mount Pangaeus and the area, to the east of it, of Crenides/Philippi, have not, he claims, revealed any traces of mining either for lead/silver or for reef gold. In the case of the Mount Pangaeus massif, according to the observations of Casson, deposits would be around rather than on it. The area is in any case ill-explored. The site, with ambiguous remains, of Askytotrypo on the south-east of the massif is probably not a mine; there are no traces of working on the north side or on the summit. There are said (doubtfully) to be workings on the southern spurs at Asemotrypai. Geologically speaking, the actual mountain massif is unlikely to produce gold: quartz occurs only on or near the foot of the mountain. The possible presence of galena needs investigation.[42]

In summary it may be said that ancient records speak only in general terms of the great wealth of the area.[43] How it was produced is a great puzzle. It is difficult to explain it all by placer deposits or the phenomenon mentioned by Strabo on the inland Paeonian region.[44] There is a certain amount of information on Roman and medieval activity in the area, of greater or less reliability, most of it relating to iron-mining.[45]

THE AEGEAN: SIPHNOS

In this island there are the evidences of rather crude mine workings at Ayios Sostis and Ayios Silvestrios.[46] There may be other indications of mining elsewhere in the island not to be confused with the exploitation of iron mines in modern times. Further, ancient stories tell of the wealth of the Siphnians in the later sixth century B C. Herodotus,[47] in narrating the exploits of the exiled Samian opponents of Polycrates of Samos, after their repulse from that island, tells of their attack on Siphnos, before they took themselves off to Cydonia in Crete, at the time of the maximum prosperity of the Siphnians. He goes on to mention the gold and silver mines, the income from which the Siphnians distributed among themselves, except that from a tithe they erected a splendid treasury at Delphi and sent to Apollo each year the offering of a golden egg. Their wealth is indicated by the statement that the Samians, after defeating them, were able to exact the sum of a hundred talents. The effect of this wealth was to fill the Siphnians with sinful pride so that they sent to Delphi, at the last, a gilded silver egg, to the wrath of Apollo who caused their mines to be flooded. Indeed the cavities on the sea cliffs at Ayios Sostis are at and below the sea level, obviously the effect of subsidence. It may well be that whatever disaster overtook the Siphnians is reflected in the contributions they made to the Greek fleet at Salamis in 480 B C, when, if they were not unwilling allies of the Greeks, their wealth was much reduced, as indicated by the small number of ships they provided.[48] And it may be noted that silver coins of Siphnos do not in fact survive in great numbers. At this early date there was no tradition of gold coins in Greece, and despite the talk of the metal in Siphnos it is interesting to note that when the Spartans needed a supply of it for a religious purpose, they had to turn to Lydia. Was there no gold in Siphnos, or only a limited amount for a short time from 'placer' deposits? Even in the case of silver production Siphnos may ultimately have suffered from scarcity of water and wood fuel, like other islands.

ATTICA (LAURIUM)

Mining was being pursued in Attica from the Bronze Age. This is demonstrated by the Belgian excavations at Thoricus north of the Laurium area where the interior road from Athens to the east coast of Attica descends to the sea. The excavations at Thoricus, a site already well known for its theatre and Mycenaean tombs, are currently taking place at several points on or near the Velatouri Hill. On the summit shoulder of Velatouri, in a Middle Helladic stratum, dated towards the end of the sixteenth century B C, there were found fragments of litharge, i.e. oxide of lead, the by-product of the cupellation of argentiferous lead in the process of extracting the silver, which seem to indicate a refining activity already present at the end of the Middle Bronze Age.

In a cemetery area (West 4), in use from Protogeometric times (eleventh century B C and later) to the Post-Classical period, in the remains of a Protogeometric structure were found remains of litharge. The excavators are quite assured as to the dating of these remains. Thus, refining activity is established also for the ninth century B C at latest, though there is no indication of the volume of the industry.[49]

It is not proposed here to discuss the technical aspects of the installations (still, in part, present on the ground) or the processing of the ore, except to mention the workings: the rather rude burrowings of what is called the First Contact, and the deeper workings of the Third; the washing tables and cisterns;[50] the rare evidence of smelting ovens, and the large and impressive vertical shafts which appear in places.

It is difficult to believe that these regular and often profound shafts were the work of those who took on the mining leases (see below). The suggestion to be preferred[51] is that they are a separate system created, against payment for use from the actual mine operators, by a separate set of people. There is an analogy in those contractors who, for example, in Derbyshire, England, constructed the elaborate channels which drew off the intrusive water from the lead mines (a well-known example is Calver Sough). There was no problem of water in the case of the Laurium mines, but there must have been one of the difficulty of evacuating spoil and ore, and another of ventilating the increasingly extensive and complicated workings.

These installations, as they may be called, are firmly connected with land and land-owners in a permanent, not a transient fashion. From a study of the names which appear of those who were land-owners or owners of industrial establishments it seems that a strong local element was involved.

The Attic mines are of paramount importance from two aspects: the part they played in the history and economy of Athens, and the fact that from literary and epigraphical sources more is known of their organization and administration than about any other group of Greek mines or, indeed, any other Greek industry. These two aspects must now be considered.

Whatever the problems of the earlier exploitation of the mines, at least the terrain is open to inspection. The area of the Attic silver mines lies in south-east Attica, and is of triangular form, its apex at Cape Sunium, modern Cape Kolonnaes, pointing south-east. The mining area proper is some eleven miles long from north-west to south-east, and some five-and-a-half miles broad. It is hilly, the hills rising to some twelve hundred feet, divided by small valleys and gullies; the whole rather stony and today definitely the least attractive portion of Attica, except on the coast near Cape Sunium. It is rendered still less attractive by the signs of modern industry (production of zinc). It is significant that the main town is called Ergastiri. The name of the whole region is Laurium, perhaps from *laura*, a 'narrow lane' or 'alley' which must here mean either a stream bed or a mining gallery.[52] In modern times there are few signs of cultivation. If there was tree cover in earlier Antiquity this must have disappeared to a great extent in the Classical period, providing fuel for smelting. It seems to have recovered under the Turks and still survives to some extent. The free population[53] cannot have been great and was concentrated in town centres, of which Thoricus, as the Belgian excavations show, with its theatre, houses and ore-washeries, and mining galleries beneath, was clearly important. In the fourth century BC the surface land was certainly parcelled out, for cultivation or pasture, as the records of the *Poletai* show: 'plot' (*chōrion*) boundaries are used to mark out the surface areas of the mining concessions. It is difficult to decide what the area looked like in the Classical period; probably industrially blasted.[54] Whatever the use of the land, trees would have gone for charcoal-making, for domestic and industrial fuel, as in so many other accessible areas of Greece. But under the unpromising surface lay Aeschylus' 'treasure of the earth':[55] that is, galena (sulphide of lead) and cerusite (carbonate of lead), the former with a very high silver content and some traces of gold; there were also iron pyrites and zinc, little used in Antiquity, if at all. These deposits, in origin volcanic water-borne, were situated at the so-called First and Third Contacts between strata of limestone and schist. The deposits varied from two to three centimetres to several metres in thickness, and some very large concentrations, and the deeper were the richer. The first workings were on or near the surface, where the upper deposit appeared and manifested its presence by the signs provided by an admixture of iron, the deposits of mineral being exposed by the weathering of the superimposed schist. The earliest workings were here. Penetration to the lower deposits took place later, exactly how is not clear. The Athenians are unlikely to have worked out the geological theory; more probably the First and Third Contacts were in places connected by geological faults, or the Third Contact emerged in places on valley sides.

The earliest history of the Laurium mines is unknown except from archaeology. Attempts have been made to connect them with Pisistratus but the arguments are not convincing.[56] They first emerge historically in the early fifth century. Herodotus, in narrating the events of the war with Aegina,[57] says the Athenians borrowed war-ships from the Corinthians to assist the Aeginetan democrats, 'for they did not happen to possess ships fit to combat those of the Aeginetans'. Only a few years later they had the best fleet of all the Greeks, and in the Athenian tradition it was believed they gained such a fleet thanks to the Laurium mines and the inspired leadership of Themistocles.

There are two chief accounts of the event. Herodotus[58] puts it that 'the Athenians received a large quantity of money into the public treasury, which came to them from the Laurium mines, and they plan-ned to distribute it 10 drachmae per head, but Themistocles persuaded them to build with it 200 ships, ostensibly for the Aeginetan War.' The writer of the *Constitution of Athens*[59] gives the date as 483/2 BC (when Themistocles was a plain member of the *Boule* or even just of the *Ekklesia*), and the place of this mining activity as Maronea. He infers an exceptional find of silver which produced 100 talents for the State. According to this authority Themistocles brought it about that a talent was handed to each of one hundred citizens – each to build a warship. Taking 30,000 (an excessive figure?) as the number of the citizens, Herodotus' 10 drachmae per head represents 50 talents. There are thus disparities in the amount (50 and 100 talents) and the number of ships (200 and 100), but the Greeks were never very accurate in figures. The curious procedure of the hundred citizens may have been followed to secure personal supervision of ship construction in the absence of state machinery.

An important point is that neither author makes clear whether the proposal changed a repeated (? yearly) practice or initiated an excep-tional one. Something exceptional is inferred, perhaps the sum, the size of which is certainly striking. We are as much in the dark about the proportion received by the State of the whole production as we are on the basis of the State's claim to it. It may be reflected that the nature and effect of a 'lucky strike' would not wholly be confined to one year. Plutarch[60] speaks of a regular distribution and Cornelius Nepos[61] of an annual one – neither is a particularly reliable informant. Some similar distribution may have taken place elsewhere,[62] and it is a fair conclusion that the exceptional increase in silver production in the period in question justified and gave point to Themistocles' proposal.[63]

Of interest is the fact that Maronea formed part of the deme of Besa.[64] A concession boundary stone, inscribed Hephaistiakon, which belonged to this deme, was found at Kamareza, which will probably be the Maronea region. Whatever may be the connection of Pangaeus in

Thrace with Pangaion in Laurium, Maronea in Laurium is unlikely
to have a mining connection with Maronea in Thrace since no mining
activity is indicated in the latter. The site of Maronea/Besa as being the
same as that of Kamareza seems to be confirmed by the source[65] which
refers to Besa as a place for a fortress halfway between Anaphlystus and
Thoricus, more or less in the vicinity of Kamareza. Here have been
found both large shafts, and, as Ardaillon describes them, 'huge
cavities' in the Third Contact, indicating considerable mining activity.

Evidence on the surface in the Laurium region is not easy to date, but
Thoricus[66] emerges as a place of considerable importance,[67] and
other such centres might have existed in the mining area (though a
monument like its theatre is hardly likely to have disappeared totally
if one existed elsewhere). The excavations present certain problems.[68]
At Thoricus there is some obscurity in connection with chronological
gaps in the sequence of finds, especially the second gap (480–450 BC)
and the third. The dating of material finds is probably responsible
for the second. It is unlikely that the importance of Thoricus was
diminished in this period. There is clear evidence of development in
the second half of the fifth century, and it increased in size c. 350 BC. Its
history, therefore, follows in some measure the periods of prosperity
of the mines. Excavation has revealed houses, washing tables, cisterns
and probably accommodation for slaves. The construction date is
given as the second half of the fifth century BC. The site is taken as
abandoned in the last years of the Peloponnesian War and restored in
the second and third quarter of the fourth century (cf. the enlargement
of the theatre). The dating is based on well stratified and dated pottery.
The excavator suggests that washing table I was constructed before
413 BC and the Spartan occupation of Decelea, and was then abandoned
by the slaves gradually from 413 BC, as was the whole area: a process
which was accelerated by the mobilization of slaves for the fleet, and
the ultimate defeat of Athens. Because of the third 'gap' (c. 404–375 BC)
it is not clear how soon the recovery took place in the fourth century.
The masonry and mode of construction at Thoricus is very similar to
the walls of cisterns and other buildings elsewhere in the mining area. A
question of similar dates, therefore?

It is not easy to disentangle the structures of different periods at
Thoricus, or determine the exact area of the settlement at any one time,
but an interesting picture is suggested of town life, with free inhabitants whose graves, set out with modest enough burial furniture, have
been excavated in close proximity to the theatre and to houses. These
latter were grouped in blocks with streets between (this does not mean

there were no open spaces), and mixed up with washeries, cisterns and presumed slaves' barracks. The finds of litharge, though admittedly of much earlier date and the slag associated with clay nozzles (*tuyères*) for the introduction of a forced draught, brought down, as the excavator suggests, from higher up on the Velatouri Hill, indicate that smelting and cupellation took place at a higher level, as might certainly be expected in the latter process since it produced noxious lead fumes; and the same seems likely to be true of the smelting process which removed the sulphur from the galena, and so produced other fumes, in the preparation of the crude lead. Or did the harm done by such fumes weigh as heavily in this arrangement as the obtaining of a good circulation of air? However, the practice of smelting in elevated areas, characteristic of the Derbyshire lead-mining area in England[69] was not necessarily followed at Laurium.[70]

Not far away from the theatre quarrying has revealed mine workings, and there are vertical shafts on the seaward side not so very far above the shore line. Extensive mine workings beneath the town have been known since the 1860s, and access to them must have been given from the open spaces even in the town itself. We have here an illustration in material fact of what can be read in the mine leases (see below, p. 181).

Elsewhere, for the period from 483–413 BC, little detail is known.[71] There are a few minor references on this subject made by Diodorus;[72] Plutarch[73] mentions *metalleis* among those participating in the Periclean building programme, but since *metallon* can mean a quarry, these may be quarrymen. That is all, and these authorities, if they can be so called, are late. Further, persons enriched by the mines are not so numerous as is sometimes thought, or to be surely interpreted. The Greeks had certain stock figures of wealthy men, some connected with 'industry'. Callias II, of whom the story of the Persian treasure is told,[74] can be conjecturally associated with mining. His son Hipponicus II is so connected only by his possession of six hundred slaves leased out to miners.[75] He is otherwise just a traditionally wealthy man.[76] His son Callias III, while mentioned again on the score of wealth, is not connected with mining. Nicias is the one clear example. He appears in Lysias' list[77] of rich men; so too in Plutarch. Xenophon quotes him (i)[78] as owner of a thousand slaves hired out to Sosias the Thracian; and (ii)[79] as purchasing an overseer for his silver mines. Plutarch[80] from these and other sources refers to his 'ownership' of silver mines, stating on the authority of one of Pasiphon's dialogues that Nicias consulted diviners about them: 'for he possessed many in the Lauriotic region, of great importance as to the revenue from them, not without risk in their working; he also maintained a body of slaves in the same place, and had the bulk of his fortune in silver mining.'[81] Of uncertain date is a lesser man, Philemonides, the owner of three hundred miner slaves. In view of Nicias' engagement in mining matters, it is natural to think of other wealthy men in the same terms (though it never seems to happen in the case of Alcibiades). Such men might also suffer, as did the family of Nicias in another connection, the reduction, within a period, of great fortunes, though Lysias (loc. cit.) warns of popular exaggeration of wealth, whether obtained, as it was believed, from peculation in public office, or from some other source. Thus popular belief put the fortune of Nicias at 100 talents (in the Peloponnesian War he had some good excuse for divination in relation to his mining interests!). His son Niceratus on his death left only 14 talents to his son ('no gold and silver'). There was also the reduced fortune of Callias III, richest of Greeks on his father's death as Lysias asserts (loc. cit.), and the reported possession by Callias II of 200 talents. Yet the war-tax (?) assessment of Callias III did not amount to two talents. This, however, uncharitable gossip said, was due to profligacy! Lysias also instances the fortune of Stephanus, son of Thallus reported to be 50 talents, but found to be 11 on his death. Similarly Ischomachus was supposed to possess 70 talents; in fact his two sons each inherited less than 10. No profligacy here (if he was the hero of Xenophon's *Oeconomicus*!) Aside from the exaggeration of popular imagination the war-tax and other burdens on the rich in the latter part of the Peloponnesian War and after must have been the cause of reduction, to some extent. One is led to wonder, however, whether damage to the mines and the loss of slave labour were not also causes, and possibly the lack of mining activity in the obscure period of the first half of the fourth century, with agriculture as a strong competitor for capital, not to mention lending on trade ventures abroad. That is to say, competition for what capital there was available. And how great really was the overall product of the mines?

Certainly the Peloponnesian War strongly affected the mining area (as seen above, on Thoricus). In this connection our information from good sources increases again. The second Peloponnesian invasion of Attica (in 430 BC) penetrated to Laurium. The Peloponnesians stayed in Attica forty days, 'and laid waste all the land'. Thucydides' words are: 'They penetrated into the Paralus region so-called, as far as Laurium, where the Athenians have their silver mines.' The fourth invasion, of 427 BC (the third was a minor one) may also have penetrated to Laurium, since the land which had been covered before was laid waste, and any that had been missed, as Thucydides puts it. It was aggravated by an earthquake, of which it is thought traces can be detected in the mining area.

The invasions ended with the minor one of 425 BC, the same year which saw the increase of the tribute. It cannot be demonstrated that there was a connection (though Ardaillon vaguely suggests there might be). From 425 BC and the capture of the Spartan hostages on Sphakteria the mining area was safe until 413 BC and the establishment of the Spartans at Decelea. Did the mining area in this period (425–413 BC) undergo considerable development, of increased importance in view of the war expenditure? It is natural to connect the undertakings of Nicias and perhaps of Hipponicus with this time. We have no mine-lease lists of the *Poletai*, but there are references in Aristophanes: so in the *Knights*[82] the Sausage-seller in a slanging-match with Cleon says:

> But *mines* I'll purchase when I've first devoured
> my ribs of Beef,

whatever that may mean. Then in the *Birds*[83] comes the following:

> 'First, whatever judge amongst you most of all
> desires to win,
> Little Lauriotic owlets shall be always flocking in.
> You shall find them all about you, as the dainty
> brood increases,
> Building nests within your purses, hatching little
> silver pieces.
> (Trans. B. B. Rogers)

And again Xenophon[84] comments on the number of slaves 'before the events at Decelea'; information probably taken from Thucydides.[85] The reference in the *Knights* is obscure in the extreme, and *metalla* need not refer to Attica at all, but the reference in the *Birds* is a clear connection of coinage and the mines of Laurium. It belongs (in 414 BC) to the end of a period when the Laurium mines might have undergone special development.

Whatever this degree of development, the Spartan occupation of Decelea in 413 BC must have gravely affected the mines as it did all other life in Attica. When Thucydides makes Alcibiades suggest to the Spartans the establishment of a permanent base in Attica,[86] he (Alcibiades) stresses the potential economic damage:

Whatever property there is in the country will most of it become yours, either by capture or surrender; and the Athenians will at once be deprived of their revenues from the silver mines at Laurium, of their present gains from their land and from the law-courts, and above all of the revenue from their allies, which will be paid less regularly as they lose their awe of Athens ...

It is pointed out by Alcibiades that the Athenians always feared this type of military action, but it is not clear that they took any steps to prevent it, or damage to the mining area if this was important, in the fashion that they took care earlier to construct the Long Walls. Efforts were made at fortification – extensions at Sunium in 413 BC, but for maritime reasons (to protect the corn route). Thoricus was fortified in 408/7 BC, as was Anaphlystus, according to the writer of *On Ways and Means*. Of interest are the comments of Xenophon (if the writer was the real Xenophon, a military man rather than a mining expert), who writes: 'I reckon that even in the event of war it would be possible to safeguard the continuance of the silver mines', and goes on to suggest an additional fort at Besa, halfway between the forts at Thoricus and Anaphlystus, in the sixty-stadia gap. He infers that no such attempt was made before.

Among the disasters arising from the Spartan occupation of Decelea was the desertion of mining slaves. Thucydides mentions, as a result of the now permanent (not seasonal) presence of the enemy, that the Athenians were entirely cut off 'from the land'.

They were deprived of the whole countryside, and more than twenty thousand slaves went over to the other side, the great part of whom were 'craftsmen'. And they lost all their cattle and draught animals.

The loss of the silver mines contributed to that impoverishment and financial difficulty to which Thucydides refers: 'in financial matters they lost their power'. This led, finally, to the emergency coinage after the battle of Notium (407 BC), consisting of a special issue of gold, in the archonship of Callias, 406/5 BC, 'the new gold of excellent quality and stamp', followed very shortly afterwards by the silver-coated copper coins, Athens' last desperate effort, which Aristophanes[87] compares so unfavourably to 'the ancient currency'. The silvered-bronze coinage, which frequently lost all its silver coating, was redeemed probably by 393 BC, the date of Conon's return to Athens, after the battle of Cnidus, with great quantities of Persian gold. It appears from an inscription of 375/4 BC, concerned with the testing of coins, that a good deal of coinage was, in the first quarter of the fourth century, unacceptable in commerce (? plain forgeries and satrapal issues).[88]

Thus the 'vile bronze'[89] disappeared, thanks to Conon and the Persians, not to any demonstrable revival of the mines; for, from the *Memorabilia* of Xenophon (its dramatic date in the late fifth century; its actual date in the first half of the fourth) we learn that mining was reduced,[90] and this seems to be borne out by the scant information available, though now forensic speeches, such as those of Lysias, afford increased potential sources of material. Ardaillon (in his book on Laurium) maintains that the confiscations of the Thirty Tyrants included mines, but it is difficult to see how, since they were in no clear sense private property, at any rate in the fourth century. It is true, however, that the confiscations and disturbances of the end of the fifth century would not encourage mining or any other speculative activity. Whether for this cause or another, despite the restoration of a silver coinage, *c.* 394 B C, Lysias in 389 B C mentions a shortage of 'silver' or of 'money'. We have already seen that the tone of the private speeches, of Lysias for instance, is that large fortunes were of the fifth century, and had been spent in the service of the State, an undoubted allusion to the 'Squeeze the Rich' policy of the later democracy, parallel to and replacing the 'Squeeze the Allies' policy of Cleon. The war-tax (*eisphora*) and the trierarchy (*trierarchia*) were financial burdens on the well-to-do. The tradition thus established continues in the fourth century and replaced the income from the empire. The tendency was to conceal wealth; to invest it or part of it, not in real estate, if it could be avoided, though of necessity land remained the main form of wealth, but in mercantile loans. Thence came undoubtedly some of Athens' difficulties in raising money, and perhaps some reason for the neglect of the mines.

The mines, however, later came into renewed prominence, and our evidence improves. The earliest yet discovered record of the *Poletai* (the officials concerned with confiscations, sales and contracts) relating to mining transactions comes to hand for the year 367/6 B C,[91] the only complete example known. Only seventeen mines were leased in that year, whereas in the record of *c.* 342/1 B C[92] more than eighty leases are entered. This difference of numbers and the increasing evidence, inscriptions, references in contemporary literature to mines and mining, actual forensic speeches concerned with mining, or references to such, of the period 345–323 B C, confirm the impression conveyed by the pamphlet *On Ways and Means*. Here among suggestions to increase the revenues of Athens most space is devoted to the mines, and though the writer argues from past greatness and immemorial activity in mining, it is also clear that in the immediate past it had not been a favoured activity. For he mentions poverty and risk in connection with it, and unwillingness to speculate, and refers to a recent recovery.[93] From mid-century to the death of Alexander the Great mining appears important, though uneven in volume.

The size of a mining undertaking cannot in any relevant sense be determined. We hear of an *ergasterion* (therefore an establishment for the treatment of ore, which could be sold, not a mine) which employed thirty slaves (?) at Maronea.[94] It may have been sold for three talents and 2600 drachmae, a price probably exaggerated. There is mention in the same speech (in the text of a charge (*enklema*)) of a *kenchreon*, which, arguably, appears to be a washery.

It is not recorded that free men worked personally in the mines for wages, but, apart from engagement through one slave or more[95] small concessionaires certainly directed their own leased mines,[96] both citizens and metics. The hard and unpleasant work would be done by slaves, as the author of *On Ways and Means* argues, with division of labour and technical supervision, of which we hear something.[97] There may have been day and night labour, possibly in shifts of ten hours. Plutarch[98] condemns mining 'the greatest part of which is done by malefactors and barbarians, some of them bound and perishing in those close and unwholesome places'. He is thinking of Roman mining particularly in Egypt, but there is no reason for believing conditions were much better in the Attic mines. There were, to be sure, few risings, but then it would be difficult for the slaves to combine.[99]

Calculations of numbers of slaves employed are idle. There was no such thing as 'an average mine'. Ardaillon's supposition that there were more than a hundred establishments employing more than thirty workers, and that 'in the greatest period of prosperity' thirty-three workers was the average for a washery, are baseless. Equally idle is the calculation of an over-all figure either from Thucydides[100] or from the muddled and hypothetical figures of (Xenophon).[101] Ardaillon suggests 'more than twenty thousand' for the period of Pericles, and infers from (Xenophon's) figures a number greater than ten thousand in the period before 413 BC.

Much detail comes from literary sources and inscriptions on the administration of the mines. The mines stood in many respects in a class by themselves. They were excavated in the subsoil of private property (*edaphos*), but the owner of the surface land did not own the mineral rights beneath it, at any rate in the fourth century. There was no private possession of mines and no sale or inheritance of them. They were the perpetual property of the State, though terms of buying and selling were used. Therefore non-citizens, even without the right of land acquisition, could work them.[102]

The mining concessions were entered, as already mentioned, in the records of the *Poletai*, which were inscribed on a stele (hence the phrases 'from the stele' and 'having a stele' in reference to mines). Each concession had a name from a deity (Artemisiakon, Hermaikon), or from heroes or persons (as Leukippeion). Its location was accurately recorded by deme location (valuable information on tribes and demes is thus given in the *Poletai* records), the plot in the *edaphos* of which it was placed, and by adjacent plots, which have their owner's name, roads, natural features, and *ergasteria*. Boundary stones of mines also occur, though it is far from clear how subterranean activities were bounded by surface limits (or did they denote an area for the deposit of spoil?). There may also have been underground boundaries.[103] The following is an example of these *Poletai* records called *diagraphai*. It is of 367/6 BC:[104]

At Sounion in the land of the sons of Charmylos, of which the boundaries are, on the north, the property of Kleokritos of Aigilia, on the south the property of Leukios of Sounion; the lessee Pheidippos, the price twenty drachmae.

Another reads:

At Laureion, the same Artemisiakon and the cuttings, of which the boundaries are, on the north the property of Diopeithes of Euonymon and the furnace of Demostratos of Kytheros, on the south the workshop [*ergasterion*] of Diopeithes and the wagon road, and the ravine of the Thorikioi; the lessee Kephisodotos of Aithalidai; the price twenty drachmae.

The following inscription[105] seems to illustrate a succession of holders of the same mine:

From the stele of the archonship of Theophilos Lysanias the son of Lysikles of Kephale declared a mine being worked at Laureion [called] Hermaikon, having a stele, from the stele of the archonship of Theophilos, which had been worked, which Antixenos of Euonymon held [?].

The latter part is obscure; and it is not clear why the stele of Theophilos is mentioned twice (= the *Poletai* list of that archon year).

Some historical figures appear in the lease lists: so Meidias, the rival of Demosthenes.[106] Demosthenes says of him:[107] 'He imported timbers for his silver-mining undertakings', on which the Scholiast observes: 'for he had rented mines, which were silver-producing, from the State.' In the *Poletai* list of the year 367/6 BC,[108] of the twenty-four men mentioned in the text as lessees of mines or as property owners in the mining district, sixteen are known persons, and of these eleven are members of wealthy families, wealthy enough, at least, to serve as trierarchs or to present an *agora* (market-place) to their deme. Among them was Nicias II of Kydantidai,[109] grandson of the great Nicias and owner of considerable property in Nape. Thrasylochus of Anagyrous, the brother of Meidias, belonging to one of the richest families of the time, was a lessee of two mines.[110] Callias III of Alopeke was owner of property in Sunium and father of Hipponicus III, who is known to have bought two workshops in Melite, having nothing to do with mining, yet certainly with industry.[111] It is to be noted that the mining area of Besa was the site of a farming estate of the Callias family, and that Epicrates of Pallene, mentioned by Hyperides[112] appears here[113] as a property-owner in Nape.

The mining concessions varied in size, making them available for rich and relatively poor; parallel therefore in more modern times to examples in Spain, and in Derbyshire, England, not so very long ago. Among the small concessions is one referred to by Andocides,[114] unless this relates to a slave hired out on the *apophora* system. An example of a very large concession appears to be that mentioned by Hyperides.[115] Moreover concessions could be expanded not only by taking other leases but also by the purchase of more slaves;[116] more economical, however, from the standpoint of those engaged in mining, as also in other economic activities, was the use of hired slave labour. These could also be an important capital investment as Nicias I showed. For the user of labour hired slaves were very convenient in view of the variations in need – more being required when driving shafts and productive galleries, and fewer when a seam diminished or mining from time to time became less profitable. The pay for these hired slaves[117] remained the same in the fifth and fourth centuries BC, namely one obol per day net (replacements, food and clothing involving no extra expenditure). The income was low in comparison with that of artisan slaves,[118] but good for untrained slaves (as far as these miners were untrained), representing, as it probably did, an average covering women and old men.

In the mining records of the *Poletai* occurs the phrase 'they themselves declared [or put on record] these mines', where the verb indicates the recording (*diagraphe*) of a 'purchased' mine with the state officials. It is explained by the *Suda* (s.v. *anapographōn* (*agraphōn*) *dike*) thus: 'by reason of [or arising from] the payment to the State of a twenty-fourth part [of the product] of a new mine'. In the *Poletai* record of the year 367/6 BC mines of the category 'from the stele' (i.e. already in the *Poletai* records = old mines) have prices set against them ranging from

1550 to fifty drachmae. The other group with no inclusion of this phrase must be formed of new concessions. Twelve of these are recorded compared with five of the others; they are all let uniformly for twenty drachmae. It may be concluded from the evidence of the leases that there were four categories of mines: first, new mines (*kainotomiai*) – the earliest (metaphorical) use of the word appears in Aristophanes, *Wasps* 876 (of 422 BC), but it should be pointed out that this metaphorical use might be derived from quarrying not mining; second, going concerns (*ergasima*); third and fourth, *anasaxima* and *palaia anasaxima*. As the last category of these types of concession costs no more than a new mining concession, it is reasonable to suppose its productivity was equally uncertain. *Anasaximon* is a term the meaning of which can only be conjectured. *Anasattein* appears to mean 'to pile up' – so 'to block up', and thus *anasaximon* means 'blocked up' and abandoned for a shorter time or a longer (*palaion*) and then reopened; the risks being much the same as for the *kainotomia*. Hence the concession period in each of these latter cases was seven years, it would seem, and the payment to the State a low one. On the other hand 'going concerns' permitted an estimate of profitability (though this might not continue), and their continued renting a matter of competitive bidding. The renewed leases were also for a shorter period – three years.

The question then arises of the nature and definition of the payment made to the State. The *Poletai* records of 367/6 BC show, as Ardaillon sought to argue long ago, that the payment for a mine was a rent, which he calls a *fermage*, paid in advance, as opposed to a proportional payment and a fixed tax, or a proportional payment only, which would have to be levied retrospectively. In the case of new mines there was paid some agreed sum sufficiently low to induce risk-taking and an outlay of capital. Then when the mine was a going concern, and when the first lease came to an end, either the previous concessionary (continuing the undertaking) or a new lessee paid a sum based on the previous profits, though how these were checked it is impossible to say. There was room for dishonesty – the possible explanation of a passage in Demosthenes:[119] 'Why is it you prosecuted Moirokles for misappropriating twenty drachmae out of the sums paid by each of the lessees of the mines?' Perhaps some principle like that of *antidosis* (exchange of properties) was adopted. The finding of a rich vein could hardly be concealed – either its working, the treatment of the ore, or the disposal of the silver – and thus there would be counter-bidding for the concession. It is not easy, on the other hand, to see how the payment of one twenty-fourth on a new mine (mentioned by the *Suda*) was calculated, *unless*, in addition to the initial payment (of twenty drachmae) there was a proportional payment subsequently. The proportion, it may be pointed out, is less than on public or sacred land, 4·16 percent compared to 8 percent, but the latter calculation was easier, certainty of return greater, and except on the occasion of a 'lucky strike' mining concessions were probably less sought after than land for cultivation.

The payment of a predetermined rent is an assumption which explains the obvious desire of (Xenophon) and Hyperides to see an increase in the number of the mines worked. The severe punishment of those cutting down supporting pillars[120] arose not only from a desire for safety, but also from a wish to prevent an attempt to increase the amount of ore produced beyond that reckoned from the previous lease periods. The predetermined rent best explains the one hundred talents of the State's share in 483 BC. If, as Ardaillon points out, we seek to connect this with the one twenty-fourth of the *Suda* on a proportional basis, then we reach astronomical figures for mined material (according to Ardaillon, in this case, a hundred talents = 945,000 tons of ore). Such an idea and the calculations are to be viewed with extreme doubt. It is far better to regard the hundred talents as income from rents of concessions, many of which came to nothing. Here again, however, there is a difficulty. Was this income that of one year or spread over a number? It is perhaps better to ignore the events of 483 BC in discussing the procedures of the fourth century.

This idea of rent in advance might adversely affect small and poor potential concessionaires if it was collected in advance and not paid in instalments. On the other hand for new or re-opened mines the sum required was not great. In the case of going concerns (*ergasima*) partnerships could be formed (*koinoniai*) of several persons, one of whom was responsible to the State (cf. Epikrates in Hyperides' speech). This, being common elsewhere in tax-collecting contracts,[121] is probably the explanation of a reference in Demosthenes:[122] 'the three talents for which I became liable' – the liability of a chief contractor (*archones*) who like all debtors to the State owed double if the original sum was not paid on time.

The manner of collecting sums due is obscure in the extreme. There *is* an example of a slave being sent somewhere with a sum due.[123] It would seem that the money could be paid at once to the *apodektai* (receivers of finance), but the collecting seems also to have been bid for, like the collection of other State dues, under the name of *aponomai*, obscurely defined by Harpokration as a portion of the proceeds of the mines received by the State, or as being divided among a number of contractors (*misthotai*) in order that each may receive some portion.

The increased importance of the mines necessitated the development of regulations to control their exploitation and to serve as a basis for the regulation of the inevitable disputes which arose from them. The whole is summed up under the term *metallikos nomos*, giving rise to *metallikai dikai* (cf. the *emporikos nomos* and *emporikai dikai*) tried in the *metallikon dikasterion*,[124] presided over by the *Thesmothetai*. The code dealt with special not general offences. Some of the offences are given as follows:

If a man ejects another from his [mining activity . . .]; if a man fills the workings with smoke . . . ; if he takes up arms . . . ; if he engages in additional excavation within [another man's] boundaries [*metra*].

Again:

the *metallikai dikai* are concerned with those who share in a mine, and those who bore through to another mine into the works of those adjacent; and in general with those working the mines and doing one or other of those acts defined in the law—but not the ordinary disputes and actions which arise out of any relation . . . transgressing the common laws, according to which it befits all men to give and receive justice . . .[125]

It should be noted that filling workings with smoke is not necessarily malicious, since fire was used for breaking down the rock. There is an alternative reading (*hyphapsēi*), which may be underground arson directed against timbering or ore for destructive purposes. We may add the charge of operating an unregistered mine (*anapographōn metallōn dike*).

To avoid dishonest or clandestine exploitation of the mines the State had to rely on informers. If we may believe Hyperides the Athenian courts were careful not to pay too much attention to informers lest prospectors hesitated to take on new mines. He argues that this enlightened policy of the courts had led to an increase in new mines. This is difficult to understand since it can hardly be reconciled with the principle that a preliminary payment at a standard rate was made for *kainotomai*. He surely is referring to *ergasima* or *anasaxima*. This seems to follow from the case he cites, of the discomfiture of the informer Lysander in connection with the mine of Epikrates of Pallene, which he charged Epikrates with having dug '*entos tōn metrōn*' (which must mean 'going beyond the proper limits'). This mine Epikrates had worked for 'three years already' in partnership, Lysander stated, 'with pretty well the richest of those in the city'. Lysander went on to promise that he would benefit the city to the tune of three hundred talents, 'for so much have they received from the mine'. It is natural also to assume that the previous reference in the same speech (*For Euxenippos*):[126] 'And Teisis of Agryle having first registered the property of Euthycrates as being the property of the State [confiscate], which was more than sixty talents', also refers to mining, as the following case is expressly said to do: 'promising to register [i.e. for confiscation] the property of Philippos and Nausicles, and asserting that they have become wealthy through unregistered mines . . .'

Some of the sums mentioned are obviously an exaggeration, on someone's part, like Lysander's three hundred talents. There is not quite the same reason to suspect an exaggeration, let alone a gross exaggeration, in the above mentioned sixty talents or more, as a total fortune. We cannot be sure that this instance refers to mining only and not to other sources of wealth. Any estimates turn on the manner of calculation of the income from *ergasima* and the State share prepaid on the basis of the previous income from such mines. If the 1/24 of the *Suda* is accepted, in the case of the *Poletai* lists of 367/6 BC, where payments range from 1550 to 50 drachmae, the total incomes from these mines would range from 6·2 talents to 12 minae, providing no account is taken of competitive bidding. The examples from the speeches are much the same. The plaintiff in Demosthenes xlii owes three talents to the State = double 30 minae for himself and two partners in connection with a confiscated mine. In another speech (unfortunately in one of those 'documents' which pepper the speeches of the Demosthenic *corpus*) there is mention of a mine 'bought' for 90 minae. Does this represent a total silver production of 22 talents 50 minae? Some high prices appear in the *Poletai* lists:[127] one is given as 2 talents 5550 drachmae (or 17,550), and is designated *palaion anasaximon* (its original state); but as M. Crosby points out (loc. cit.) it must surely be *ergasimon*). Other prices are 6100 drachmae, 3500 drachmae and 2000 drachmae. On the basis of the *Suda* proportion (1/24) these would represent total production in the first (*ergasimon*) concession period of 73 talents 7·5 minae; 25 talents 25 minae; 14 talents 25 minae; 8 talents 20 minae. These figures are impressive even if spread over a working period of three years, rather than seven. They make the 22 talents 50 minae (above) less unconvincing! And the whole question turns on the *Suda*'s 1/24. There we must leave it.

That mining was not on all occasions profitable seems to be the meaning of the grant of *ateleia* (freedom from public financial obligations and war-tax) on the income from mining activity. It is not known when it was instituted. Less easy also to evaluate are the lamentations of those engaged in mining activity. When *ateleia* was instituted mining was freed from the disability which still lay on income from land which could not be concealed and enjoyed no *ateleia* (while investment in trade overseas could be concealed, but was a chancy business). Whenever possible, land cultivation seems to have been preferred for its better and safer return. For the fluctuations of the fourth century and the relationship of cultivation to mining activity the evidence is clear.[128] Such fluctuations were mainly influenced by the price of foreign corn. In Demosthenes xlii the speaker, a man with mining interests, opposed to a cultivator in an issue of *antidosis* (a challenge to exchange of property) has the following points to make probably at a date late in the fourth century BC. He admits that reversals of prosperity are universal, but embarks on a tale of woe in connection with those engaged in mining:

For my own part I would have been only too glad to see myself in prosperous circumstances, as I used to be, and remaining in the Three Hundred [i.e. of the richest citizens]. But since I have shared the general misfortunes of all those engaged in the mining works, and have also incurred special losses of a ruinous nature in my own business, and now on this last occasion I have to pay to the State three talents, a talent for every share – for I was a partner, I am sorry to say, in a confiscated mine – I am under the necessity of trying to take the place of a man who is richer than myself . . .

Elsewhere he adds:

I have in former times by my own bodily labour and exertions reaped considerable profits from silver-working – I acknowledge it, but I have lost all my gains, except a small fraction. Phaenippus should now take his turn, since the people in the mining works have been unfortunate, and you agriculturists enjoy more than your fair share of prosperity.

He goes into more detail on this:

You, who are now selling from your farm barley at eighteen drachmae and wine at twelve drachmae, are a rich man, as one might expect, when you produce more than fifteen hundred bushels of corn and above seven thousand measures of wine.

There is special pleading, of course, but such situations are manifest in a number of sources, including the *Poletai* lists. Much the same idea is clear from the pamphlet *On Ways and Means*:

Why then, someone might say, do not many people now too, as they did formerly, open new mines? Because those concerned with the mines are poorer. For [only] lately are they being developed again. There is a great risk for one who opens a new mine. On the one hand he who finds success becomes rich; he, on the other, who does not, loses all his outlay. The men of the present day have little urge to tackle this risk.

This tendency clearly was even more pronounced than the writer liked to admit; hence the establishment of *ateleia*.[129]

What the nature of this *ateleia* exactly was cannot be said with certainty. Holders of mining concessions do not always seem to have been free of *eisphora* (war-tax) and *leitourgiai* (public financial burdens). It has been suggested that the capital engaged in the mines and *ergasteria* and the *current* year's income from them were not liable to these imposts, but an accumulated fortune from those sources was. We do not really know, but the important point is that the idea of *ateleia* was introduced as an encouragement to mining, though it had not always been so, and the date of its introduction is uncertain.

In the fifth century B C the mines had been exposed to a military peril, in the late fourth to an economic one. The latest *Poletai* records belong to the later part of the fourth century and the beginning of the third. The speech of Hyperides quoted above belongs to the year 324/ 3 B C. Until towards the end of the fourth century the mines seem to have been of a fair importance, but then the decline of Athens, and the flood of Alexander coin-issues, much reduced the incentive to mine precious metal, and produce a universally acceptable coinage. On the other hand the later elaborately produced New Coinage probably used the silver of earlier coins.[130]

The author of the pamphlet *On Ways and Means*, in urging the further development of the mines, frequently emphasizes, like Aeschylus, this great god-given resource of Athens. He asserts that the mines are capable of infinite expansion. Silver is universally acceptable, especially as a return cargo. Men can never have enough of it. He believes, rather naïvely, that the ordinary effects of supply and demand do not operate in the case of this precious metal, unlike other natural and industrial products of which a surplus produces a fall in price and in production. The reverse, he says, is true of silver. For him silver was the superior metal; for good reason, as he observes of the return cargoes of the merchants: 'wherever they sell it, they gain more than their outlay'. This, in addition to the policy of keeping the coinage at a high level of weight and fineness,[131] made Athenian coinage famous over a wide area, and the head of Athena and the owl familiar even on the outskirts of the Greek world. Athens gained in many ways from this, as from her position as a banking centre in the fourth century. Xenophon clearly felt that this state of affairs would last for ever, but the same power which struck a mortal blow against the political basis of the State of Athens removed also this prop of Athens' economic importance, first when Philip II of Macedon developed the resources of

Crenides (Philippi), throwing on the market, it was said, a thousand talents yearly of gold and silver, followed then by Alexander's distribution of the treasures of Persia, even as this had been preceded by the distribution of four thousand talents of gold and six thousand talents of silver, the pillage of the Delphic treasure in the Third Sacred War.

The importance, it may be said in conclusion, of the Attic mines, is not only their wider economic aspect, but, in comparison to other activities, the unique amount of information available on this one Greek industry.

CHAPTER TEN

STATES OTHER THAN ATHENS:
A BRIEF SURVEY INTO
THE HELLENISTIC PERIOD

THE TRADE AND INDUSTRY of other Greek states, less well documented than that of Athens, were similar in nature if not in dimensions.[1] A great interest in precious metals and in mining, and certain State commercial arrangements existed, as, for example, those relating to the wine trade of Thasos or the *miltos* of Cea. Unfortunately, no systematic treatment deals with the trade of, say, Corinth or Miletus – this would have been alien to the Greek approach. The principal interest, in food supplies and particularly corn, was underlined by the concern shown to facilitate commercial relations by means of *proxenia*, *asylia*, contracts, the expediting of the settlement of disputes, freedom of movement and, especially in the fourth and following centuries, problems of safety on the seas.

After the defeat of Athens in the Great Peloponnesian War her former subjects were no longer dominated by her, but very often appear, despite her efforts in the Second Athenian League, as her rivals in attempting to deal with the manifold problems of the fourth century B C.

There was no change in technological methods and no introduction of new materials.[2] As a source of power human force remained paramount, though there was later, very much later, some development of the use of animal and water-power. There was also an improvement in lifting tackle. Hiero's steam engine, however, remained a toy: its potential was not realized or exploited. The main issue was the efficient employment of human labour, the means of marshalling and controlling it. Such labour came from a free peasantry, from an urban proletariat, and from slaves. Agriculture and other cultivation was capable of being organized into units of a larger size, but not very large, and in the Hellenistic period it could be bureaucratically controlled, as in Egypt and Pergamene Asia Minor, but not in Greece. Cattle raising could be conducted on a considerable scale as the Romans later showed, but it is unclear how far manufacturing industry could be organized into large units.

The main objective of the Successors of Alexander was the raising of revenue, not the well-being of the subject, and the securing and extension of personal dominion. Following on the decay of the Achaemenid Persian power and Alexander's conquests, Greeks, Greek culture and Greek arts spread far to the East, to Afghanistan and north-western India, and exercised influence even farther afield. These developments were to the advantage of craftsmen and traders, dispersing the former widely in the East, and, with the formation of very large political units, facilitating the travel of the latter – mainly by sea, since the means of transport by land remained primitive and slow even when roads were available.[3] Ships seem not to have been conspicuously larger than before, and the means of propulsion were the same. The limited references in our sources to large ships indicate that they were a rarity; harbour accommodation and facilities made smaller ships more useful.[4] Apart from the carriage of corn, cargoes were mixed, in small packets, and determined by the prevailing nature of coasting trade, as is indicated by undersea archaeology – witness (for imperishable objects) the fourth-century ship found off the coast of northern Cyprus (Kyrenia), and the later vessel found off Marseilles.[5]

Maritime trade-routes were gradually extended to the Red Sea, the Persian Gulf and the Indian Ocean, ultimately with the use of the south-west monsoon. In the reverse direction there were the two Silk Routes, north and south of the region east of the Black Sea, and the incense route from southern Arabia. Mainland Greece gradually declined as an area of trade: the Romans destroyed Corinth in 146 BC. The route to the Black Sea remained, and the great cities of western Asia Minor flourished, despite the problem of the silting of harbours. The main east–west trade-route moved southwards to the open seas to replace that by way of Corinth. A particular phenomenon from the fourth century BC was the development of Rhodes as a mercantile centre and great naval power, until the animosity of Rome caused her decline, and the establishment of Delos as a free port in 166 BC, the centre of the slave trade and of the Italian merchants until it was destroyed by Mithridates VI of Pontus (88 BC). Contact with the Middle East and farther east meant the development of the commerce of the Syrian cities, and the increased importance, under the Ptolemies, of Egypt and particularly of Egyptian Alexandria. Wholly decisive was the rise of Rome and her victories over the Hellenistic monarchs and Carthage, the final effect of which was the unifying of the Mediterranean under her control.

Some interesting material can be extracted from the mercantile speeches of the Demosthenic *Corpus* on non-Athenian business in the later fourth century when, as it makes clear, travel, trade and financial arrangements had become increasingly complicated, and the objects of trade very diverse.

The speech of Demosthenes against Xenothemis (xxxii) which concerns a ship and its cargo of corn, involves not only Athens, but Syracuse, Massilia and Cephallenia and not only Athenians but also Massiliotes, and the magistrates of Cephallenia.[6] Again, the speech against Apaturius (xxxiii) concerns not only Athens, but also Byzantium, Sicily, Ophrynium on the Hellespont and the Thracian Chersonese; two of the principals are Byzantines.[7] The speech against Phormio (xxxiv) relates to Athens, Bosporus (= Panticapaeum) and Acanthus. It is characterized by snippets of information, as is so often the case (cf. xxxv below). Among those involved is a Phoenician; reference is made to corn and bread distribution in Athens, to gifts of corn, to the harbour-masters' records at Panticapaeum, and to the fact that around the time of the transactions dealt with in the speech business in South Russia (Panticapaeum) was slack on account of a war between Paerisades and the Scythians[8] – indicating the vulnerability of both the corn trade in South Russia and of life in general (see below on Olbia, n. 41). There are even more of such snippets in the speech against Lacritus (xxxv). It concerns not only Athens but Mende, the Scythian Bosporus, the Black Sea coast to the mouth of the Dnieper (Borysthenes), Theodosia, Hieron (Teichos) in Bithynia; and not only an Athenian, but a Carystian, three Phaselites, including Lacritus a pupil of Isocrates, a Cypriote, a Chian moneylender in Pontus, and, if one of the depositions is genuine, a further lender, a Halicarnassian.[10] The speech contains also a wide variety of other mercantile information.[9] Finally, in the speech against Dionysodorus (lvi) the ship involved was engaged in the Egyptian corn trade via Rhodes. The issue was its halting at Rhodes – illegally since the loan on it was made at Athens: how much interest was to be paid on the loan? Points of interest mentioned include the manoeuvres of Cleomenes in Egypt[11] and the organized transmission of commercial information across the Aegean.[12]

These speeches provide some interesting details on cargoes. Corn is, of course, predominant,[13] but there are other items: possibly three hundred passengers[14] and a deck cargo of one thousand hides;[15] on another occasion a proposed cargo of three thousand jars of Mendean wine.[16] We hear (in the South Russian coasting trade) of salt fish and sour Coan wine,[17] two or three bales of wool, eleven or twelve jars of

fish and two or three bundles of goat-skins – minor tramp-shipping
cargo indeed, in contrast to the great convoys of corn ships.

Important for the fourth century and later is the ever-increasing
body of inscriptions relating to 'Greece' in the sense this term is used in
the title of this book – therefore excluding the great source (relevant
for Egypt) represented by the papyri. Some of the information they
supply will now be considered.[18]

(a) FOOD SUPPLIES AND OTHER COMMODITIES

Many sources of information[19] indicate suppliers of commodities and
state preoccupation with them. Macedonia, 'the timber yard of
Athens',[20] held a strategic position as a supplier, its importance is indicated by the treaty between Athens and Perdiccas (423/2 BC),[21] and
that between Amyntas and the Chalcidians (between 389 and 383 BC),
on the export of wood and pitch.[22]

Some details survive about other important materials, such as wool
from Miletus,[23] flax from Amorgos,[24] Phasis and Carthage,[25] but such
information tends to be sporadic. There is a clear emphasis on marketing regulations and the control of prices. The Thasian wine trade has
been dealt with already (above, pp. 94–95). Evidence for the wine
trade, by reason of the imperishable nature of the amphorae with their
stamps, is provided by the remains of sunken ships.[26] Apparently there
could be state intervention in wine importation as in that of corn. This
must be the meaning of one section of a decree of the Olbiopolitans
(c. 230 BC) in honour of a certain Protogenes who came to their aid
when they had purchased a quantity of wine for three hundred
staters and then found they had no money to pay for it![27]

Other examples of commodity and price control relate to the
marketing of wool at Chios in the second half of the fourth century,[28]
to the sale of wood and charcoal in Delos,[29] and of fish at Acraephia.[30]
What amounts to commodity control (of corn, wine and olive-oil)
figures (together with the manipulation of coinage) among the rather
desperate devices adopted by impoverished states in the later fourth
century.[31] Control of prices was essential in the fourth century BC and
later. There are some scattered references to actual prices, for example
at Delos for various categories of cattle – oxen, sheep and goats.[32] Corn
prices are widely given in honorific decrees to demonstrate the gener-
osity of those who sold corn in a crisis at a price below that in the
market. This is certainly, as at Athens, an index of the economic
difficulties of the times, and it is tempting also to deduce from the

cattle prices at Delos, for example, a considerable decline in the value of money between the earlier and later fourth century.[33]

Obviously connected with the control and facilitation of trade was the control of currency, represented earlier by the well-known Athenian imperial currency decree, and a later one which may have the same meaning.[34] A clear example is the currency decree of Olbia, of the first half of the fourth century BC.[35]

In some respects opposed to facilitation was the urge to tax imports and exports of commodities and property in order to raise revenue, as with the two percent tax (*pentekoste*) at Athens and elsewhere. It was a universal practice (for its collection see n. 94 below) except in free ports, and started at any early date, as appears to be indicated by an inscription probably of the mid-sixth century from Ephesus.[36] As time passed such taxes were very frequently remitted by grants of immunity to win the favour and co-operation of merchants.

Epigraphical sources make clear the paramount pre-occupation with corn supply, not only at Athens but everywhere else also, from the fifth century onwards, occasioned by such happenings as the universal grain shortage of 357 BC. In each century it was bound up closely with inter-state hostilities and piracy, which ultimately involved the Roman corn trade until in 67 BC Pompey the Great produced the more or less final solution. At all times the corn supply was vital and corn-shortage (*sitodeia*) was the menace. In the fifth century, apart from the operations of the Imperial Athenians, there is the inscription of about 470 BC declaring public imprecations at Teos on those hindering the importation of corn by land or by sea (this in fertile Ionia!), and appropriately enough on those carrying out brigandage or receiving pirates by land or sea in what may have been a disturbed period in that area.[37] From the fourth century onwards this problem of *sitodeia* remained, making the sea lanes difficult and dangerous, particularly the main corn route from South Russia to the Aegean. On it at the narrow Hellespont was Sestos, called 'the corn bin of the Piraeus'.[38] Some of the causes of these dangers have been explored in connection with Athens. Natural disasters and the effects of war produced devastation and neglect in the fourth century and later.[39] Among those preoccupied about their corn supply are some where this would not be expected, in the Black Sea area, such as Istros,[40] and Olbia. Olbia lay in a very fertile area of South Russia; none the less an inscription of exceptional interest, already mentioned,[41] of around 230 BC indicates impoverishment, corn shortage, and neglect of fortifications and the State merchant ships. This led Protogenes, who must have been very wealthy – there is repeatedly a contrast between wealthy individuals and poverty-stricken states – to come to the city's aid in connection with both corn supplies on a number of occasions and the repair of fortifications. There was a threat of barbarian attack, such as might often menace a city on the outposts of Hellenism, and in consequence its customers. What was true of Olbia could be true of other places and periods, and dangers both in South Russia and at the Hellespont would have profound effects on the corn supply.[42] The following inscriptions show the diverse involvement of cities and peoples in this matter:

Fourth Century. Gyges of Torone (at the end of the fourth century) was honoured for the importation of corn.[43] A decree of Mytilene relates to corn import from South Russia (not much before mid-fourth century) as a benefaction of the ruler Leucon and his sons.[44]

Third Century. The Coans thank the cities of Thessaly for sending corn in a time of scarcity.[45] Citizenship was granted to a Rhodian for services to the Ephesian corn supply c. 300 BC; the same man is named *proxenos* and benefactor about the same date by Arkesine in Amorgos.[46] The needs of Olbia have already been mentioned. A decree of Histiaea was set up at Delos in honour of Athenodorus of Rhodes (230–220 BC), granting citizenship for services in contributing money free of interest, and expediting the work of corn-purchase commissioners.[47] Two inscriptions of this period are of special interest. The first relates to an oath to be taken at Chersonesus (Cherronesus) in the Crimea (= Chersonesus Taurica), which deals with the restriction of corn export, c. 300–280 BC, from the *pedion* and elsewhere, to the city only – not so much a matter of conserving supplies locally as establishing a closer check on exports and the revenue from them.[48] The other records the importation of corn into Samothrace (228–225 BC) from the Chersonese with the permission of the Ptolemaic commander Hippomedon. Which Chersonese this is, Tauric or Thracian, is unclear; more important is that the Ptolemies rarely permitted unrestricted trade in corn – to protect the interests of Egypt?[49]

Second Century. A reference to corn shortage appears in an inscription of Methymna[50] and there is also the corn law of Samos.[51]

(b) PIRACY AND WAR

An important factor in trade and travel was safety on the seas. Less is heard of the dangers of travel by land; perhaps these were regarded as easier to guard against. The background of the whole problem was the ancient concept of the stranger as having no rights except in his own state; elsewhere he was the object of justifiable depredation and protected only by guest friendship and Zeus Xenios. The robbery of strangers was no crime and the pursuit of piracy bore no stigma. All this is apparent from the Homeric poems and implicit much later (around 450 BC) in the treaty of the Ozolian Locrian towns of Oeanthea and Chaleum which shows an early effort to regulate such matters between two states.[52] It is to be noted that something like a state form of piracy could be practised, as by the Samians under Polycrates and earlier.[53] The battle against piracy was an up-hill one, indeed never decisively concluded. The powers effective to check it or put it down had to combine mercantile interest and naval strength, as did Athens and Rhodes. Athens crushed the pirates of Scyros, and as a great imperial power policed particularly the Black Sea–Aegean trade-route. Clearly she was not so effective in the fourth century, though she attempted to do something in that period about the Adriatic pirates.[54] Her successor was Rhodes in the eastern Mediterranean until her decline, and ultimately Rome. Of outstanding interest and importance is an inscription which makes clear the function of the Rhodian republic in the keeping down of piracy. This is a treaty between Rhodes and Hierapytna in Crete[55] of 220 BC. The Cretans were notorious as pirates. Hierapytna is to provide harbours and bases; in the case of operations by the Rhodians against pirates or against those harbouring or cooperating with them, Hierapytna is to aid by land and sea. Rhodian naval commanders are to come to the aid of Hierapytnians, and to protect them.

For all that was done, piracy was rife in the fourth century and later. Their haunts included Halonesus (and the pirate Sostratus) in the northern Sporades,[56] the Gulf of Argos,[57] and Alopeconnesus (on the west coast of the Thracian Chersonese) where pirates were associated with wreckers (*katapontistai*).[58] No private travellers were safe.[59] Among others Plato suffered the fate of being captured and was ransomed. The ransoming of those captured by pirates was a meritorious act.[60] Furthermore, there was not necessarily safety on land from pirates, as a fragmentary decree of Amorgos (possibly of the third century) shows: pirates raided Amorgos, seized free men, women and slaves, took one ship and sank others in harbour.[61] A natural recourse was to reach agreement not to engage in piracy or to harbour pirates.[62] 'Admitting' pirates, however, might mean their use as part of military operations (privateering). In this connection an inscription of 200–197 BC is of considerable interest, praising the Rhodian naval commander, Epicrates, in the war of the Rhodians, Islanders and Athenians against Philip V of Macedon, for taking care of the safety of sailors and the protection of the islands, including Delos. There is a reference to a *diagramma* ordaining that 'those privateering against the enemy shall operate from their own harbours, but no one shall use a base of operations in Delos'.[63]

There were also dangers for sailors from the land. The Thracians went in for wrecking on an organized basis.[64] There was also the danger to shipwrecked sailors from wild coastal inhabitants especially in the Black Sea. For instance safety is guaranteed (*c.* 250 BC) to Coan sailors by a king of Bithynia: both a general assurance of safety, and protection to those shipwrecked on the coast.[65]

For some of these dangers there was the solution of convoying,[66] which in turn led to convoy protection by fleet commanders of Athens for personal gain, the so-called 'benevolences' (*eunoiai*)[67].

Finally, there were dangers to trade from regular military operations, which sometimes had to be dealt with by a military reaction.[68] There was also general danger to property, which could be tackled in the way indicated by an agreement between Erythrae and Hermeas of Atarneus, providing for the deposit with him of goods during a military emergency.[69]

All of this made commerce difficult. There was also the problem of the barriers, political and legal, which stood between the citizens of different states. Exclusiveness died hard, and the 'stranger within the gates' suffered from various disabilities, both as visiting and resident aliens. The attitudes and procedures of Athens have been dealt with in Chapter V above. The same preoccupations are present in other Greek states and the same means to meet them, characterized by the same self-interest. There is also a distinct tendency at times among neighbours to relax the stance of rigid independence.

(c) Facilitation of Movement and Intercourse

A variety of general political associations or 'customs unions' (to use a modern term) are in evidence – significantly in the Hellenistic period for the most part.[70] The following illustrative examples may be listed in order of date:

(i) Cea and Histiaea (before 363/2 BC). Mutual rights of citizenship and commerce, and unimpeded freedom of import and export were established.[71]

(ii) Miletus and Sardis (before 334 BC?). Freedom of movement and trade for citizens of both cities.[72]

(iii) Miletus and Olbia (a little after 334 BC). *Isopoliteia.* Equality of status in both states; freedom from payment of duty; the contracts of the Milesians in Olbia to be dealt with in the same way as those of the Olbiopolitans.[73]

(iv) Teos and Lebedus (around 303 BC). Synoecism (city union). Promoted by letters and a *diagramma* of King Antigonus. General regularization of *proxenia* arrangements, plaints, debts and contracts. New system of laws, and regulation of the movement of commodities. Establishment of a formal general agreement (*syntheke*), with Mytilene as *ekkletos polis* (arbiter) in case of difficulties.[74]

(v) The Messenians and Phigalea (250–222 BC). *Isopoliteia* and right of intermarriage. No actual mention is made of commercial arrangements or the like, but there is reference to *symbola*.[75]

(vi) Chios and the Aetolian League (mid-third century). Citizenship of Chios to the Aetolians; Aetolian *asylia* for the Chiotes. It looks at first like an empty gesture, but it could have potential benefits.[76]

Apart from these fairly complete arrangements involving whole communities, there were those privileges accorded to individuals which must have been of significance. The frequently repeated formula was:

To X, who ever says and does what he can for the benefit of [name of state]; to be proxenos and benefactor, with the right of acquiring land and house ... with freedom from seizure [*asylia*] in war and peace, entering the harbour and leaving it, with freedom from duty [*ateleia*] on exports and imports ... approach to the Council and the Assembly.[77]

They are the same privileges which were accorded by the Athenians, but *politeia* (citizenship) which is rare at Athens appears more frequently elsewhere. It is to be noted that non-Greeks also could adopt the same system. Thus Paerisades of Bosporus and his sons grant the same honours to a man of Euxine Piraeus (Amisus).[78]

Proxenia was an office of old standing. The earliest known proxeny decree belongs to Eretria (of the first third of the fifth century), and is by a quarter of a century older than the next, of about mid-fifth century.[79] The office was even earlier if Alexander I of Macedon was really *proxenos* of Athens.[80] As at Athens, distinguished men received *proxenia* (with other honours) elsewhere, so Conon at Erythrae and Mausollus.[81] We have already seen (Chapter V) that at Athens *proxenia* could be a real and onerous office; the same is apparent elsewhere, as is shown by the *proxenia* given by the Cnidians to Iphiades of Abydos, at a time (before 360 BC?) when there was only one *proxenos* of a state in another, and so this was a supernumerary *proxenia* for practical purposes. Later grants of *proxenia* became very numerous,[82] and there were also grants of hereditary *proxenia*.[83] But it must be doubtful that it ever became a 'joke', augmented as it was by other privileges, some of them carefully detailed.[84] These curious generosities occur from time to time, as at Zeleia (the Troad),[85] a grant of citizenship is attended by a plot of land, a house, two hundred amphorae and freedom from market taxes – in effect the setting up of the new citizen in business. It may be observed, finally, that where *proxenia* might be expected (or where it has already been granted) commendation and a crown takes its place.[86] But the basic principle is always there, the encouragement of inter-state service.

Asylia has been commented on already, in relation to its opposite, the right of seizure (*sylān*).[87] It was a relatively ancient institution (see on Oianthea and Chaleum above),[88] and at a later period it was much lavished on individuals and on communities, as by the Aetolian League.[89] In practical terms it could be a considerable advantage to merchants, giving them freedom from internal seizure, and in certain cases a right of seizure, as is clear from honours given by Ilium to three Tenedians (around 300 B C): 'And if they are wronged by some stranger, seizure is permitted from the Ilian territory'.[90] In reverse this may explain the meaning of Demosthenes XXXV 13: 'unloading the goods where there is no right of seizure against *Athenians*'.

Ateleia was a privilege that represented a loss of revenue to the state granting it, unless it was reciprocal between two states. It might grant freedom from public financial burdens,[91] or be total (*ateleia hapantōn*),[92] or more restricted and detailed.[93] It was all part of an effort to conciliate aliens, including metics.[94]

Further, judicial treaties and the suits based on them (*dikai apo symbolōn*) have been discussed at length in connection with Athens. They were widely used, as in the Cretan *koinon*, in the Aetolian League and elsewhere.[95]

Certain recurring problems militated against trade: debt and debt-settlement,[96] the intervention of the Hellenistic kings and their commanders, and chronic impoverishment like that of Arkesine in Amorgos, pledging everything for a loan of three talents from a private individual,[97] piracy and war. In fact little remained favourable for trade after the time of the Athenian Empire.

I Italy, Sicily and the Western Mediterranean

II   The Eastern Mediterranean and the Black Sea

III *Greece and the Western Aegean*

IV   The Aegean and Western Asia Minor

ABBREVIATIONS

ANCIENT TEXTS

Aesch.	Aeschines
Andoc.	Andocides
Appian, *BC*	Appian, *Bellum Civile*
Arist. *Constit. of Athens*	Aristotle, *Constitution of Athens*
Pol.	*Politics*
Rhet.	*Rhetoric*
Aristoph.	Aristophanes, *Acharn*(ians), *Birds*, *Clouds*, *Eccles*(iazusae), *Frogs*, *Knights*, *Lys*(istrata), *Peace*, *Plutus*, *Thesm*(ophoriazusai)
Athen. *Deipn.*	Athenaeus, *Deipnosophistae*
Bekker, *Anecd. Graec.*	Bekker, *Anecdota Graeca*
Dem.	Demosthenes
Didymus	Didymus, *Commentary on Demosthenes*
Dio. Sic.	Diodorus Siculus
Dion. Hal.	Dionysius of Halicarnassus
Eur.	Euripides (followed by title)
Her.	Herodotus
Hyper.	Hyperides
Isocr.	Isocrates
Lyc.	Lycurgus
Lys.	Lysias
Ox. Hist.	*Oxyrrhynchus Historian*
Paus.	Pausanias
Pliny Sen. *NH*	Pliny Senior, *Naturalis Historia*
Plut.	Plutarch, *Lives* given by name of subject
	Mor. = *Moralia*
	Vit. X Or. = *Vitae X Oratorum*
Polyb.	Polybius
Pollux	Pollux, Julius, *Onomasticon*
Ps.-Arist, *Oec.*	Pseudo-Aristotle, *Oeconomica*
Ps.-Xen. or (Xenophon)	Pseudo-Xenophon, *Athenaiôn Politeia* = *The Old Oligarch*
Soph.	Sophocles (followed by title)
Theophr.	Theophrastus: *Charac.*, *Characters*
	Hist. Plant., *Historia Plantarum*
Thuc.	Thucydides
Xen.	Xenophon: *Cyr.*, *Cyropaedia*
	Hell., *Hellenica*
	Oec., *Oeconomicus*
	Mem., *Memorabilia*
(Xen.)	Pseudo-Xenophon = *Peri Porôn* = *De Vectigalibus* = *On Ways and Means*

MODERN PUBLICATIONS

AA	*Archäologischer Anzeiger* (see *JdI* below)
AR	*Archaeological Reports* (Hellenic Society and the British School at Athens)
AJA	*American Journal of Archaeology*
BCH	*Bulletin de Corréspondence Hellénique*
Beloch	Beloch, K. J., *Die Bevölkerung der griechisch-römischen Welt* (1886)
BMQ	*British Museum Quarterly*
Boeckh	Boeckh, A., *Die Staatshaushaltung der Athener*[3] (1886)
CAF	Kock, T., *Comicorum Atticorum Fragmenta* i–iii (1880–88)
CAH	*Cambridge Ancient History*
CIA	*Corpus Inscriptionum Atticarum*
CP	*Classical Philology*
CQ	*Classical Quarterly*
Ditt. *Syll.*[3]	Dittenberger, *Sylloge Inscriptionum Graecarum*, ed. 3 (1915–21)
Edmonds	Edmonds, J. M., *The Fragments of Attic Comedy* (1957–61)
EHR	*Economic History Review*
FdD	*Fouilles de Delphes* (1902–77)
FGH	Jacoby, F., *Fragmente der griechischen Historiker* (1954–55)
FHG	Müller, *Fragmenta Historicorum Graecorum* (1860–81)
GDI	Collitz-Bechtel-Hoffmann, *Sammlung griechischen Dialekt Inschriften* (1884–1915)
Gernet	Gernet, L., *L'approvisionment d'Athènes en blé au Vième et IVième siècles* (1909)
Jardé	Jardé, A., *Les céréales dans l'antiquité grecque* (1925)
JdI	*Jahrbuch des Deutschen archäologischen Instituts* (Berlin)
IG	*Inscriptiones Graecae*
JHS	*Journal of Hellenic Studies*
NC	*Numismatic Chronicle*
OCT	*Oxford Classical Texts*
PA	Kirchner, J., *Prosopographia Attica* (1901–03)
PEQ	*Palestine Exploration Fund Quarterly*
RE	Pauly-Wissowa-Kroll, *Realencyclopädie des classischen Altertumswissenschaft*
RFC	*Rivista di Filologia Classica*
RM	*Rheinisches Museum*
SEG	*Supplementum Epigraphicum Graecum* (1923–)
TAPA	*Transactions of the American Philological Association*
Tod, GHI i, ii	Tod, M.N., *Greek Historical Inscriptions* i (1946), ii (1948)

NOTES

INTRODUCTION

1 Her. ii 167.2.

2 'Pale cobblers', Aristoph. *Eccles.* 385–87.

3 Probably of mid-fourth century date. The author is variously given as Xenophon, (Xenophon) or Pseudo-Xenophon. See Chap. iv, n. 66.

4 See M. I. Finley, *Studies in Land and Credit* 254, notes on text.

5 C. H. V. Sutherland, 'Overstrikes and Hoards', *NC* (1942) 1–18.

6 Ibid.

7 Currently in process of study. They are for the earlier period the so-called SOS amphorae. They have of late been noted much more than formerly, e.g. in the western Mediterranean; *AR* (1976–77) 56, 57, 61–62, 65, 67, 71, 73–74. A variety of shapes of amphorae has been studied by Virginia Grace on the basis of the finds from the Athenian Agora. On the SOS amphorae see R. M. Cook, *Greek Painted Pottery* 76, 303, which also gives an excellent account of painted pottery.

8 Originally 'to do with craftsmen', then acquiring a pejorative sense as in modern usage.

9 See n. 2 above. For rivalry of potters and carpenters, see Hesiod, *Works and Days* 25, and Arist. *Rhet.* 1381 b 17.

10 On painted and scratched inscriptions, see R. M. Cook, op. cit. 356; R. Hackl, *Münchener Archäologische Studien* (1919) 1–106; D. A. Amyx, *An amphora with a price inscription*; a recent study of a particular group (from Rhodes) by A. Johnston, *BSA* (1975) 145ff.

11 See R. M. Cook, *JdI* (1959) 118–21. On pots and trade see also R. M. Cook, op. cit. n. 7 above, 271–75, 277.

12 And for heavy textiles (including ship's canvas) not much comes from these sources, as Alison Burford points out, *Craftsmen in Greek and Roman Society* 70 and nn. 153–54.

13 Aristoph. *Knights* 1382ff.

14 Isocr. vii 44–45.

15 Plato, *Laws* 846dff.

16 Xen. *Oec.* iv 2.

17 Ibid. vi 5.

18 Arist. *Rhet.* 1367 a 30.

19 Thuc. ii 38.

20 Plut. *Life of Pericles* 12.

21 Plut. *Life of Cimon* 4.

22 IG^2 678.

23 Menander, *The Peplos Bearer*, fr. 68 (K).

CHAPTER ONE

1 V. R. d'A. Desborough, *The Last Mycenaeans and their Successors* (1964) (hereafter 'Desborough'); A. M. Snodgrass, *The Dark Age of Greece* (1971) (hereafter 'Snodgrass'); R. J. Hopper, *The Early Greeks* (1976) (hereafter 'Hopper').

2 Desborough, passim: Hopper 63–64.

3 Desborough, Gen. Index, under 'New settlers (non-Mycenaeans)'; Snodgrass 142–64; 170–84, 314–17, 323–84; Hopper 64.

4 Thuc. i 12; Hopper 53ff.

5 The most important general work, J. N. Coldstream, *Greek Geometric Pottery* (1968) (hereafter 'Coldstream').

6 The standard work on Protogeometric: V. R. d'A. Desborough, *Protogeometric Pottery* (1952); on Athens and the migration question, J. Cook, *CAH*³ ii 2, 773ff.

7 Thuc. i 2.6; J. Cook, op. cit.; Hopper 68ff.

8 *Istanbuler Mitteilungen* (1958) 126–30; *AR* (1972–73) 39.

9 Thuc. i 2.6; J. Cook, op. cit.

10 Snodgrass, Index under 'Iron'; useful points in Snodgrass, 'The First European Body Armour', in *Studies in honour of C. F. C. Hawkes* (1971) (hereafter 'Hawkes Studies'). Further: iron first from Cyprus, Snodgrass 326; K. R. Maxwell-Hyslop, 'Assyrian sources of iron', *Iraq* (1974) 139ff; D. H. F. Gray 'Metal-working in Homer', *JHS* (1954) 1–15.

11 See preceding note.

12 V. R. d'A. Desborough, op. cit. n. 6 above, 296–305.

13 J. Cook, op. cit. n. 6 above; Hopper 68ff.

14 Coldstream, passim.

15 Coldstream 10ff.

16 On this, Snodgrass, *Hawkes Studies* 41–43.

17 Cf. also the Argive panoply, Snodgrass, *Hawkes Studies* 42ff; Lefkandi, moulds, M. R. Popham, and L. H. Sackett, *Excavations at Lefkandi, Euboea, 1964–66* (1968) 28–29; Coldstream 363f.

18 Coldstream 348–49.

19 Cf. V. Karageorghis, *Salamis in Cyprus* (1969) passim and 28–29.

20 Hesiod, *Works and Days* 219–21; 250–51 and following.

21 Hopper, Chap. 6.

22 See below, p. 104.

23 There is an extensive literature: Hopper 83ff., 235.

24 J. Boardman, *The Greeks Overseas* (1964) 57ff. (hereafter 'Boardman'); T. J. Dunbabin, *The Greeks and their Eastern Neighbours* (1957) 30–31; Hopper 98ff.

25 T. J. Dunbabin, *The Western Greeks* (1948) 211–99.

26 Theophr. *Hist. Plant.* i 7.2; Dioscurides i 1 (*Iris Illyrike*); M. I. Finley on Beaumont, *JHS* (1936) 167, in *Second International Conference of Economic History, Aix-en-Provence 1962* (1965) vol. i, 15 (hereafter 'Finley, Aix-en-Provence 1962*).

27 R. M. Cook, *JdI* (1959) 114–23.

28 T. J. Dunbabin, op. cit. n. 25 above, 7f., metals of Etruria; for Elba and copper, Arist. *de mir. auscult.* 93, 837b. R. M. Cook suggests agriculture, *Historia* (1962) 113–14.

29 D. Ridgway, in C. F. Hawkes, *Greeks, Celts and Romans* (1973) 17–18; Snodgrass, *Hawkes Studies* 43; Coldstream 371.

30 It is to be wondered if the sorrows of Miletus for Sybaris (Her. vi 21) have anything to do with such a route across the 'toe' of Italy. On the whole it is unlikely.

31 Coldstream 352–54 (Ithaca); 228, 367, 370 (Corcyra).

32 Snodgrass, *Hawkes Studies* 42–44.

33 Hesiod, *Works and Days* 630–38.

34 See below, p. 43.

35 See below, p. 45.

36 A. Blakeway, 'Prolegomena to the Study of Greek Commerce with Italy, Sicily and France in the eighth and seventh centuries B.C.', *BSA* (1932–33) 170–208; Coldstream 373–74.

37 G. Vallet and F. Villard, 'Dates de la fondation de Megara Hyblaea et de Syracuse', *BCH* (1952) 289ff.

38 Finley, *Aix-en-Provence 1962* 1ff.

39 Coldstream 370ff.

40 Coldstream 373.

41 D. Harden, *The Phoenicians* (1962) 44ff. For Phoenicians in the West, see *JRS* (1976) 212; *JdI* (1974) 85. For interactions of Greeks, Phoenicians and Carthaginians in Sicily, *AR* (1976–77) 74.

42 *II Chronicles* viii 17–18 (Ezion-Geber); ix 21 (Tarshish).

43 *Iliad* xviii 478ff.

44 See D. Harden, op. cit. 57ff.

45 R. D. Barnett, 'Phoenician and Syrian Ivory Carvings', *PEQ* (1939) 4–19; *A Catalogue of the Nimrud Ivories in the British Museum* (1957); M. E. L. Mallowan, *Nimrud and its Remains* (1966); there are others from Arslan Tash, and fine decoration of a throne from Cypriote Salamis, V. Karageorghis, op. cit. n. 19 above, 82.

46 J. W. and G. M. Crowfoot, *Samaria-Sebaste 2, Early Ivories* (1938). Ahab's wife, Jezebel, was daughter of Ithobaal of Tyre.

47 F. Salviat, *BCH* (1962) 95ff. Samos, *JdI (AA)* (1964) 494.

48 T. J. Dunbabin, *The Eastern Greeks* (1957) 39; Coldstream 361.

49 Fine photographs, E. Akurgal. *Die Kunst Anatoliens* (1961) figs 17–28, The best account of the whole subject: O. W. Muscarella, 'The oriental origins of Siren Cauldron attachments', *Hesperia* 31 (1962) 317–29 (good refs); griffin absent from Urartu (321); assoc.

of Urartu and n. Syria until 742 B C (321, n. 20); origin of 'Siren' attachments in n. Syria (322). There is a division of opinion on origins: K. R. Maxwell-Hyslop and R. D. Barnett, pro-Urartu; O. W. Muscarella, pro-Syria.

50 Gordion: E. Akurgal, op. cit. 70ff; Coldstream 378–80; Hopper 146–48.

51 See below pp. 33–34.

52 Coldstream 347–48.

53 See V. Karageorghis, op. cit. n. 19 above, pl. 5; Attic exports, Coldstream 349, 361, 422–23.

54 Coldstream 320–21, 385–86; Boardman passim; G. Hanfmann, *Hetty Goldman Studies* 165–84.

55 Rhodes: Coldstream 380ff., 418; Rhodian faience, Boardman 144; Crete, Coldstream 415–17.

56 E. Kunze, *Kretische Bronzereliefs* (1931); ivories, Coldstream 347–48, 357.

57 E. Kunze, op. cit.; jewellery, J. Boardman, *BSA* (1967) 57ff.; Coldstream 361; R. A. Higgins, *BMQ* xxiii 101–7; *Greek and Roman Jewellery* (1961) 95ff., for types and general; E. L. Smithson, *Hesperia* (1968) 77ff.

58 Coldstream, see n. 55 above.

59 Homer, *Odyssey* xv 403ff.

60 *Odyssey* iv 615–19.

61 *Odyssey* xviii 290–300. The earrings were probably thought of as of the type known in the Near East, though at a 15th–14th century date, cf. K. R. Maxwell-Hyslop, *Western Asiatic Jewellery* (1971) 116.

62 On early Etruscan jewellery, R. A. Higgins, op. cit. n. 57 above, 133ff.

63 M. Guido, *Sardinia* (1963); B. H. Warmington, *Carthage* (1964) 1ff.; W. F. Albright, *The Archaeology of Palestine* (1949) 123; R. Carpenter, *AJA* (1964) 178. See also n. 55.

64 In the possession of the Hispanic Society of America. W. F. Albright, op. cit. 123; Boardman, 219.

65 Boardman, 219. The question of the earliest Phoenician penetration of the West is again involved with Spain and the site of Almunecar (ancient Sexi?), where, in the earliest cemetery seventh-century material occurs, including Protocorinthian pottery, which seems to provide a date for the earliest settlement. It has been suggested that 'Egyptian' influence is present, which may relate to scarabs from Tanis in the Egyptian Delta. It is obscure whether these scarabs are to be dated to 870–847 or later (the difficulties of dating late scarabs are notorious); the prevailing opinion is that the Protocorinthian pottery gives the date. The site is called, by J. Heurgon, 'the earliest Phoenician necropolis in Spain' ('first half of the seventh century'), 'd'un caractère fortement égyptisant'. See *Madrider Mitteilungen* iv (1963) 9–38; the most convenient references, *Fasti Archaeologici* xviii–xix (1964) 8299–301 and xxiii (1968) 5533.

66 Margaret Guido, *Sardinia* (1963), Chap. VII, Bibliography 229. Ischia (Pithecussae): scarabs, G. Buchner, and J. Boardman, *JdI* (1966) 1–62; D. Ridgway, in C. F. C. Hawkes, op. cit. n. 29 above, 15–16.

67 T. J. Dunbabin, op. cit. n. 48 above, 31.

68 Tell Sukas: Coldstream 312, 333.

69 Coldstream 312; for following dates see D. Ridgway, op. cit. n. 66 above, 8–9.

70 Coldstream 423; Boardman 61–79.

71 Earliest pottery and influences, Coldstream 312. See also J. Boardman, *Historia* (1958) 250.

72 Motya: Coldstream 388, 428. For refs to English and Italian excavation reports, see *AR* (1976–77) 74.

73 The Lelantine War, Hopper 121–23.

74 T. J. Dunbabin, op. cit. n. 25 above, passim; Thuc. vi 3–5; note Thuc. vi 2.6, on the Phoenicians, 'about the whole of Sicily' followed by withdrawal to the West. For Phoenicians in the West, see *JRS* (1976) 212; *JdI* (1974) 85. For interactions of Greeks, Phoenicians and Carthaginians in Sicily, *AR* (1976–77) 74.

75 G. Vallet and F. Villard, *BCH* (1952) 289ff.

76 See above n. 26.

77 Boardman 77–78, and fig. 11.

78 See above pp. 31–32, and nn. 49ff.

79 J. Boardman, *BSA* (1967) 57ff.

80 D. Ohly, *Griechische Goldbleche* (1953) passim.

81 See above n. 57.

82 Coldstream 29ff.

83 See above pp. 35–36.

84 Hopper 179; Coldstream 361, and n. 10 (a problem here of Pheidonian Chronology?)

85 Hopper, Chap. 6, 109ff.

86 The Crowe Corselet, J. Boardman, *The Cretan Collection in Oxford* (1961) 142.

87 The Aegean groups, and Argive and Protoattic are restricted in distribution. SOS amphorae are now more carefully noted, e.g. in the West. For a considerable variety of other oil and wine containers (Corinthian, Chiote, Cypriote, Lesbian and other Ionian, Massiliote or Etruscan (?), see graves at Camarina, *AR* (1976–77) 71. For SOS, ibid. 56, 57, 61–62, 65, 67, 71.

88 Demaratus (Livy i 34) was one of the Bacchiads of Corinth. He fled at their overthrow by Cypselus to Tarquinii, taking a body of followers, including exponents of the graphic arts, such as the painter Cleophantus, and Eucheir and Eugrammus, whose names sound bogus, but there is no reason to doubt his historicity, as one of those Greek emigrants who account, in part at any rate, for the presence of such quantities of Greek pottery in Etruria. A palmette-antefix of the mid-fifth century from the Refrisco-

Iaro cemetery at Camarina shows the name Diopos, borne by a clay worker associated with Demaratus in Pliny Sen., *HN* xxxv 152, *AR* (1976–77) 71.

89 H. G. G. Payne, *Necrocorinthia* (1931) 216–19; R. Joffroy, *Le trésor de Vix* (1954) 22ff.

90 Coldstream 353, on the connection of Hera Akraia and Megara; T. J. Dunbabin, *BSA* (1951) 61ff.

91 See below, Chap. ix, pp. 165–69.

92 Hopper 126.

93 Hopper 94; *JdI* (*AA*) (1959) 8ff.

94 Boardman 76–77.

95 Her. ii 152, 3–4.

96 Naucratis: Her. ii 178ff.; faience manufacture, Boardman 144–45.

97 Her. iv 150ff.

98 Her. iv 152, 1–4.

99 Her. i 163ff.

100 E. S. G. Robinson, *NC* (1956) 1–8; C. M. Kraay, *Archaic and Classical Greek Coins* 20ff., 312ff., Hopper 110ff.

101 C. M. Kraay, op. cit. 41–43 (Aegina); 79–81 (Corinth).

102 C. M. Kraay, *JHS* (1964) 76–91; R. M. Cook, *Hesperia* (1958) 257–62.

103 Hopper 179–80, 189ff.

104 See above p. 37.

105 See below, Chap. ix, p. 170.

106 Arist. *Constit. of Athens* 5–12; Plut. *Life of Solon*, passim.

107 Cf. the Attic bowl and stand, signed by Sophilos, *BMQ* xxxvi 107–10.

108 See below, Chap. iv, pp. 96–98.

109 The question of the pottery trade, and Mediterranean trade in general, is made more personal by the *apparent* appearance of Sostratus of Aegina as a trader in Attic pottery. He is mentioned by Herodotus (iv 152.3) in the same context as Colaeus of Samos, as having made a fortune *somehow* in trade, where or how is unknown. He appears as the dedicator of a stele to Aeginetan Apollo found in Etruria at Gravisca, the port of Tarquinii, and belonging to the later

sixth century. The inscription is translated 'Sostratus caused me to be made'. It might equally mean that 'Sostratus made it'. The script is Aeginetan. His name has been connected (as trader) with mercantile inscriptions (appearing as SO=Aeginetan script) on early Attic red-figure pottery exported to Etruria in the later sixth and earlier fifth century. There would thus emerge a personality who illustrates the early multi-state nature of trade (here an Aeginetan dealing in Attic pottery). The diligent study, however, of the following will reveal the weak links in the chain of argument: A. Johnston in *PdP* (1972) 416ff.; F. D. Hardy, *PdP* (1976) 206–14 and refs in these articles. Inscription illustrated *AR* (1973–74) 50.

110 See G. Devereux, *Hermes* (1966) 129–34.

111 Dates of Stesichorus: birth *c.* 632–629, death *c.* 556–553 BC. See *CQ* n.s. xix (1969) 207–21.

112 Her. i 163ff.; foundation of Massilia i 13–14. On the Phocaeans in the West, *BCH* (1975) 854–96.

113 Her. i 166; see V. Merante, *Kokalos* (1970) 98–138. See n. 74 above.

114 Her. vi 17.

115 Tocra, 'the richest deposit outside Naucratis'; J. Boardman and J. Hayes, *Excavations at Tocra 1963–1965* (1966, 1973). See the suggestion in *AR* (1971–72) 40, by J. Boardman (in connection with Tocra) that merchants gradually exhausted their cargoes and thus restricted their (more distant?) customers' choice. That there may have been a systematic assembling of pottery (and other cargo?) at one centre as a preliminary to a trading voyage seems indicated by what is called 'the trader's complex' at Corinth where (*AR* (1973–74) 7) in a building and a dump a wide selection of pottery was found, *including Etruscan*. Cf. the Gravisca shrine (*AR* (1973–74) 49–50) which produced the inscription of Sostratus (see n. 109 above). Here again there is a diverse selection of pottery, the later of which may have come from the stock-in-trade of this merchant.

116 Catania: G. Rizzo, *Bolletino d'Arte* (1960) 247ff. Compare Taranto? See E. Will, in Finley, *Aix-en-Provence 1962* 45, n. 2, 460 + pots from end of eighth century to mid-sixth: PC and Cor. 390, the rest Aegean, East Greek and Attic (from second quarter of sixth century).

117 See R. Joffroy, *Le trésor de Vix* (1954); the route, 51ff. Joffroy assigns the gold diadem to Scythia, 48.

118 Boardman 77–79.

119 There are some difficult issues. Are we to suppose the 'sorrows' of Miletus over Sybaris and of Athens over Miletus (Her. vi 21) have anything to do with commerce?

CHAPTER TWO

1 Aristoph. *Knights* 129, 254.

2 Ibid. 132.

3 Aristoph. *Knights* 130 and scholia.

4 Scholia to Aristoph. *Peace* 631; *Wasps* 1007; *Clouds* 1065.

5 Plut. *Life of Pericles* 24.

6 Hesychius, *s.v. probatopoles*; Thuc. iii 19.

7 Olives, exported from the eighth century.

8 Paying an agreed sum to his owner, and working on his own.

9 Aristoph. frag. 299 (Edmonds).

10 Aristoph. *Knights* 852–54.

11 Theophr. *Charac.* vi (xxiii) 26 (Jebb).

12 Thuc. vi 91. 7; vii 27.5.

13 See below, Chap. vi, p. 120.

14 See above n. 8.

15 Finley, *Aix-en-Provence 1962* 66–67, 118ff.

16 But note, admittedly at a late date (first century AD), traces of iron working and the sludge of marble polishing in South Stoa II (*Hesperia* (1960) 360ff.).

17 *IG* ii² 1672, 9–10.

18 Cf. Rogers' note on Aristoph. *Acharn.* 187ff.

19 Scholia to Aristoph. 979; Harpocration *s.v.*; Dem. i 33; *Knights*; Lys. fr. 45 *apud* Dion. Hal. vi 983 (Reiske); Dem. xxxv 35; Xen. *Hell.* v 1. 21; Polyaenus vi 2.2.

20 Thuc. ii 38.

21 Cf. (Xenophon) ii 5–6; Isocr. iv 42.

22 Isocr. xvii 20.

23 Ibid. 52.

24 Ibid. 35ff.

25 Ibid. 52, 53, 57.

26 Ibid. 42.

27 *Acharn.* 901.

28 Thuc. ii 97. 3.

29 Lists of foreign specialities: see below Chap. iii, n. 1.

30 Thuc. vii 28. 1.

31 Thuc. iii 86. 4.

32 Thuc. iii 2. 2–3.

33 Aristoph. *Acharn.* 141–47. B. B. Rogers's trans.

34 See (Xen.), *On Ways and Means* below, Chap. ix, 188.

35 Note also the reverse, the traders who come to the country, for example the fish-dealer in the *Boutalion* of Aristophanes, Athen. *Deipn.* viii 358d=Edmonds ii 195, no. 68.

36 Thuc. vi 22. 1.

37 See above p. 50. and n. 12.

38 Theophr. *Charac.* xiv.

39 Arist. *Rhet.* 1367a30.

40 Plato, *Laws* 847d.

41 *Laws* 849a.ff.

42 *Laws* 914d.ff.

43 *Laws* 918c.ff.

44 *Laws* 919e.ff.

45 *Laws* 849e.

46 *Laws* 920a.ff.

47 Aristoph. *Frogs* 1386–87.
48 Athen. *Deipn.* iii 76d.
49 *Deipn.* xv 700b.
50 *Deipn.* xv 700b.
51 For a good example, see Athen. *Deipn.* vi 224c; Edmonds ii 327, 30.
52 Aristoph. *Wasps* 1388.
53 Aristoph. *Frogs* 857.
54 Aristoph. *Wasps* 1390–91.
55 Aristoph. *Plutus* 426–27.
56 Aristoph. *Plutus* 435.
57 As in the *Frogs* of Aristophanes. 550ff.
58 Speech lvii.
59 lvii 34.
60 lvii 30.
61 lvii 36.
62 Aristoph. *Thesm.* 445ff. B. B. Rogers' trans.
63 *Acts* xix 24–28.
64 Aristoph. *Thesm.* 400.
65 Plut. *Life of Demosthenes* 60.
66 Theophr. *Charac.* xvi (vi) 24.
67 Isocr. vii 49.
68 Cf. Dem. xviii 169.
69 Aristoph. *Knights* 144ff. B. B. Rogers' trans.
70 Aristoph. *Acharn.* 33ff.
71 Cf. *IG* ii² 1177 and 1362, for a reference to the 'ancient laws' which related to wood-gathering.
72 Aristoph. *Acharn.* 272–75.
73 Aristoph. *Acharn.* 180ff.
74 Aristoph. *Acharn.* 333; coaldust, ibid. 348ff.
75 Athen. *Deipn.* viii 358d.
76 (Xenophon), *Constitution of Athens* ii 7–8.

77 Thuc. ii 88.
78 Pollux ix 47; cf. Edmonds i (Eupolis) 304.
79 Aristoph. *Plutus* 1155 and Rogers' note.
80 *IG*² ii 2403.
81 Aristoph. *Wasps* 680.
82 Aristoph. *Clouds* 766ff.
83 Aristoph. *Plutus* 175.
84 Edmonds i (Eupolis) 243.
85 Aristoph. *Eccles.* 757.
86 Aristoph. *Lys.* 557ff.
87 Aristoph. *Wasps* 789; *Frogs* 1068.
88 Eupolis, in schol. *ad loc.* (Edmonds i 418)
89 Pollux ix 47 (rather late).
90 Aristoph. *Eccles.* 303.
91 Aristoph. *Thesm.* 445ff.
92 Hyper. *Against Athenogenes*, col. 5, 12 (OCT).
93 Aristoph. *Birds* 14; 1079. B. B. Rogers' trans.
94 Aristoph. *Knights* 1247.
95 Lys. xxiii 6.
96 Ibid. 3.
97 Xen. *Oec.* viii 22.
98 Aristoph. *Frogs* 1350.
99 Lys. i 24.
100 Hyper. *Against Athenogenes*, col. 3, 6 and 9 (OCT).
101 Ibid. col. 9, 19.
102 Ibid.
103 *Hesperia* vii 127. 27.
104 Aristoph. *Thesm.* 348ff. B. B. Rogers' trans.
105 Aristoph. *Clouds* 636. B. B. Rogers' trans.
106 *IG*² ii–iii 1. 230.

CHAPTER THREE

1 See K. J. Beloch, *Bevölkerung der griechisch–römischen Welt* (1886).
2 Hermippus, fragment of the *Phormophoroi* (*CAF* 63); Aristoph. *Acharn.* 870ff.; *Peace* 999ff.; (Xenophon), *Constitution of Athens* ii 11–13.
3 Xen. *Hell.* vi 1. 11; Dem. *Olyn-*thiac i 22; Ps-Arist. *Oec.* ii 27; Xen. *Hell.* v 4. 56 (Thebans buy corn from Pagasae); Dem. i 22 (on market dues of Thessaly).
4 Dem. i 32.
5 Thuc. viii 95. 2; 96. 2.
6 Andoc. *De Pace* 9.

7 Gernet 307.

8 Dem. xviii 241, 301; Xen. *Hell.* v 4. 6.

9 Cf. *IG* ii² 1. 401.

10 Dem. xxiii 155.

11 Strabo xiv 3. 22.

12 Xen. *Hell.* ii 1. 18–19; Ps-Arist. *Oec.* ii 2. 7.

13 Xen. *Hell.* iii 2. 17.

14 Andoc. ii 20–21 (late fifth century); *IG* ii² 1. 407 (330–326 BC).

15 Gernet 306.

16 Strabo xiv 6. 5.

17 *IG* ii² 1. 407.

18 Dio. Sic. xi 90. 3; xii 9. 2 (Sybaris); Cicero, *In Verrem* iii 47 (Leontini); Varro, *De Re Rustica* i 44 (Syracuse).

19 Thuc. iii 86. 4.

20 Gernet 307; H. Droysen, *Athen und der West* (1882) 41.

21 Thuc. i 41.

22 *IG* ii² 1. 126; Dem. xxiii 172; Dio. Sic. xvi 34. 4.

23 *IG* i² 19–20.

24 Thuc. iii 86.

25 H. T. Wade-Gery, *JHS* (1932) 217–18.

26 Gernet 317.

27 Dio. Sic. xii 31, 36; xiv 93.

28 Plut. *Life of Pericles* xx.

29 Cf. Lys. xvi 4, for relations with the Pontus before 404 BC.

30 Her. vii 147.

31 For the fertility of Thrace, cf. Xen. *Hell.* v 2. 6; Isocr. viii 30.

32 Arist. *Constit. of Athens* lv 4.

33 M. Rostovzeff, *Iranians and Greeks in South Russia* (1922) 68.

34 Gernet 314.

35 Gernet 319.

36 Isocr. viii 28–30; cf. Xen. *Hell.* iii 2. 8.

37 Aesch. iii 82; cf. Dem. x 8.

38 Thuc. iii 2.

39 *IG* i² 57.

40 *IG* i² 32.

41 Quoted by Harpocration, s.v. 'Dekateutes'.

42 Arist. *Constit. of Athens* xxiv 2.

43 Xen. *Hell.* i 1. 22; Dio. Sic. xiii 64. 2.

44 Polyb. iv 44. 3ff.

45 Cf. Polyb. iv 38. 43, for its favourable position.

46 Xen. *Hell.* iv 8. 27 and 31; Dem. xx 60.

47 Polyb. iv 5. 47.

48 *IG* i² 57.

49 *IG* i² 58.

50 *IG* i² 133. 9.

51 *IG* i² 46. 7.

52 *IG* i² 58.

53 Thuc. i 64.

54 Philochorus in the scholia to Aristoph. *Wasps* 718.

55 Her. v 104–15.

56 Her. vii 90; Dio. Sic. xi 2–3.

57 Thuc. i 94; Dio. Sic. xi 44.

58 Plut. *Life of Cimon* 12–14, 18–19; Polyaenus, *Strategemata* 1.

59 Thuc. i 112; Dio. Sic. xii 4; Plut. *Life of Cimon* 13.

60 *CAH* v 77.

61 H. T. Wade-Gery, in Tod, *GHI* i² 57, on *IG* i² 19.

62 *IG* ii² 1. 407, of 330–326 BC.

63 Thuc. i 13. 2; Strabo viii 6. 20.

64 Thuc. iii 86. 4.

65 Thuc. iv 53. 3.

66 *IG* i² 71, of 422 BC.

67 Thuc. v 83. 4.

68 Cf. Dem. xix 123.

69 Thuc. iv 118. 5.

70 *IG* i² 93a, 11ff., of 419/18 BC or 413/12 BC.

71 Thuc. vii 27. 5.

72 Thuc. vii 28. 1.

73 Thuc. viii 4. 1.

74 Xen. *Hell.* i 1. 35.

75 Xen. *Hell.* ibid.

76 Thuc. viii 90. 5.

77 Aesch. iii 171, 223; Zosimus, *Vita Demosthenis*; *Anon. Vita Demosthenis.*

78 Aristoph. *Wasps* 715f.

79 Thuc. viii 96; Andoc. iii 7; Dem. xix 220.

80 Thuc. viii 60. 1.

81 Thuc. viii 96.

82 Lys. vii 6; Oxyrrhyncus Historian (*OCT*, col. 13).

83 Andoc. ii 11.

84 Lys. vi 49.

85 Cf. Lys. vii, *passim*, of 395 BC; Xen. *Oec*. 20–22.

86 Aristoph. *Eccles*. 547f.

87 See n. 33 above.

88 Isocr. xvii 57, of 394 BC.

89 Dio. Sic. xiv 94. 2.

90 *IG* ii² 1. 28.

91 Ibid. lines 17f.

92 Xen. *Hell*. v 1. 28.

93 Xen. *Hell*. v 1. 2.

94 Xen. *Hell*. v 1. 10–13.

95 Xen. *Hell*. vi 2. 1.

96 Xen. *Hell*. v 1. 21f.

97 Polyaenus, *Strategemata* vi 2. 2.

98 Xen. *Hell*. vi 4. 35.

99 Dem. liii 6.

100 Dem. lii 5.

101 Isocr. iv 133.

102 Dio. Sic. x 95; Polyaenus vi 2. 2; Xen. *Hell*. vi 4. 35.

103 Dem. l 5.

104 Xen. *Hell*. v 4. 60–61; Dio. Sic. xv 34. 3.

105 Aesch. ii 79.

106 Dem. vii *passim*.

107 Plut. *Life of Pericles* 19.

108 Xen. *Hell*. iv 8. 35 (387 BC); Dem. xxiii 166 (360/59 BC).

109 Dem. lviii 53 and 56.

110 Dem. xii 2.

111 Letter of Philip II to Athens, Dem. xii 2.

112 Scholia to Dem. xii 173.

113 Dem. xxi, *passim*.

114 Aesch. ii 12 and 75.

115 Thuc. vii 28; viii 95; Dicaearchus, frag. 7 (Müller, *FHG*); Strabo ix 2. 6.

116 Dicaearchus, frag. 29 (Müller, *FHG*).

117 Xen. *Hell*. v 4. 56.

118 Xen. *Hell*. v 4. 56; Strabo ix 5. 51; Hermippus, in Athen. *Deipn*. i 27f.

119 Dem. xviii 241.

120 Ditt. *Syll*.³ 212.

121 Ps.-Arist. *Oec*. ii 9.

122 Ibid. ii 17.

123 Dem. l 17. 19, 21; cf. l 5 and 7 and v 25; Ps.-Arist., *Oec* ii 11.

124 Dem. xlv 64.

125 *IG* ii² 1. 360.

126 Dem. 1, *passim*; ibid. 20 (Maronea).

127 Dem. l 19; Xen. *Hell*. v 4. 60 and 61; Dem. iv 34; Didymus, col. 10, 47.

128 Dem. lvi 9.

129 Dem. viii 24f.

130 Aesch. ii 74.

131 Dem. xx 33.

132 Dem. xviii 301 (326).

133 Dem. xviii 241 (307).

134 Dem. iv 34.

135 Dem. xviii 72–73.

136 xviii 145–46.

137 Dem. xii 5; xix 153 (389), 315 (442); i 22.

138 Dem. xviii 248 (310).

139 Dinarchus i 43.

140 Lyc. *In Leocratem* 18.

141 Dem. xxxii 26; lvi 9.

142 Dem. x 49 (144).

143 Dem. xxxiv 51; lvi 48– 49.

144 Dem. xxxii, xxxiv, xxxv, lvi.

145 Dem. xxxiv.

146 Dem. lvi.

147 Xen. *Oec*. 20, 27.

148 Dem. lvi 7–8, 10; Ps.-Arist. *Oec*. ii 34.

149 Lys. xxii 14 and 21.

150 Dem. lvi 9.

151 Dem. lvi *passim*.

152 *IG* ii² 1. 206.

153 *IG* ii² 1. 176.

154 Ps.-Arist. *Oec*. ii 34.

155 Dem. lvi 7–8, 10.

156 Lyc. *In Leocratem* 18.

157 *IG* ii² 1. 407, of 330–326 BC.

158 Ditt. *Syll*.³ 305.

159 Lys. xxxii 25.

160 Ibid.

161 Lyc. *In Leocratem* 26.

162 Dem. xxxiv 37, 38–39; for one probable cause, cf. Dem. xxxiv 8.

163 S. Ferri, *Alcune Iscrizioni di Cirene* no. 3.

164 Dem. xlii 20.

165 Dem. xxxiv 38, 39.

166 *IG* ii² 1. 342, before 332/1 BC.

167 *IG* ii² 1. 407.

168 *IG* ii² 1. 408, *c.* 330 BC.

169 *IG* ii² 1. 409, *c.* 330 BC.

170 *IG* ii² 1. 416.

171 *IG* ii² 1. 423, after 336/5 BC.

172 See below, p. 87; Ditt. *Syll.*³ 152.

173 Ditt. *Syll.*³ 280 of 333/2 BC.

174 Ditt. *Syll.*³ 280, 44–45, of 333/2 BC.

175 Dem. xvii 19 (217).

176 *IG* ii² 1. 408.

177 *IG* ii² 1. 284 of 336/5 BC, and ibid. 399, of 320/19 BC.

178 *IG* ii² 1. 398.

179 *IG* ii² 1. 401.

180 C. Michel, *Recueil d'inscriptions juridiques greques* (1900) 124, 24ff.

181 Ibid. 125.

182 Isocr. xvii 57.

183 Dem. xx 29.

184 Ibid. 32.

185 Ditt. *Syll.*³ 206, of 347/6 BC.

186 Dem. xxxiv 36.

187 G. Grote, *History of Greece* ii, pt 2, chap. 98, p. 304, of ed. 1869.

188 Dem. xxxiv.

189 Dem. xviii 86; xx 31.

190 Dem. xx 31.

191 *IG* ii² 2. 834b; Ditt. *Syll.*³ 587.

192 Beloch 96.

193 Boeckh i 128.

194 Jardé, 125.

195 Ps.-Arist., *Oec.* ii 2. 33 (1352a).

196 Jardé 123–44.

197 Gernet 296–301.

198 Dem. xx 33.

199 Strabo vii 4. 6.

200 Kocevalov, *RM* (1932) 320–23.

201 Dem. xx 33.

202 *Hermes* (1915) 24.

203 Dem. xx 32.

204 Hermippus, frag. 63 (*CAF*), from the Hellespont; Dem. xxxv 31 (from the Cimmerian Bosporus); Aristoph. *Knights* 1008 (mackerel from Byzantium); ibid. 66 for the general importance of fish as food at Athens. Cf. the market law forbidding the wetting of fish to increase its weight, Xenarchus, in Athen. *Deipn.* vi 225e.

205 Hermippus, frag. 63 (*CAF*); Plut. *Life of Nicias* 1; Aristoph. *Wasps* 838; Antiphanes, in Athen. *Deipn.* i 27e.

206 Hermippus, frag. 63 (*CAF*).

207 Ibid.

208 Ibid.

209 Ibid; Antiphanes, in Athen. *Deipn.*

210 Ibid.

CHAPTER FOUR

1 C. T. Seltman, *Athens, Its History and Coinage* (1924) 11–14. The amphora, of course, *need* not be an oil container.

2 Dio. Sic. xiii 81.

3 *Ox. Hist.* xii 4 (*OCT*); Lys. vii passim.

4 Aristoph. *Wasps* 252.

5 Ibid. 297–99.

6 *IG* ii² 903, of 176/7 BC; E. Ziebarth, *Seeraub und Seehandel*, Appendix ii 73.

7 In the view of the historian Beloch, on the basis of (Xenophon), *On Ways and Means* v 3; cf. the scholia to Pindar, *Nemean Odes* x 64.

8 Dem. xxxv 35.

9 E. Ziebarth, *Seeraub und Seehandel*, 75, 124, 133.

10 *IG* ii² 1100; E. Ziebarth, op. cit., Appendix ii 73a.

11 On the problem of the middleman, see above, Chap. Two.

12 *Hesperia* (1934) 297 n. 3, published by Virginia Grace.

13   M. Rostovzeff, *CAH* viii 628.

14   Archestratus, in Athen. *Deipn.* i 29e.

15   For its value, cf. Plut. *Mor.* 470f.

16   *Hesperia* (1934) 297, n. 3.

17   Aristoph. *Acharn.* 901.

18   E. H. Minns, *Scythians and Greeks in South Russia* (1913); M. Rostovzeff, *Iranians and Greeks* (1922), for full accounts.

19   Isocr. vii 117; Aristoph. *Acharn.* 519.

20   Alexis, in Athen. *Deipn.* xii 540d.

21   J. Hasebroek, *Staat und Handel* 97.

22   E. Ziebarth, op. cit. 74, 78, 80.

23   *RM* (1932) 39.

24   Dem. xx 32; xxxii 18; xxxiv 34.

25   Rebutted by P. N. Ure, *Gnomon* v (1929) 220–26.

26   Assuming 12–13,000 talents.

27   Thuc. ii 13. 3.

28   Tod, *GHI* (1946) i² 56.

29   In Tod, op. cit. 46, iii 33.

30   See Thuc. vii 28.

31   Andoc. *De Mysteriis* 133.

32   Cf. Thuc. vii 28.

33   Andoc. *De Mysteriis* 133.

34   Ibid.

35   Dem. xxxiv; lix 7.

36   Andoc. ibid.

37   Plato, *Republic* 8; Lys. xii 8, 19; Plut. *Vit. Dec. Or.* 835 b–c.

38   Lys. xii 19.

39   Dem. xxxvi 11.

40   K. J. Beloch, *Griechische Geschichte* iii (2) 1, 318.

41   J. Hasebroek, *Staat und Handel* 77.

42   Lyc. *In Leocratem* 58.

43   Dem. xxvii 9; cf. ibid. 33.

44   Aesch. i 97.

45   *Isocr.* in *Vit. Dec. Or.* and Dion. Hal. *Isocr.* 1.

46   Xen., *Mem.* ii 7. 6; Dem., xlviii 12.

47   Thuc., vii 27. 5. It must be noted that skilled agricultural workers such as vine-dressers could be called 'craftsmen'.

48   Xen. *Mem.* ii 3. 3; Lys., xxiv 6.

49   Scholia to Aristoph. *Knights* 44.

50   Xen. *Apol. Socr.* 29; scholia to Plato's *Apology* 18b.

51   *IG* ii² 2. 971.

52   Aristoph. *Clouds* 876.

53   Scholia to Aristoph. *Clouds* 876.

54   It will be useful at this juncture to point out that a great deal of writing has been produced at a high intellectual level on this question of Greek trade and industry, sometimes in a wider context. There may be instanced, K. Bücher, *Beiträge zur Wirtschaftsgeschichte* 1–97; E. Meyer, *Die wirtschaftliche Entwicklung des Altertums* (1895) and *Kleine Schriften* (1910) 79ff.; K. J. Beloch, *Conrads Jahrbücher* lii (1899) 626–31 and *Zeitschrift fur Sozialwissenschaft* v (1902) 92ff., 169ff.; A. Boeckh, *Jahrbuch für Nationalökonomie und Staat* xviii (1899) 626ff.; M. Weber, *Wirtschaft und Gesellschaft*; H. Francotte, *L'industrie* (1900), and 'Handel und Industrie' in *RE*; F. Oertel in his Appendix to R. von Pöhlmann, *Soziale Frage*; J. Hasebroek, *Staat und Handel* and *Griechische Wirtschafts . . . -geschichte*.

These writers may be divided between three different groups: the first denying the capitalistic and international character of Greek trade and industry (Bücher); the second affirming it (Meyer, Beloch, Pöhlmann); the third a middle and on the whole eminently reasonable view taken by Oertel and Hasebroek. In Finley, *Aix-en-Provence 1962* (1965), the approach is rather different, and the observations, for Greek Antiquity, not particularly inspired, apart from Finley's excellent introduction ('Classical Greece') pointing out the anachronistic approaches of some other scholars.

55   Timaeus, in *Athen. Deipn.* vi 264d.

56   Plato, *Laws* viii 12, 846 d–e.

57   Dio. Sic. i 74 (on Egypt).

58   Xen. *Cyr.* viii 2. 5.

59   Dem. xxvii.

60 *IG* ii² 1122.

61 Cf. F. Oertel's note on the fortune of Demosthenes' father, Appendix to R. von Pöhlmann, *Soziale Frage*³ 532–33; and R. Schwahn, *RM* (1931) 253ff.

62 R. von Pöhlmann, op. cit. 174ff.

63 Aristoph. *Eccles.* 815–22.

64 Xen. *Mem.* ii 7. 2.

65 For war-contributions (*eisphorai*) cf. Dem. xiv 24–27.

66 Which is ascribed on grounds of style to Xenophon. It has also been suggested that it is a pamphlet of Eubulus and his party.

67 Dem. xx 40 (Leucon); Ditt. *Syll.*³ 206 (Spartocus and Paerisades).

CHAPTER FIVE

1 (Xenophon), *On Ways and Means* iii 14.

2 See *RE* ix 2, 1404–05.

3 Lys. vi 28–29.

4 J. Hasebroek, *Staat und Handel* 115; cf. Dem. xxxiv 52.

5 Aristoph. *Knights* 347 and A. A. Neil's note *ad loc.*

6 Dem. vii 9; Hitzig, *Zeitschrift der Savigny Stiftung für Rechtsgeschichte* xxviii 218–31; R. J. Hopper, *JHS* (1943) 35–51; *Oxford Class. Dictionary*², s.v.

7 *IG* i² 16.

8 Arist. *Constit. of Athens* 59 17.

9 Ibid. 58.

10 Ibid. 53.

11 Ibid. 58.

12 M. Clerc, *Les métèques athéniens*, 260–74.

13 Aristoph. *Frogs* 569.

14 Aristoph. *Peace* 684.

15 Arist. *Pol.* iii 2.

16 Dem. xxv 58.

17 Dem. lix 37.

18 Hyper. *Against Aristagoras*, in the *Suda*, s.v. 'prostates' (*Oratores Attici* ii 335, frag. 26).

19 Isocr. vii 53.

20 Hesychius, s.v. 'aprostasiou dike'.

21 Cf. Arist. *Constit. of Athens* 58; Dem. xxxv 48.

22 Lyc. *In Leocratem* 21.

23 Lys. xxxi 9 and 14.

24 The *Suda*, s.v. 'aprostasiou dike'; cf. Bekker. *Anec. Graec.* i 201, 11,

where the *prostates* is defined as a guarantor (*engyetes*).

25 Cf. Dem. xxxii–xxxvi; lii; lvi; lix.

26 Lys. v, a public action for impiety; Isaeus, frag. B.

27 For various theories, see M. Clerc, op. cit. n. 12 above, 267–70.

28 Dem. xxv 59; lix 37; and Hyper. *Against Athenogenes.*

29 Isocr. viii 53.

30 Arist. *Constit. of Athens* 58 2.

31 M. Clerc, with Hitzig, *Zeitschrift der Savigny Stiftung für Rechtsgeschichte* xxviii 219; Meier-Schöman-Lipsius, *Das attische Recht und Rechtsverfahren* (1905–15) i 65, n. 49.

32 Lys. xxiii 4.

33 Isocr. xvii 16.

34 Cf. M. Clerc, op. cit. n. 12 above, 80.

35 Aesch. i 158.

36 Dem. lix 66.

37 Dem. xxxv 51.

38 M. Clerc, op. cit. n. 12 above, 188–92.

39 *IG* ii² 1. 336.

40 Arist. *Constit. of Athens* 59, 15.

41 Ibid. 59, 17.

42 Cf. the fragmentary *IG* ii² 1. 144 (before 353/2 BC) for a reference to *proxenoi.*

43 J. Hasebroek, *Staat und Handel* 134ff., particularly 136.

44 Hitzig, *Altgriechische Staatsverträge*, 33–44.

45 J. Hasebroek, op. cit. 137.

46 M. Clerc, op. cit. n. 12 above, 218–20.

47 *IG* i² 36, 70, 72, 82, 83, 103; *IG* ii² i 5, 13, 39, 49, 53, 63, 76, 82, 86, 95, 162, 180, 193, 205, 265, 285; and Ditt. *Syll.*³ 199.

48 *IG* i² 145, 154; *IG* ii² 105 13, 39, 49, 53, 63, 76, 83, 86, 95, 162, 180, 193, 205, 265, 285, 287, 288, 344.

49 *IG* ii² i 130, 174, 186, 189, 285.

50 *IG* ii² i 83, 288.

51 *IG* i² 106, 154, 245.

52 Ditt. *Syll.*³ 126.

53 Ditt. *Syll.*³ 168.

54 Ditt. *Syll.*³ 258.

55 Cf. C. Michel, *Recueil d'inscriptions juridiques grecques* 321, 332.

56 Ditt. *Syll.*³ 332.

57 Ditt. *Syll.*³ 179.

58 Ditt. *Syll.*³ 187.

59 Ditt. *Syll.*³ 110.

60 Ditt. *Syll.*³ 219.

61 Ditt. *Syll.*³ 217.

62 Cp. *IG* i² 93; *IG* ii² 1. 12, 18, 286.

63 Cp. *IG* ii² 1. 342, 363, 398, 400, 401, 407, 408, 409, 416.

64 *IG* ii² i 176.

65 *IG* ii² i 206.

66 *IG* ii² i 229.

67 *IG* ii² i 252.

68 *IG* ii² i 339.

69 *IG* ii² i 343.

70 *IG* ii² i 398.

71 *IG* ii² i 399.

72 *IG* ii² ii 401.

73 *IG* ii² i 416.

74 *IG* ii² i 12 (*asylia*) 81 (*asylia*) 286 (complete freedom from tax, *asylia*).

75 Dem. xx 14–18.

76 Ditt. *Syll.*³ 119; *IG* ii² i 61, 180.

77 Dem. lii.

78 Dem. lii 19.

79 Tod, *GHI* i² 34, lines 8–9 (c. 450 BC).

80 Cf. the phrase in decrees: 'approach to the Council and People', and the further privilege of 'precedence' (*prodikia*), 'first after the sacrifices'.

81 Dem. lii 19, 24.

82 Cf. Dem. lii 4.

83 Pollux, *Onomasticon* (Bethe) iii 59.

84 Confirmed by R. Schwahn, *RM* (1931) 273, but see J. Hasebroek, *Staat und Handel* 138.

85 *IG* ii² i 401 and 407.

86 *IG* ii² i 373.

87 Dem. lii 10.

88 Thuc. iii 70.

89 *BCH* xv 412.

CHAPTER SIX

1 For general works, see *Bibliography*, under 'Banking', particularly J. Hasebroek, 'Zum griechischen Bankwesen', *Hermes* (1920) 114–15, n. 2, and R. Bogaert, *Banques et banquiers dans les cités grecques* (1968).

2 J. Hasebroek, op. cit. 113.

3 B. V. Head, *Historia Numorum*² 4ff. The table surely bears coins not grapes.

4 Cp. Dem. xxiv 212.

5 On this, see J. Hasebroek, op. cit. n. 1 above, 116.

6 Arist. *Oec.* ii 1346b, 24.

7 See R. S. Stroud, 'An Athenian Law on Silver Coinage', *Hesperia* (1947) 157–88.

8 The question here arises of other ways of transferring funds.

9 Dem. xlviii 12.

10 Ibid. and Dem. xxxiv 6.

11 See below also J. Hasebroek, op. cit. n. 1 above, 140–41.

12 On our relative ignorance of Classical banking, see J. Hasebroek, op. cit. n. 1 above, 113. It is also clear from R. Bogaert, op. cit. n. 1 above, which also clearly demonstrates the even lesser amount known of centres out-

side Athens. It is not clear how far temples (which used their real property to produce income) used other assets in a banker-like fashion. On the Hellenistic period, see R. Bogaert, passim. He gives (61–94) an excellent account of what is known of Attic banking.

13 See below.

14 See below.

15 See J. Hasebroek, op. cit. 140–41. There is the nice point how, in detail, Pasion's eleven talents were employed (see below, p. 120: 'on land and lodging houses'). Indeed it is claimed that he had 'more than fifty talents lent at interest'. Was this sum also similarly disposed? Note that in Dem. xxxvi 5–6, it sounds as if the eleven formed part of the fifty.

16 See above, 9.

17 See *BSA* (1953) 200–54.

18 Tod, *GHI* ii (1948) 123, lines 25–31. There is the problem of an investment, in Peparethos, Dem. xlv 5.

19 See n. 12 above.

20 Isocr. xvii.

21 *Prosopographia Attica (PA)*, s.v.

22 Dem. xxxvi 23.

23 Dem. xxxvi 45, 46, 49, 50, 51, 52, 53.

24 *PA* 1411; Dem. xxxvi, delivered in his defence. Such assistants (cf. Kittos in Isocr. xvii) were essential, to sit at the table, cp. J. Hasebroek, op. cit. n. 1 above, 154, n. 3.

25 *PA* 2876; Dem. xxxvi 28.

26 *PA* 1947; Dem. xlv 63.

27 Dem. xxxvi 28, 29.

28 Dem. xxxvi 45.

29 Dem. xxvii 11; add Blepaios, in Dem. xl 52.

30 Dem. xxxvi 5 and 11; J. Hasebroek, op. cit. 147–49.

31 See n. 15 above.

32 Ibid.

33 Dem. xxvii 11. A parallel is Stratocles in Isaeus xi 42. For money kept in the house, see n. 69 below.

34 Cp. the shield-factory of Lysias and his brother, Lys. xii 8, 12, 19; Plut. *Vit. Dec. Or.* on *Lysias*.

35 It must be admitted Demosthenes' arithmetic or his description is not perfect: the sword-factory appears to be valued at 190 minae, i.e. 290 less 100 = 190. The rate of income is given separately as 30 minae, but if the aggregate income is 50 minae and other investments bring in 17 minae, the income from the sword-factory should be 33 minae. Interest/income rate therefore is 16 percent or 17·4 percent approx.

36 In fact if the sword-factory is correctly valued at 190 minae, it all adds up to 656 minae (14 talents = 840 minae). There is probably here a manuscript corruption of figures, a warning against basing too close calculations on such.

37 Dem. xxxvi 45.

38 Dem. xxxvi, Argument and Summary.

39 Ibid.

40 Dem. xxxvi 18.

41 Dem. xxxvi 11.

42 Dem. xxxvi 13.

43 Cf. Isocr. xvii.

44 Dem. xlv 5.

45 Dem. l 56.

46 Dem. xxxvi 45.

47 Dem. xlvi 3, 5, 15; liii 18; lix 2.

48 Dem. xlv 28.

49 Dem. lii 13.

50 Dem. xxxvi 7; xlix 42; lii 14.

51 E.g. Lys. xix 46.

52 See above.

53 Dem. xxxvi 5 and 11. See the obscurity in 5 which is mentioned in n. 15 above.

54 The trierarchy, the provision of choruses for festivals, the war tax and its prepayment (*eisphora* and *proeisphora*), as a group called *leitourgiai*.

55 Cp. Dem. l 61.

56 Dem. xxxvi 36–43.

57 Dem. xxxvi 40–42. For the public

services of his father, see R. Bogaert, op. cit. 70.

58 Dem. xxxvi 43–44.

59 Dem. xlv 33; xlix 5, 8, 30; lii 6; lii 5, 19. J. Hasebroek, op cit. n. 1 above, 130–32. For a private record of a financial transaction, cp. Aristoph. *Clouds* 18ff. There is a similar stress sometimes on witnesses to transactions, Dem. xlvii 64; xlix 25, 26, 28; lii 4, and 7; J. Hasebroek, op. cit. 123. Contrast Isocr. xvii 2.

60 See J. Hasebroek, op. cit. 117ff. A good example is provided by Dem. lii. It is uncertain whether such transactions could be carried out purely by written documents, J. Hasebroek, op. cit. 123–24. It could be combined with deposit banking, see J. Hasebroek, op. cit. 141.

61 Dem. xxxvi 50–51. Note what is said, ibid. 11, that a shield-factory is safer than a bank.

62 See p. 151..

63 Dem. xxxiv 28 and passim.

64 Dem. xlix 5ff.

65 Dem. xlix 22–24.

66 Dem. liii 9–10.

67 See above, p. 123.

68 Dem. xlix 5–6 and 29.

69 Which may not be so important, it is suggested by J. Hasebroek, op. cit. n. 1 above, 147, who compiles an interesting list of examples of money kept in the house, op. cit. 144. If this is so there is a contradiction.

70 See above p. 122. There is the case of Pasion and S. Russia, the theme of Isocr. xvii.

71 Dem. lii 3.

72 The speech Isocr. xvii deals with the financial problems of a young man from Pontus (S. Russia), son of Sopaios, minister of the ruler Satyros. He came to Athens and used Pasion as his banker, who subsequently attempted to deprive him of the money deposited in the bank.

73 Some cases, such as Dem. l 56 would sound like it.

74 J. Hasebroek, op. cit. 137, would deny it on the basis of Isocr. xvii 35, where the son of Sopaios asks Stratocles, who was about to sail to S. Russia, to leave his money in Athens and collect the corresponding amount from Sopaios in S. Russia, to avoid the risk of loss on the way. There are, however, examples of the conveyance of actual cash – the son of Sopaios on his first coming to Athens provides an example. So, too, Pasion proposed to sail with him to Pontus and return the disputed money there. Possibly there was a mixed procedure in the case at any rate of important centres: the actual conveyance of sums to form the basis of long-distance giro-banking, with documentary accounting for transactions.

75 More in the Hellenistic period than earlier.

76 Dem. xxxvi 30.

77 (Xenophon), *On Ways and Means*.

78 36, 45, 46, 49, 50, 51, 52, 53.

79 G. Baiter and H. Sauppe, *Oratores Attici* (1850).

80 See R. Bogaert, op. cit. 62–84. Epigenes and Konon (Dinarchus i 43); Eucles (*IG* ii² 2741); Heracleides (Dem. xlvii 12); Kittos (Dem. xxxiv 6); Philios (Lys. ix 5), is dubious; Satyros and Timodemos (Dem. xxxvi 39); Sosinomos and Timodemos (Lys. fr. 38, 1–4).

81 32, 33, 34, 35, 37, 50, 56.

CHAPTER SEVEN

1 Xen. *Cyr.* viii 2, 4.

2 Xen. *Mem.* ii 7, 3.

3 Xen. *Mem.* ii 7, 6.

4 Xen. *Mem.* ii 7, 2ff.

5 Xen. *Mem.* ii 7, 7.

6 Pherecrates, frag. 134 (Edmonds 256).

7 Lys. xxiv.

8 Andoc. i 40.

9 Lys. xii 8; Dem. xxxvi 4. See also Chap. vi.

10 Dem xxxvi 11.

11 Dem. xxvii passim; 9ff.

12 Dem. xlviii 12.

13 Aesch. i 97.

14 Lyc. *In Leocratem* 58.

15 Ibid. 22–23.

16 Loc. cit.

17 Andoc. i 40.

18 Lys. xxiii 2.

19 Cf. Lys. iii 15 and xxiii 2.

20 *IG* ii² 2677, 2746, 2750, 2752, 2759, 2760.

21 *IG* ii² 2747, 2748, 2749, 2751.

22 *Hesperia* (1948) 170ff.

23 Dem. liv 7.

24 *Hesperia* (1937) 343; *Hesperia* (1951) 135ff., 187ff.

25 *Hesperia* (1960) 360ff.

26 Pherecrates, frag. 24 (Edmonds 218).

27 Theophr. *Charac.* xvi (vi) 8ff.

28 Theophr. *Charac.* xxxix 6.

29 Andoc. i 133.

30 Plato, *Laws* xi 918d.

31 Dem. xix 272.

32 Aristoph. *Frogs* 114.

33 Dem. lvii 45.

34 Ibid. 35.

35 Dem. xlv 71.

36 From *IG* ii–iii² 3. ii, 11681; 12948.

37 Dem. liii 14.

38 *IG* ii–iii² 3. ii, 11689; 11804 12372; 13179; 13180; 12073; 11954.

39 Ibid. 12423; 12433.

40 *IG* i² 408ff.; 436; 442; 751; 428; 672; 473; 501; 631; 645; 720.

41 Ibid. 483; 516. *Hesperia* (1935) 152.

42 *IG* ii–iii² 3. i, 4320; *PA* 4048.

43 *IG* ii–iii² 3. i, 4334. Cf. the wreath-maker of Aristoph. *Thesm.*

44 *IG* i² 424 (*SEG* (1949) 311).

45 Ibid. 650.

46 Hesiod, *Works and Days* 25; cf. Arist. *Rhet.* 1381 b 17.

47 *IG* ii–iii² 3. ii, 6320.

48 *IG* ii–iii² 3. i, 2934.

49 Aristoph. *Lys.* 407ff.

50 Aristoph. *Eccles.* 385–87.

51 Lucian, *Voyage to the Underworld* (*Kataplous*), trans. H. W. and F. G. Fowler, *Works of Lucian* (1905) 239

52 Eur. *Bacchae* 1067.

53 Aristoph. *Clouds* 766f.

54 Cf. *IG* i² 313–14, from Eleusis, 408/7 B C.

55 *Hesperia* (1938) 209, 250.

56 Cf. *Hesperia* (1932) 142ff.

57 *Hesperia* (1955) 68.

58 *BCH* (1957) 349, fig. 36. See *ILN* 23.1.1954 114, for a fine linen cloth, embroidered with diaper pattern and lions, from Koropi, Attica, of late fifth century B C. On such textiles see J. Beckwith, *ad loc.*

59 As indicated by the 'couch' factory of Demosthenes' father.

60 *SEG* (1949) 41 (*c.* 435 B C) = *IG* i² 74=Bannier, *RM* (1928) 278–80.

61 *Hesperia* (1939) 239.

62 *IG* ii–iii² 2, 1382, 15–16 (*c.* 400 B C, Hekatompedon Inventories).

63 Ibid. 1421, 27 (272/1 B C, Hekatompedon Inventories).

64 Ibid. 1438, 33.

65 Ibid. 1443, 131.

66 Ibid. 1456, 41.

67 Thuc. vii 25, 5.

68 E.g. Aristoph. *Knights* 315–21, leather for shoes; Dem. xxvii passim (on the workshop of his father): ivory, iron, galls, copper.

69 Plato, *Laws* 921a and ff.

70 Plut. *Life of Pericles* xii 6; *JdI (AA)*, (1943) 106ff.
71 Xen. *Cyr.* viii 2, 4.
72 Cf. *AJA* (1953) 199–210.
73 *IG* i² 373, 54.
74 Ibid. 59.
75 Ibid. 61.
76 *IG* i² 374, 260ff.
77 Ibid. 95ff.
78 *IG* i² 374, 248ff.
79 Ibid. 248ff., 318.
80 *SEG* (1949) 286.
81 *IG* i² 374, 27–34.
82 *SEG* (1924) 285 (restored).
83 *IG* ii–iii² 1672, 9ff.
84 *Hesperia* (1938) 263 and (1943) 12.
85 *IG* i² 371, 5 (see also *SEG* (1949) 267); 374, 286ff.; 371, 12.
86 *IG* ii–iii² 1672, 9–10.
87 Ibid. 13, 14, 15; cf. 66ff., passim.
88 Ibid. 70–71, 78, 160–61.
89 *IG* i² 374, 282ff.
90 *IG* ii² 356; cf. *JHS* (1914) 282.
91 *IG* ii–iii² 1675, 17.
92 *IG* ii–iii² 1668, 58 and 1672, 188.
93 *IG* ii–iii² 1658, 5 (394/3 BC).
94 *IG* ii–iii² 1659, 6ff. (394/3 BC).
95 *IG* ii–iii² 1662, 5 (392/1 BC).
96 *SEG* (1949) 245.
97 *IG* i² 336, 339, 347–49; *IG* ii–iii² 1665.
98 *IG* ii² 88, 2.
99 *IG* i² 336, 8ff.
100 *IG* i² 338, 24, 46.
101 *IG* i² 367, 7.
102 *IG* i² 371 (III), 2.
103 *IG* i² 374, 279–81.
104 *IG* ii² ii. 463, 72, 89.
105 *IG* ii–iii² 1668, 16, 58.
106 *IG* ii–iii² 1670, 12.
107 *IG* ii–iii² 1672, 12–14.
108 Ibid. 71.
109 Ibid. 102.
110 Ibid. 104.
111 Ibid. 105.
112 Ibid. 125.
113 Ibid. 146.
114 Ibid. 157; cp. 168.
115 Ibid. 204.

116 *IG* ii–iii² 1673, 45ff.
117 *IG* ii–iii² 1672, 191.
118 Ibid. 304. Cp. *IG* i² 313–14, 101. As an example of timber import of a special sort, see Ditt. *Syll.*³ 129, after 394 BC, gift by an Eteocarpathian and his sons of cypress wood 'for the temple of Athena Polias at Athens'.
119 J. G. Frazer, *Pausanias's Description of Greece* (1898), vol. ii: on Hymettus i 32, 1, Notes i 423–26; on ancient roads, 424–25; on Pentelikon, i 32, 2; see also Notes i 418ff., with mention of 'an ancient road, very steep and rugged'.
120 Sheila Adam, *The Technique of Greek Sculpture* (1966) 5, and pl. 1 (Pentelikon and Paros); for chisel marks, J. G. Frazer, op. cit. 418 (Pentelikon).
121 *BSA* (1968) pls 12–13; C. Blümel, *Greek Sculptors at Work* (1955) figs 2–4.
122 See A. T. Hodge, *The Woodwork of Greek Roofs* (1960), on primary and secondary timbers, 45ff. On various kinds of wood, 124–25.
123 On wagons and road-making, see Alison Burford, 'Heavy Transport in Classical Antiquity', *EHR²* (1960) 1–18; R. J. Forbes, *Studies in Ancient Technology* ii (1955) 79ff., 126ff.; vii (1963) 139–49, 162–77.
124 For lifting, see J. J. Coulton, 'Lifting in Early Greek Architecture', *JHS* (1974) 1ff.
125 See on Pentelikon, J. G. Frazer, op. cit. 418: 'The quarries are situated in the gullies above the monastery of Mendeli. An ancient road, very steep and rugged, leads up the eastern side of the principal gully to the quarries. The road is roughly paved; the blocks of marble were probably brought down it on wooden slides. Square holes may be seen at intervals cut in the rock at the side of the road; the beams which supported the wooden slides may have been fastened in these holes.'

126 On heavy transport, see A. Burford, op. cit. 1–18. This covers a number of important points: use of large teams with multiple yoking (as for moving heavy blocks of stone, *IG* ii² 1673); the ox as the principal source of traction (R. J. Forbes, op. cit. n. 123 above ii 82, calls it too slow); the moving of large beams and stones, including column-drums; inscriptions on quarrying and transport; size and cost of animal teams. An important source of information is Alison Burford, *The Greek Temple Builders at Epidaurus*: 252–53 for preparation of heavy transport at Eleusis in 327/6 BC (*IG* ii² 1673, 11–43), for the transport of heavy column drums from the Pentelic quarries to Eleusis. For points on transport see 184–88. Note especially from the Parthenon accounts (*IG* i² 352, 12) the use of wheeled trolleys for stone transport.

127 Such as Eudemus of Plataea, honoured, *IG* ii² 351, for providing a thousand yoke of oxen, A. Burford, op. cit. 11.

CHAPTER EIGHT

1 Passim in Ps.-Xen.
2 Ibid. ii 11–12.
3 Ibid. ii 7.
4 Ibid. ii 6.
5 Ibid. ii 14–15.
6 Thuc. ii 38.
7 Thuc. ii 16; Isocr. iv 42.
8 Cf. D. M. Lewis, *CQ* (1961) 63.
9 Dinarchus i 71.
10 Tod, *GHI* ii 123, 25–31.
11 Ps.-Xen. ii 16.
12 For example, in Thasos; cf. *IG* i² 376=*SEG* x 304, around 424 BC (farms in Euboea, Chalcis, Histiaea, Eretria). Cf. i² 375.
13 Thuc. viii 63.4.
14 Plato, *Euthyphro* 4 c.
15 Xen. *Oec.* iv 4.
16 Ps.-Arist. *Oec.* i 1343a30.
17 *Ox. Hist.* xii 4–5.
18 Thuc. vii 27.5.
19 *Ox. Hist.* xii 5.
20 Aristoph. *Peace* 629.
21 See B. B. Rogers' note *ad. loc.*; Thuc. ii 21; Aristoph. *Acharn.* 183; Andoc. iii 8; for the convention see Plato, *Rep.* v 471.
22 Lys. vii 7–8.
23 Dem. lv 11.
24 Ibid. 24.

25 Aristoph. *Plutus* 223.
26 Xen. *Oec.* xix 6.
27 Ibid. xx 22ff.
28 Ibid. xx 26.
29 Lys. vii 4–10.
30 Harpocration s.v. *eschatia*.
31 See Dem. lv.
32 Dem. lv 3.
33 Ibid. 11.
34 Cf. Eupolis fr. 14 (Edmonds, p. 320).
35 Dem. lv 22.
36 Dem. xlvii 53, 60.
37 Xen. *Oec.* xvi 7.
38 Xen. *Hell.* vi 2. 36.
39 *IG* i² 615.
40 *IG* i² 684.
41 Cf. *Hesperia* (1948) 243ff.
42 *Hesperia* (1956) 122ff.
43 *Hesperia* (1953) 225ff.; (1956) 178ff.
44 Tod, *GHI* i² 197–200 (nos 79–80).
45 See n. 18 above.
46 Aristoph. *Eccles.* 651–52.
47 Aristoph. *Wasps* 712.
48 R. C. Jebb, *The Characters of Theophrastus* xiv (iv), ed.² (Sandys) (1909) 7.
49 Xen. *Mem.* ii 7, passim for employment of free persons; for 'artisan' and 'liberal' in the case of the employ-

ment of a steward, op. cit. ii 8.

50 Plato, *Euthyphro* 4 c–d.
51 Xen. *Oec.* xvi 8ff.
52 Dem. lv 13.
53 Dem. xliii 15–16.
54 Cf. ibid. 15–16.
55 Plato, *Laws* 844dff.
56 Dem. xxix 3.
57 Dem. xxx 28.
58 Dem. xlii 5ff.
59 Ibid. 20.
60 Ibid. 20.
61 Ibid. 20.
62 Ibid. 21.
63 Ibid. 19.
64 Plut. *Life of Pericles* xii 6–7. See R. H. Randall, 'The Erechtheum Workmen', *AJA* (1953) 194–210, also Alison Burford, 'Heavy Transport in Classical Antiquity', *EHR*² (1960) 3–4, in particular on inscriptions relating to workmen and building operations: at Athens, see above (Randall); Epidaurus, *IG* iv² 102–20; Delphi, *FdD* iii 5, 19ff.; Delos, *IG* xi² 142ff., *Inscr. de Délos* 499–509.
65 *IG* ii² 1672, 252ff., the Eleusinian

accounts of 332/1–329 B C
66 Plut. 849d; Hyperides the Orator: Eleusinian accounts 332/1–329/8 B C, *IG* ii–iii² 1672, 252ff.
67 Lys. vii 4–8, especially 6 and 7. Cf. Lys. xvi 10; Aesch. ii 147.
68 *IG* ii² 2491.
69 Ibid. 2492.
70 Ibid. 2493.
71 Cf. Ditt. *Syll.*³ 963, 7.
72 Cf. *IG* ii² 1241, 21.
73 Cf. *IG* ii² 1241, 21. Note Theophr. *Hist. Plant.* viii 7. 2: 'the best fallow follows after beans.'
74 Cf. Hesychius, and Xen. *Oec.* xix 11.
75 Cf. *IG* ii² 2499, 16.
76 Ibid. and Ditt. *Syll.*³ 963, 31.
77 *IG*² 2494.
78 Cf. Ditt. *Syll.*³ 986, 3 (Chios).
79 *IG*² 2498.
80 Ibid. 2499, of 306/5 B C.
81 Ibid. 2500 of the end of the fourth century B C; 2501.
82 Dem. xlvii 52.
83 Aristoph. *Birds*, 714.
84 Xen. *Oec.* xix 6.

CHAPTER NINE

1 J. D. Muhly, *Copper and Tin* (1969) passim.
2 Ibid.
3 See above, 54, 60.
4 On Melos and its mineral products, *BSA* (1975) 191–97.
5 J. T. Bent, in his *Aegean Islands*, gives an interesting account of his own observations of Greek island mining activity: 18 (Seriphus), 38–40 (Siphnus), 55 (Cimolus), 359 (Naxos), 383ff. (Paros), 464 (Cea), (cf. *AR* 1973, 29).
6 Her. vi 47. See *BCH* (1962) 108, n. 7.
7 Ainyra appears in a fragment of Archilochus (Lasserre-Bonnard, fr. 307) and in a third-century inscription, *BCH* (1964) 278; maps, ibid. 277, 279.

8 Loc. cit. 284; milestone, 267–87.
9 Ibid. 282, n. 5.
10 See Bibliography.
11 See J. M. F. May, *The Coinage of Damastion*.
12 See J. N. Svoronos, *L'hellénisme primitif de la Macédoine* passim; and *A Guide to the Principal Coins of the Greeks* (1932) nos IB, 3, 5, 14–17; IIB, 6.
13 Here a direct export, as seems indicated by the die-links: C. F. A. Schaeffer, 'Une trouvaille de monnaies grecques archaïques à Ras Shamra', *Mélanges R. Dussaud*, i (1939) 461–87.
14 Her. iv 107. 3; at Megabazus' warning nipped in the bud by Darius.

15 Her. v 23.

16 See below, pp. 166–69. on the Athenians in the North.

17 Gold mines are specifically mentioned by Herodotus (ix 75) in connection with the general Sophanes, at the time of one of the fruitless attempts to found a colony on the Strymon.

18 Her. vi 44; vii 108, 109, 110, 112–21.

19 Arist. *Constit. of Athens* 15, 2. Nothing is expressly said of a settlement in the Pangaean region or of mines.

20 Her. i 64.

21 See S. Casson, *Macedonia, Thrace and Illyria* 218, 222.

22 Thuc. i 100–101.

23 Ibid.

24 Thuc. i 100. 2. Trans. *Everyman Library*, Richard Crawley. The tribute of Thasos initially (452/1–447/6 BC) was three talents (an irregular figure for 448/7 (List vii)), indicating the reduction of its possessions; then from 446/5 BC (as far as tribute lists are preserved) it becomes 30 talents, which must indicate a restoration of responsibilities for the mainland region (?) (*Athenian Tribute Lists* iii 259. On Drabescus, see *ATL* iii 106ff.; on 'the mine', 259, n. 76).

25 Thuc. iv 102.

26 Thuc. iv 108. Brasidas proposes to build warships there in the Peloponnesian War, Thuc. iv 109. 7.

27 It would seem, according to the estimates of West, *TAPA* (1930) 217–39 that Athens lost 50–75 talents as the result of the loss of Amphipolis, Scione, Torone and Acanthus (cf. Thuc. iv 108); he also suggests (219) that there was income lost which did not appear in the Tribute Lists, as from Eion on the Strymon.

28 Thuc. iv 105. 1.

29 Her. vi 46. Cf. Theophrastus, *De Lap.* 17.

30 *IG* i² 184–85 and Suppl. 33–34.

31 P. Perdrizet, *Klio* (1910) 1ff.; not from mines, but from pockets of broken-down auriferous quartz, which may therefore have been relatively soon exhausted (see below, n. 35)

32 Appian *BC* iv 106.

33 Dio. Sic. xvi 8, 6.

34 G. F. Hill, *Historical Greek Coins* (1906) 78–83, no. 41.

35 See V. Martin, 'La durée d'exploitation des gisements aurifères de Philippes en Macédoine, 21, in *Études dédiées à la mémoire d'André M. Andréades* (1940). Other bibliography, *BSA* (1953) 200, n. 1 *a*; (1968) 292, n. 2. Crenides is called by Casson 'the central mining town of the whole Pangaean area'.

36 Strabo 331, 36.

37 Cf. Appian *BC* iv 106. 'Philippi is a city which was of old called Datos, and Crenides before Datos.'

38 *A Guide to the Principal Coins of the Greeks* (1932), IIIB, 16, 19, 20.

39 See for definition, S. Casson, op. cit. n. 21 above, 59–60.

40 Pliny Sen. xxxiii 66.

41 For *chrysou psegmata*, gold dust, see S. Casson, op. cit. n. 21 above, 16, n. 3; 62 and 104.

42 See below, on S. Casson, op. cit. 59. This part of O. Philippson, *Die griechische Landschaften*, appears unpublished as yet.

43 See above the references of Herodotus, Strabo and others; also Eur. *Rhesus* 921 and 970.

44 Strabo 331, 34.

45 S. Casson, op. cit. n. 21 above, 59; C. J. Sagui, *Journal of Econ. Geology* (1928) 671–80.

46 Not to be confused with the nineteenth-century iron workings, on the same site. See *BSA* (1968) 315 and pl. 64(a) and (b); O. Philippson, op. cit. n. 42 above, 76–79.

47 Her. ii 58–59.

48 It *could* be they were not sea-goers. Like Seriphus they provided one fifty-oared ship, less than Cythnus, Herodotus viii 48; contrast Aegina which provided 30 (viii 46) triremes ('ships' in the parlance of Herodotus) if this type had been developed at this date.

49 *BSA* (1968) 293ff.

50 See for illustrations *BSA* (1968), pls 56–63 and pls 48–50 in the present work. For a new and rare type of washing device (found so far at three sites in Laurium) see *Proceedings of the Athens Academy* (1970) 3–21, pls i–xxii; Healy, 279, n. 93.

51 *BSA* (1968) 315ff.

52 Laureion (an adjective with *oros* understood) is used in the *Poletai* account of 367/6 BC.

53 In the time of Strabo the area was 'rough and poor'.

54 The reference of Sophocles in the *Ajax* (1218ff.): 'O to be wafted where the wooded sea-cape stands upon the laving sea, O to pass beneath Sunium's level summit, that so we might greet sacred Athens' (trans. Jebb), probably refers only to the vicinity of the temple, the area of the modern 'Green Coast'.

55 *Persae* 237–38; cf. Eur. *Cyclops* 293–94 for 'the rock of Sunium with silver beneath'.

56 As P. N. Ure, *The Origin of Tyranny* (1922) 37ff.; see *BSA* (1961) 194, n. 49.

57 Her. vi 89–90.

58 Her. vii 144.

59 *Constitution of Athens* 22, following the *Atthis*, and followed by Polyaenus.

60 Plut. *Life of Themistocles* 4.

61 Cornelius Nepos, *Themistocles* 2.

62 Cf. Siphnos, Her. iii 57. 2 and perhaps Thasos, Her. vi 46. 3.

63 Note that Thuc. i 14 mentions only the increase in the Athenian fleet and not the source of the money.

64 Dem. xxxvii 4 and 25; Aesch. i 101; *CIA* ii 780, 5; Harpocration, s.v. '*Epi Thrasyleōi*'.

65 (Xenophon), *On Ways and Means* iv 44.

66 See *Miscellanea Graeca*, fasc. 1, *Thorikos and the Laurion in Archaic and Classical Times*, ed. H. Mussche, P. Spitaels, F. Goemaere-De Poerck, the proceedings of a seminar held in Ghent in March 1973 (published Ghent, 1975), which gives (208–11) a list of the publications relating to Thoricus. See also *BSA* (1968) 293–95, and the details and comment given there.

67 It appears also in literature in the play of Antiphanes (date 408 or 405–334 or 331 BC), which is part of the Middle Comedy, and therefore belongs to the fourth century. It has the title *Thorikioi ē Dioryttōn*, which, however, need have no connection with mining, except in so far as the inhabitants of Thoricus, in their calling as miners, might also be expert sappers or burglars.

68 See H. Mussche, 'Thorikos in Archaic and Classical Times', *Miscellanea Graeca*, fasc. 1, 45–54 for an excellent summary.

69 See *BSA* (1968) 304ff.

70 See H. Mussche and K. Konophagos, 'Ore-washing Establishments and Furnaces at Megala Pefka', *Thorikos* vi (1969).

71 Cf. E. Ardaillon, *Mines du Laurion* 141ff.

72 Dio. Sic. xi 41, 43, 70.

73 Plut. *Life of Pericles* 12.

74 Plut. *Life of Aristides* 25.

75 (Xenophon), *On Ways and Means* vi 15.

76 Andoc. 1 130; Plut. *Life of Alcibiades* 8.

77 Lys. xix 47–48.

78 (Xenophon), *On Ways and Means* iv 14.

79 Mem. ii 5. 2.

80 Plut. *Life of Nicias* iv 2.

81 Or is it 'in silver'? Cf. Lys. xix 47: 'the greater part of his fortune in his house'.

82 *Knights* 362, of 424 BC.

83 *Birds* 1105–06, of 414 BC.

84 (Xenophon), *On Ways and Means* iv 25.

85 Thuc. vi 91 and vii 19 and 27.

86 Thuc. vii 27. 5.

87 Aristoph. *Frogs* 720: 'the new gold'.

88 See *Hesperia* (1969) 157–88.

89 Aristoph. *Eccles.* 815ff.

90 Xen. *Mem.* iii 6, 12.

91 *Hesperia* (1941) 14ff.

92 *IG* ii² 1582 and *Hesperia* (1936) 10.

93 iv 28: 'for lately again (the mines) are being organised.'

94 Dem. xxxvii, of 345/4 BC.

95 Like the man (Andoc. i 38) who walked from Athens to Sunium to collect the wages of one mining slave on the *apophora* system.

96 Cf. Dem. xlii 20: 'formerly I myself in my own person laboured [in mining]'; Theophr. *de Lapid.* 58; (Xenophon), *On Ways and Means* iv 22.

97 Xen. *Mem.* ii 5. 3; Aesch. i 37.

98 Plut. *Comparison of Nicias and Crassus.*

99 E. Ardaillon, *Mines du Laurion* 92–93, points out that no record of troubles exists for the time of the Persian Wars or in the Peloponnesian War until 413 BC, and ascribes the revolt later recorded by Athenaeus (vi 272 e) and possibly by Diodorus (xxxiv 2. 19) to the period of the Second Slave War in Sicily and not to 413 BC as Mommsen does.

100 Thuc. vii 27.

101 (Xenophon), *On Ways and Means* iv 3, and 26.

102 (Xenophon), *On Ways and Means* iv 12.

103 Cf. Bekker, *Anecd. Graeca* i 205: 'Hormoi (limits) were like pillars in a mine. These served as boundaries also of each unit which he (the mine operator) rented from the State'.

104 *Hesperia* (1941) 14ff.

105 *IG* ii² 1582, 340–47.

106 *IG* ii² 1582, 44.

107 Dem. xxi 167.

108 *Hesperia* (1941) 14ff.

109 Loc. cit. lines 41–42, 58–65.

110 Loc. cit. 49, 51–52.

111 *Hesperia* (1936) 10, line 110.

112 Hyper. *Against Euxenippus* 35.

113 Loc. cit. lines 70–71.

114 Andoc. i 38.

115 Hyper. *Against Euxenippus*, *OCT.* coll. 44–45.

116 There seems to have been no lack of these. There is in the fourth century some basis for the calculation of their price: the better ones at 150–160 drachmae, the inferior much lower (Xen. *Mem.* ii 5. 2). For slaves the property of concessionaries, cf. Dem. xxxvii 4, 22, 26. They appear on mortgage stones, as *CIA* ii 1122, 1123 show: 'boundary of a workshop [*ergasterion*] and slaves, sold with option of redemption [*prasis epi lusei*] to Pheidon of Aixone.' But these relate to washeries and the like, not to mines which it was not possible to pledge.

117 If (Xenophon), *On Ways and Means* iv 14, is to be believed.

118 Cf. Aesch. i 97.

119 Dem. xix 293.

120 *Vit. dec. Or:* Lyc. *In Leocratem* 34.

121 Andoc. i 133.

122 Dem. xlii 32.

123 Dem. xxxvii 22.

124 Dem. xxxvii 37–38.

125 See *BSA* (1968) 304–6 for a discussion of these, and comparison with the Derbyshire mining regulations.

126 iv 34.

127 See *Hesperia* (1957) 14.

128 See the writer's article, *BSA* (1953) 247–54.

129 See Dem. xlii 18, where the undeclared property 'in the mines', must include *ergasteria* (workshops) since mines could not be *owned* in any case; see also xlii 31, which appears in an interesting context: 'If one fails, Men of the Jury, to get your verdict, what is one to have recourse to – when wealthy men, who have never done any good to you, who produce a large quantity of corn and wine and dispose of it for treble the price they did formerly, obtain undue advantage in your courts.'

130 See Margaret Thompson, *The New Style Silver Coinage of Athens* (American Numismatic Society (1961),

Text and Plates). On interesting indications of either mines or mint-workshops on the reverse of this coin-age, see American Numismatic Society, *Museum Notes* (1952), 25–48: M. Thompson, 'Workshops or Mines?' (which was possibly some form of bullion check).

131 For the official tester (*dokimastes*) see the inscription of 375/4 BC, *Hesperia* (1969) 157–88.

CHAPTER TEN

1 This should be qualified: note the importance of Megara (Isocr. viii 117) and of Lampis, a native of Aegina, 'the largest shipowner of Hellas' (Dem. xxiii 211).

2 On the question of silk, see G. M. A. Richter, 'Silk in Greece', *AJA* (1929) 27ff.

3 Movement was speedier by sea, Dem. xix 163; passage-ways of importance were the Hellespont for sea-travel and Thermopylae by land, Dem. xix 180; for open-sea sailing (*pelagios*) as from Cape Malea to Melos, cf. Thuc. viii 39, 3; for speed, an example from Athens to Mytilene, 'the third day after leaving Athens (=48 hours?), Thuc. iii 3, 5; the dangers of the sea, Andoc. i 137–38; later, in early second century, Ditt. *Syll.*³ 591, 13 and 40.

4 There *were* large ships. A ship of 10,000 talents burden was used by the Athenians in the Great Harbour at Syracuse (Thuc. vii 25, 6); Xen. (*Oec.* viii 11) mentions a great Phoenician merchantman which (significantly) carried arms and fighting men for defence. The unique *Alexandreia* of Hieron II could carry perhaps 1600 tons, and the Alexandrian grain ship *Isis* of the second century AD measured roughly 180 by 45 feet, with a depth of 44 feet and a carrying capacity of

1200 tons (see *Oxford Class. Dictionary*² (1970) 984). The average Roman merchant ship had a capacity perhaps of 50 tons and earlier probably the same. See *CQ* (1977) 331ff.

5 On this aspect of underwater archaeology, see J. du Plat Taylor (ed.), *Marine Archaeology* (1965).

6 The speech *might* be a literary exercise; Dem. xxxii 4ff., 8, 9.

7 Dem. xxxiii 5, 13, 20.

8 Dem. xxxiv 8; note that at Athens Sidonian merchants (between 376 and 360 BC) were granted freedom from the *metoikion*, *choregia* and *eisphora* 34, 36, 37, 38–39.

9 Dem. xxxv 6–7, 9, 10 – a document; these are not always genuine; 31, 32, 52; the disreputable character of the Phaselites (xxxv 1–2), the varying interest rates on passage from the Black Sea to the Aegean before and after the rising of Arcturus, and in the region of the Hellespont after the rise of Sirius, the former in early September, the latter at the end of July (xxxv 10), reference to discharge of cargo at a friendly port 'where the Athenians have no right to reprisals' (xxxv 13), use of the term *sylān* (xxxv 26), jettison by consent of the passengers (xxxv 11), payments to enemies (ibid.); on breach of contract, distraint on *all* the property of the defaulters

'whether on land or sea, where ever they may be.'
10 Ibid. 20 and 23.
11 Dem. lvi 7.
12 Ibid. 8.
13 Dem. lviii 53–56; because of the importance of the South Russian trade.
14 Dem. xxxiv 15; like an overloaded Caribbean schooner!
15 Ibid. 15.
16 Dem. xxxv 18, in jars (*keramia*) of six gallons, theoretically valued at a talent – a useful indication of price – but only 450 were loaded in fact.
17 Ibid. 31–32, food for a farmer's slaves.
18 Two modern published collections are cited, less cumbersome than the various sections of *IG*: *GDI* (1884–1915), and Ditt. *Syll.*³ (1915–24), and some additional material from *SEG*. A written document of a unique sort was found on the island of Berezan, off the coast of Olbia in South Russia. It is a private letter written on *lead* from Achillodorus to his son Anaxagoras, describing the organization of trading operations in the region at the end of the sixth and beginning of the fifth century BC. See *AR* (1971–72) 49, from *Vestnik drevnei istorii* (1971) 4, 74–100.
19 See H. Michell, *Economics of Ancient Greece*² 170–298.
20 Xen. *Hell.* vi 1, 11; cf. Dem. xvii 28.
21 *IG* i² 71, 22–23: limitation on the sort of export engaged in by Andoc. (ii 11). Wilhelm (see *SEG* x 86) suggests that corn may also have been mentioned.
22 *GDI* 5285 b.
23 Aristoph. *Lys.* 729.
24 Ibid. 735. See n. 2 above; it might be some form of silk.
25 Xen. *Cynegetica* ii 4.
26 E.g. *Archaeology in Greece 1961–62*, 5, amphorae from Chios, Lesbos and Mende.

27 Ditt. *Syll.*³ 495, 19–23.
28 *GDI* iv, Suppl. no. 52.
29 Ditt. *Syll.*³ 975.
30 *BCH* (1936) 11–36.
31 Ps.-Arist. *Oec.* 1346 b 3–16.
32 *IG* ii² 1635, 35–36; 1672, 89.
33 In 377/6 and 375/4 BC an ox is priced at 77 drachmae; in ? 329/8BC it costs 400 drachmae (while a goat or sheep is priced at 30 drachmae).
34 *Hesperia* xiv 119ff., no. 11 = *SEG* x 87.
35 Ditt. *Syll.*³ 218. Permission for export and import of stamped gold and silver, with sale and purchase on 'the stone in the *ekklesiasterion*.' All sales and purchases to take place through the medium of the bronze and silver of Olbia and no other. The (Cyzicene) stater to be tariffed at 10½ (? 11½) drachmae in Olbian silver, no more and no less. Other foreign currency exchange rates to be determined by bargaining. Compare Ditt. *Syll.*³ 525 (3rd century BC) of Gortyna in Crete.
36 *GDI* iv, Suppl. no. 49 A, p. 870, which seems to refer to sums raised by taxes on timber, salt (?) and ships (?).
37 *GDI* 5632; Tod, *GHI*² 23, A9–12, B20–22.
38 Arist. *Rhet.* 1411 a 14.
39 Cf. Ditt. *Syll.*³ 497 (after 229 BC) with honours to an Athenian for public services including repairs to harbours and the restoration of land which had fallen out of cultivation (lines 8–9).
40 *Dacia* iii–iv 391ff.
41 Ditt. *Syll.*³ 495, above, n. 49.
42 Ibid. 58ff. (corn supply); 100ff. (fortifications); 148 (public shipping).
43 *SEG* i 361.
44 Ditt. *Syll.*³ 212. Grant of right of corn export to the amount of 100,000 medimni (restored), with payment of only the simple 1/60 and 1/90 (?) tax.
45 *RFC* (1934) 169–93.
46 Ditt. *Syll.*³ 354. Importation of

corn and its sale, at the instance of the *agoranomos*, at a price below the market level.

47 Ditt. *Syll.*³ 493. Note that the services of a Rhodian are comprehensible enough as connected with a centre of the corn trade, but why Delos?

48 Ditt. *Syll.*³ 360.

49 Ditt. *Syll.*³ 502; see M. Rostovzeff, *The Social and Economic History of the Hellenistic World*¹ (1941) 385, 591.

50 *SEG* iii 710, p. 131.

51 Ditt. *Syll.*³ 976.

52 Tod, *GHI* i² 34 and notes and references. In the same document (8–18) is a law of Oianthea (?) regulating procedure. It is to be noted that this inscription makes clear the fine distinction between piracy and seizure (*sylān*), and mentions *proxenia* and *symbolai*, two of the devices to protect individuals and establish inter-state legal relations.

53 See Tod, op. cit. 7, on the Aeaces inscription of about 540 BC and the references to Herodotus given there. The inscription uses the word *sylē*=by brigandry or piracy. Cf. Livy v 28.

54 Mention of fighting against these (Tyrrhenians) in the Adriatic (?) appears in *GDI* 3835 of the second half of the third century.

55 *GDI* 3751.

56 Dem. vii, an issue between Athens and Philip II of Macedon.

57 Dem. lii 5.

58 Dem. xxiii 166–67; cf. 139.

59 Dem. liii 8; Aesch. ii 12.

60 *IG* ii–iii 1, 283, 284.

61 *GDI* 5364; possible ransoming of the captured, ibid. 5366.

62 *IG* i² 53+*SEG*×46.

63 Ditt. *Syll.*³ 582; cf. Livy xxxi 22, 6 and Diod. Sic. xxviii 1.

64 Xen. *Anab.* vii 5, 14.

65 Ditt. *Syll.*³ 456, 30ff.; cf. Xen. *Anab.* vi 4, 2.

66 Especially of corn ships by war-

ships, from Hieron, to protect against seizure (really piracy) by Byzantium, Chalcedon, and Cyzicus, Dem. 1, 6 and 17.

67 Dem. viii 25.

68 For example Ditt. *Syll.*³ 742, a decree of the Ephesians concerning debtors, *c.* 85 BC, in general dealing with debts and contractual obligations in the crisis of the attack of Mithridates VI. There is particular mention of maritime contracts to be remitted or suspended (*symbolaia ta nautika*).

69 Ditt. *Syll.*³ 229, of before 342/1 BC. Cf. Ditt. *Syll.*³ 633.

70 Something like them *c.* 450 BC between Cnossus and Tylissos.

71 Ditt. *Syll.*³ 172.

72 Ibid. 273.

73 Ibid. 286. Olbia was a colony of Miletus.

74 Ditt. *Syll.*³ 344.

75 *GDI* 4645.

76 *SEG* ii 258.

77 *DGI* 5310 (Eretria).

78 Ditt. *Syll.*³ 217, in the period 342–309 BC

79 *Hesperia* v 273ff. (Wallace); the next, *IG* i² 27, 28 and 36; another early example, Ditt. *Syll.*³ 110.

80 Hdt. viii 136.

81 *GDI* 5686 and 5687.

82 Cf. the list of proxenoi at Histiaea, Ditt. *Syll.*³ 492.

83 *GDI* 5464, followed by citizenship for the first recipient.

84 As for example Ditt. *Syll.*³ 282 (of 333 BC) in which Priene honours Megabyxus of Ephesus with the usual privileges associated with *proxenia*, and the right of land acquisition to five talents value – the land to be not less than 10 stadia from the frontier of Ephesus, and not in the area of the Pedieis. It should be noted that such acquisition was of great business value.

85 *GDI* 5533.

86 As in the case of Philocles, king of Sidon, for his services to the Delians in the recovery of debts (Ditt. *Syll.*[3] 391 of *c.* 280 BC=*SEG* i 363); *proxenia* and *politeia and* a gold crown appear in Ditt. *Syll.*[3] 426.

87 On which see Ditt. *Syll.*[3] 256 (Tenedos).

88 See also *MusHelv.* (1960) 21–33; an early example of *asylia* and *ateleia, c.* 450 BC, Ditt. *Syll.*[3] 55.

89 On Chios (*SEG* ii 258); on Teos (at its request) (Ditt. *Syll.*[3] 563); and on Magnesia on the Maeander (Ditt. *Syll.*[3] 554) (also on request). In this latter case (which was accepted by other states) there was a religious connection, an epiphany of Artemis (see Ditt. *Syll.*[3] 557), which recalls the granting of *asylia* to religious centres (Ditt. *Syll.*[3] 550 and 590, 15), which in turn recalls our *droit d'asile.* It no doubt served to make life easier if the provisions could be enforced.

90 Ilium decree, Ditt. *Syll.*[3] 355.

91 Such as the Athenian grant to Sidonian merchants (between 376 and 360 BC) of freedom from *metoikion, choregia* and *eisphora*).

92 A possible case to Siphians at Calauria (religious?), according to 'ancestral custom' (Ditt. *Syll.*[3] 359); an example of one community to another, Epidaurus to Astypalaea (its colony) (second half of the fourth century) (Ditt. *Syll.*[3] 357).

93 As Ditt. *Syll.*[3] 355, Ilium to three Tenedians: freedom of tax on acquisition of land, houses and anything else, and for those who purchase from them or sell to them.

94 Cf. Ditt. *Syll.*[3] 941 (third century BC), in this case to Phocaeans in Magnesia (? on the Hermus), but only for private purposes, not trade. In this way there was less loss to the import-export tax, for the collection of which (at Cyparissia) see *GDI* Suppl. no. 44= Ditt. *Syll.*[3] 952, of the fourth century BC.

95 As between Mausollus and Phaselis (*GDI* 4259). See Ditt. *Syll.*[3] 955 for the probable detail of their provisions.

96 Cf. at Amorgos, in the first half of the fourth century, *GDI* 5361.

97 Ditt. *Syll.*[3] 116; cf. Olbia pledging the city's sacred vessels to a money-lender (Ditt. *Syll.*[3] 495).

Supplementary: other relevant inscriptions: Dittenberger, *Orientis Graeci Inscriptiones* (*OGI*) i (1903): on the *sitodeia* and gifts of corn especially in the crisis of 321/20 BC; *OGI* 4: import into Ionia 'from the Satraps'; *OGI* 9: Honours to Archestratus, garrison commander of Demetrius, from the Ephesians, *c.* 302/1 BC, since 'he saved the cornships'; *OGI* 56: the Canopus monument of Ptolemy III, 239/8 BC, on the failure of the Nile to rise, and resulting corn shortage: corn supplies drawn from elsewhere: Syria, Phoenicia, Cyprus and other regions, including, probably, Sicily.

On trade organization, note *OGI* 140 and 247, the term *ekdocheis* used of agents between *emporoi* and shippers (*naukleroi*).

BIBLIOGRAPHY

TRADE

General Theory: Trade and Industry

1 Beloch, K. J., *Griechische Geschichte* (1922) iii 1, 313–45, for good notes
2 Bücher, K., *Beiträge zur Wirtschaftsgeschichte* (1922)
3 Cavaignac, E., *L'économie grecque* (1951)
4 Cloché, P., *Les classes, les métiers, le trafic* (1931)
5 Finley, M. I., *Studies in Land and Credit in Ancient Athens, 500–200 B.C. The Horos Inscriptions* (1951). Very useful bibliography
6 ——, et al., *Second International Conference of Economic History, Aix-en-Provence 1962* (1965), vol. i, 'Trade and Politics in the Ancient World'.
7 ——, *The Ancient Economy* (1973)
8 Francotte, H., *L'industrie dans la Grèce ancienne* (1900)
9 Glotz, Gustave, *Le travail dans la Grèce ancienne. Histoire économique de la Grèce* (1920)
10 Glover, T. R., *From Pericles to Philip* (1918), particularly pp. 302–36
11 Gomme, A. W., *Essays in Greek History and Literature* (1937), 'Traders and Manufacturers in Greece'
12 Hasebroek, J., 'Betriebsformen des griechischen Handels', *Hermes* (1923) 392–425
13 ——, *Staat und Handel im alten Griechenland* (1928)
14 ——, *Griechische Wirtschafts- und Gesellschafts-geschichte* (1931)
15 ——, *Trade and Politics in Ancient Greece*. Trans. by Fraser, L. M. and MacGregor, D. C. (1933) of 13 above
16 Heichelheim, F. M., *An Ancient Economic History* ii (1964). Very full bibliography on all aspects of Greek economic history
17 Jones, A. H. M., *Ancient Economic History* (1948)
18 Knorringa, H., *Emporos. Data on Trade and Trader in Greek Literature from Homer to Aristotle* (1926)
19 Michell, H., *Economics of Ancient Greece*[2] (1957). Good bibliography 394–98, 425–27. Useful appendices
20 Oertel, F., 'Zur Frage der attischen Grossindustrie', *RM* (1930) 230–52
21 Pöhlmann, R. von, *Geschichte der sozialen Frage und des Sozialismus in der antiken Welt*[3] (1925)
22 Schaal, H., *Vom Tauschhandel zum Welthandel* (1931)
23 Toutain, J., *L'économie antique* (1927)

Particular Aspects

24 Ehrenberg, V., *From Solon to Socrates*[2] (1973). The best account of the historical background

25 Gernet, L., *L'approvisionment d'Athènes en blé au Vième et IVième siécles* (1909)
26 Grace, V. R., *Amphoras and the Ancient Wine Trade* (1961)
27 Jardé, A., *Les céréales dans l'antiquité grecque* (1925)
28 Panagos, C. T., *Le Pirée* (1968)
29 Roebuck, C., 'The grain trade between Greece and Egypt', *Class. Philol.* (1950) 236–47
30 Sutherland, C. H. V., 'Corn and Coin: a Note on Greek commercial monopolies', *AJP* (1943) 129–47
31 Ziebarth, E., *Beiträge zur Geschichte des Seeraubs und Seehandels im alten Griechenland* (1929)

Facilitation and Protection: The State and Trade
See above, particularly 2–3, 6, 12–14, 31
32 Brecht, C. H., *Zur Haftung der Schiffer im antiken Recht* (*Münchener Beiträge zur Papyrusforschung* 45 (1962))
33 Cohen, E. E., *Ancient Athenian Maritime Courts* (1973). On *dikai emporikai*
34 Jones, J. W., *The Law and Legal Theory of the Greeks* (1956)
For standard works on Greek (especially Athenian) law: see Finley, 5 above

Objects of Trade
See below, on Trades and Crafts, passim, and Heichelheim, 16 above

Means of Exchange; Coinage
35 Babélon, E., *Traité des monnaies grecques et romaines* (1901–33) i 772ff., 807ff., 831ff., 874ff., 897ff., 950ff. On coins and numismatics in general
36 Cook, R. M., 'Speculations on the Origins of Coinage', *Hesperia* (1958) 257–62
37 Gunn, B., 'Export of Silver to Egypt in the Fourth Century. The Naucratis Stele', *Journal of Egyptian Archaeology* (1943) 55–59
38 Kraay, C. M., 'The Early Coinage of Athens: A Reply', *NC* (1962) 417–23. Reply to W. P. Wallace, 46 below
39 ——, *Greek Coins* (1966)
40 ——, *Archaic and Classical Greek Coins* (1976)
41 Price, M. J., ed., *Coin Hoards* i (1975), ii (1976)
42 Seltman, C. T., *Athens, Its History and Coinage* (1924)
43 ——, *Greek Coins*[2] (1933)
44 Stroud, R. S., 'An Athenian Law on Silver Coinage,' *Hesperia* (1974) 157–88
45 Sutherland, C. H. V., 'Overstrikes and Hoards', *NC* (1942) 1–18
46 Wallace, W. P., 'The early Coinages of Athens and Euboia', *NC* (1962) 23–42
47 Williams, R. T., 'The "Owls" and Hippias', *NC* (1966) 9–13

Finance and Banking
See above 5, 13, 14, 19
48 Bogaert, R., *Banques et Banquiers dans les cités grecques* (1968)
49 Calhoun, G. M., *The Business Life of Ancient Athens* (1926)

INDUSTRY

General on Technology
50   Finley, M. I., 'Technical Innovation and Economic Progress in the Ancient
       World', *Econ. History Review* (1965) 29–45
51   Forbes, R. J., *Studies in Ancient Technology* i–ix (1955/56–64). All aspects of
       industrial activity; bibliography
52   Singer, C., Holmyard, E. J., Hall, A. R., eddd., *A History of Technology.* i
       From Early times to the Fall of the Ancient Empires (1954)

Particular Aspects of Industry and Cognate Activities
See above 3, 9, 14, 23; Athenian metal-working, *Hesperia* (1977) 340ff.; for
    Corinth, ibid., 380ff.

(i) *Miscellaneous*
53   Crowfoot, G. M., 'Of the warp-weighted Loom', *BSA* (1936–37) 36–47
54   Drachmann, A. G., *Ancient Oil Mills and Presses* (1932)
55   Finley, M. I., 'Metals in the Ancient World', *Journal of the Royal Society
       of Arts* (1970) 598ff
56   Muhly, J. D., *Copper and Tin* (1969)
57   Moritz, L. A., *Grain Mills and Flour in Classical Antiquity* (1958)
58   Young, R. S., 'An Industrial District of Ancient Athens', *Hesperia* (1951)
       135–288
For electrum, silver and gold, see below under (vi) Mining

(ii) *Pottery and Potters*
59   Amyx, D. A. *An Amphora with a Price Inscription* (1941)
60   Beazley, J. D., *Potter and Painter in Ancient Athens* (1946)
61   Cook, R. M., 'Die Bedeutung der bemahlten Keramik für den griechischen
       Handel,' *Jdl* (1959) 114–23
62   ——, *Greek Painted Pottery* (1960). Good bibliography on all aspects
63   Richter, G. M. A., *The Craft of Attic Pottery* (1923)

(iii) *Quarrying, Technique of Sculpture, Building Materials*
64   Adam, Sheila, *The Technique of Greek Sculpture in the Archaic and Classical
       Periods* (1966)
65   Pritchett, M., 'The Attic Stelai II', *Hesperia* (1956) 281ff. On tiles and
       bricks

(iv) *Workers, Free and Slave*
66   Burford, Alison, *Craftsmen in Greek and Roman Society* (1972)
67   Finley, M. I., ed., *Slavery in Classical Antiquity, Views and Controversies*
       (1960); Suppl. 1968
68   Flacelière, R., *La vie quotidienne en Grèce au siècle de Périclès* (1959)
69   Glotz, G., *Ancient Greece at Work* (1926)
70   Guiraud, P., *La main d'oeuvre industrielle dans l'ancienne Grèce* (1900)
71   Lauffer, S., *Die Bergwerkssklaven von Laureion*, i and ii (1955–56)
72   Schwahn, R., 'Die Xenophontischen Poroi und die Athenische Industrie im
       vierten Jahrhundert', *RM* (1931) 253ff.
73   Westermann, W. L., *The Slave Systems of Greek and Roman Antiquity* (1955)

(v) *Agriculture*

74 Finley, M. I., ed., *Problèmes de la terre en Grèce ancienne* 1973)

75 Strauss, L., *Xenophon's Socratic Discourse. An Interpretation of the Oeconomicus* (1970)

(vi) *Mining*

(1) *Attica*

76 Ardaillon, E., *Mines du Laurion dans l'antiquité* (1897)

77 Buchanan, J. J., *Theorika. A Study of Monetary Distributions to the Athenian Citizenry during the Fifth and Fourth Centuries B.C.* (1962)

78 Hopper, R. J., 'The Laurion Mines', *BSA* (1953) 200–54; 'The Laurion Mines: A reconsideration', *BSA* (1968) 293–326

79 Labarbe, J., *La loi navale de Thémistocle* (1957)

80 Lauffer, S., 'Prosopographische Bemerkungen zu den attischen Gruben-pachtlisten', *Historia* (1957) 287–305

80a Healy, J. F., *Mining and Metallurgy in the Greek and Roman World* (1978)

80b On mining and farming, *Hesperia* (1977) 162ff.

(2) *North Aegean*

81 Casson, S., *Macedonia, Thrace and Illyria* (1926)

82 Davies, Oliver, 'Ancient Mines in Southern Macedonia', *Journ. Anthrop. Inst.* (1933)

83 Martin, V., 'La durée d'exploitation des gisements aurifères de Philippes en Macédoine', *Études Andréades* (1940)

84 May, J. M. F., works on northern coinage:
    (a) *The Coinage of Damastion and the lesser Coinages of the Illyro-Paeonian Region* (1939)
    (b) *Ainos. Its History and Coinage 474–341 B.C.* (1950)
    (c) *The Coinage of Abdera, 540–345 B.C.* (1966)
    (d) 'The Coinage of Maroneia *c.* 520–449 B.C.' *NC* (1965) 27–56

85 Philippson, O., *Die griechische Landschaften* (1950–59), on Thasos, op. cit. iv (1959) 210–13

86 Pouilloux J., *Études thasiennes* iii (1954), *Recherches sur l'histoire et les cultes de Thasos*, i

87 Raymond, D., *Macedonian Regal Coinage. Numis. Notes and Monographs* 126 (1953)

88 Robinson, D. M. and Clement, P. A., *Excavations at Olynthus* ix, *The Chalcidic Mint* (1938)

89 Sagui, C. J., *Journal of Economic Geology* (1928) 671–80. Information on Macedonia–Thrace in Roman and later times

90 ——, *The Ancient Mining Works of Cassandra, Greece*. A curious work, date and place of publication unknown; it is not included in Casson's bibliography

91 Strack, M. L. and Gaebler, H., *Die antiken Münzen Nord-Griechenlands* (1899 and foll.)

92 Svoronos, J. N., *L'héllénisme primitif de la Macédoine* (1919)

93 West, A. B., *Fifth and Fourth Century Gold Coins from the Thracian Coast. Numis. Notes and Monographs* 40 (1929)

(3) *Siphnos*

94   Bent, J. T., *Aegean Islands* (1884, reprint, 1966) 32–33, 38–40
95   Hopper, R. J., *BSA* (1968) 293–326 passim, and pl. 64
96   Philippson, O., *Die griechische Landschaften* (1950–59), 'Die westliche Reihe
      der Kykladen: Siphnos', 76–79

(vii) *Roads; Transport of Heavy Weights (Stone, Large Timbers)*
97   Burford, Alison, 'Heavy Transport in Classical Antiquity', *Economic History
      Review*² (1960) 1–18
98   ——, *The Greek Temple Builders at Epidaurus* (1969)
99   Forbes, R. J., *Studies in Ancient Technology* i–ix (1955/56–64)
100 Hodge, A. T., *The Woodwork of Greek Roofs* (1960). For dimensions of
      building timbers

NOTE The following discussions on population (including slaves) are of importance in particular for their connection with A. W. Gomme's *Population of Athens*
(1933).
 (i) Gomme, A. W., 'The Slave Population of Athens', *JHS* (1946) 127–29
      Answers to objectors to Gomme's rejection of Ctesicles' figure of 400,000
      slaves for Athens in the fourth century BC
 (ii) ——, 'The Population of Athens again', *JHS* (1959) 61–68
      In reference to A. H. M. Jones, in Appendix to *Athenian Democracy*
(iii) Salmon, P., 'La population de la Grèce antique', *Bulletin de l'association
      Guillaume Budé* (1959) 448–76

SOURCES OF ILLUSTRATIONS

ACL 8; Alinari 4; Argos Museum 10;
Athens: The American School at Athens, Agora Excavations 38, 39; British
   School of Archaeology 19; German Archaeological Institute 1, 2, 3, 44
Basle, Münzen und Medaillen, A. G. 23 (from Catalogue XXII, 1961); 27 (from
   K. Schefold, *Meisterwerk griech. Cunst*, Berne, 1960)
Berlin, Staatliche Museen 37
Boston, Museum of Fine Arts 35, 47
Lawrence, A. W. 51
Leipzig, Teubner Verlag 24 (H. Schaal, *Vom Tauschhandel zum Welthandel*, 1931)
London, British Museum 14, 15, 17a–e, 29, 34, 43, 45
Munich: Antikensammlung 8; Hirmer Verlag 7, 18, 20, 21, 22
New York: Hispanic Society of America 6; Metropolitan Museum 13, 31, 32
Oxford, Ashmolean Museum 11, 16
Paris, Société d'Edition, 'Les Belles Lettres' 26, 28, 30, 33, 46, 47
   (from P. Cloché, *Les classes, les métiers, le trafic*, Assoc. Guillaume Budé)
Rome, Soprintendenza delle Antichità dell'Etruria Meridionale 5
Schaal, H., *Bilderhefte zur Kunst und Kulturgeschichte des Altertums V, Griechische
   Vasen* II, Verlag von Velhagen und Klasing, Bielefeld and Leipzig, 1930
Toronto, Museum of Classical Archaeology 12
Utrecht, Imago: Nederlands Klassiek Verbond and Prof. J. H. Jongkees 25, 40
The following photographs were taken by the author: 48, 49, 50
The maps were drawn by Peter Bridgewater

INDEX